TRACING THE EAGLE'S ORBIT:

ILLUMINATING INSIGHTS INTO MAJOR US FOREIGN POLICIES SINCE INDEPENDENCE

GAUTAM MAITRA

2007

Order this book online at www.trafford.com/06-2428
or email orders@trafford.com

Most Trafford titles are also available at major online book retailers.

Note for Librarians: A cataloguing record for this book is available from Library and Archives Canada at www.collectionscanada.ca/amicus/index-e.html

ISBN: 978-1-4251-0670-6

We at Trafford believe that it is the responsibility of us all, as both individuals and corporations, to make choices that are environmentally and socially sound. You, in turn, are supporting this responsible conduct each time you purchase a Trafford book, or make use of our publishing services. To find out how you are helping, please visit www.trafford.com/responsiblepublishing.html

Our mission is to efficiently provide the world's finest, most comprehensive book publishing service, enabling every author to experience success. To find out how to publish your book, your way, and have it available worldwide, visit us online at www.trafford.com/10510

www.trafford.com

North America & international
toll-free: 1 888 232 4444 (USA & Canada)
phone: 250 383 6864 • fax: 250 383 6804
email: info@trafford.com

The United Kingdom & Europe
phone: +44 (0)1865 722 113 • local rate: 0845 230 9601
facsimile: +44 (0)1865 722 868 • email: info.uk@trafford.com

15 14 13 12

What the topmost foreign policy experts in the United States say about this book:

"...found the book very interesting and thus like it a lot.

James Rosenau, University Professor of International Affairs, The George Washington University

"...impressed by the wide range of analysis..."

Zbigniew Brzezzinski, Former National Security Adviser, USA.

...book is quite impressive, ... successive developments in the evolution of American foreign policy is very effective and easy to follow. My major criticism is that recent developments, particularly President Bush's attack on Iraq and the implications of that action, should be more explicit and more detailed. More emphasis on the fundamental changes in American foreign policy which the Bush Administration has made would be desirable. However, I do appreciate that an analysis and evaluation of the Bush policy innovations would be very difficult without access to the literature both supporting and criticizing these changes and especially "the Bush Doctrine". ...an impressive and thorough history of American foreign policy since independence.

Robert G. Gilpin, Professor emeritus, Politics and International Affairs at the Woodrow Wilson School of Public and International Affairs at Princeton University

...Clearly, it is a major piece of work and a contribution to understanding the role of the United States on the international scene over the long term. Indeed, TRACING THE EAGLE'S ORBIT contains "illuminating insights" into American foreign policies ... optimistic conclusions about the benefits of American hegemony contain much truth ... It deserves them and should stimulate a lot of discussion. ...concluding comments about the hope represented by the United States, despite the blemishes, were a useful antidote to total pessimism about recent events in Iraq, torture and rendition, attacks on civil liberties, etc. that we have seen under the Bush crowd....There is much food for thought in it.

Wendell Bell, Professor Emeritus of Sociology, Yale University.

...It is always interesting to read books about US foreign policy written by non-Americans,...

I particularly appreciated... listing of US advantages and disadvantages. The anti-hierarchic nature of the United States and its disposition under some circumstances to provide public goods are indeed significant advantages. The self-righteousness of many Americans, and excessive reliance on pure capitalism as the solution to all economic problems, are indeed liabilities.

We differ on a number of points. In my view, the United States is not as strong economically as it was in the 1990s, as reflected in its current account and budget deficits. The low quality of US primary and secondary education is a source of concern for the long term. Furthermore, I see unilateralism as more evidently self-defeating, and I would put more emphasis on multilateral institutions, which indeed have limitations but are not bankrupt (p. 251)... overstates the directed and farsighted character of US leadership, and its consistency. Domestic politics is more important... I see no evidence for the proposition (p. 21) that the US opening to immigration in the 1960s was designed to facilitate US expansionalism and imperialism in future decades... seems to me to understestimate the extent to which the presidency of George W. Bush departs sharply from the foreign policy consensus of presidents from Truman to Clinton, including George Herbert Walker Bush.

Professor Robert Keohane, Professor of Political Science at the Woodrow Wilson School at Princeton University

"Gautam Maitra has created one of the few good foreign policy books as an outsider to the United States. He weaves an interesting set of common values in foreign policy that often go unnoticed by Americans. He addresses the issues of power and domination in a new way that I think readers will find intriguing. This is a book for all good students of American foreign policy precisely because it does come from an outsider. You may not agree with all he says, but the work does provoke thought."

M. Gene Aldridge, Board Member, New Mexico Research Institute.

PREFACE

Dealing with a subject like the US foreign policies since independence is by itself a very exhaustive and trying job that can hardly be captured in a single book like this. Moreover, there are several aspects to any single foreign policy matter pursued by a nation. The problem remains what to keep and what to leave out. As the title of the book suggests, it is not quite like other books on the American foreign policies. It is neither too descriptive nor is it overtly analytical. It rather seeks to focus on major developments in America's foreign policy history in important crossroads in that nation's life. But it has a specific methodology.

This book has a *purpose*. The twenty-first century happens to be the era of unprecedented interdependence between nations of the world. Contemporary international politics is defined by two conflicting developments: on the one hand, there are efforts towards the building of a more inclusive and global type of civilization while some ominous developments in the international arena portend to reverse such a process, on the other. Free world led by the United States and the forces of traditionalism led by the forces of orthodoxy and fundamentalism are now pitted against each other in what can be construed as a repeat of the ideological rivalry of the just bygone era. As a result, people in many parts of the world now like to know more about a nation, like the United States, that controls the destiny of every other nation.

Yet such an interest in the American foreign policy in these nations follows a distinct pattern. Barring the academics and scholars in international politics, common masses everywhere- friends and foes alike- rather prefer to have a concise knowledge about America's political history and foreign policies. Since contemporary era happens to be the era of the media, the line of demarcation between journalistic and academic styles and approaches has become thinner. Politically conscious people, everywhere, like to hear more about the salient points, like the news headlines. Likewise, a book written with that purpose in a living and flowing style catches the fancy of common readers and academicians alike. Therefore, it is the selection of the appropriate style and methodology that is more important for a topic like this. Readers are drawn by happenings of recent phenomena like, globalization, terrorism etc. Then they like to know more about the causes that gave rise to such phenomena until they develop a keen interest in the whole of the topic. This is best done by anyone writing in a dispassionate and impartial way.

Since foreign policies of nations rove round the same set of national interests and priorities, it is better to focus attention on some major American foreign policies, like, the Neutrality, the Manifest Destiny, and the Truman Doctrine etc. This book proceeds from several important assumptions. First, the successive American foreign policies served to complete the unfinished jobs of the Declaration that, over time, set the rules of the games in international politics. Secondly, the American Declaration, in its turn, rested on the premise of creating a new and a different type of international political order – an alternative to the political order established by colonialism-imperialism. As a result, the values and principles as enshrined in the Declaration come in the way of America's adopting a 'different' role in the contemporary era. This conflict with its parent political philosophy required the incumbent American policy makers to frame appropriate policies either to strike a balance or to shed off its past. The third assumption is that it is the remoteness of America's geography and culture that had fostered a sense of isolation in the minds of the early American policy makers and that still shapes that country's foreign policies. Neither the Declaration nor America's ideological battle with the forces of totalitarianism, conservatism and dictatorship is free from this 'fear'. The fourth assumption is that the messages of the Declaration are dialectical and are continuously evolving that imparts a sort of 'eternity' to the American values and elasticity to the American foreign policies, at the same time.

This book has been possible because of access to the inexhaustible sources in the major libraries in India and of course, the Internet. All these render the arduous job of verification of facts and data relatively easy. I hope that the readers everywhere will find this book interesting and useful. It may open a new horizon for the international political scholars, especially the second chapter dealing with the politics of Domination that is extremely timely and novel.

Gautam Maitra

FOREWARD

Mr. Gautam Maitra's book is not only a learned interpretation of US foreign policy and its impact on the global arena during the last two hundred years but also a very interesting intellectual experiment. The reader has the chance to get an informed analysis of the nature and history of US foreign policy written by an author who, by his own account, is a "non-Westerner", who lives "far away from North America" and whose take on his topic is different from the standard interpretations popularized by the Western mass media and pundits. Even more remarkable, while avoiding the risk of being a mere echo of the standard Western rhetoric, the author also manages to circumvent the clichés associated with the non Western, "Third-world" perspective's contrived interpretations of international affairs. The result is a truly fascinating document: a complex international relations analysis and at the same time a case study in non-orthodox thinking in foreign affairs analysis and commentary. The alert reader is surprised to discover a unique combination of original insights and reinterpretations of traditional themes in the literature. Yet, the author does not strive to be original for the sake of being original. He has an argument to make and he makes it with talent, insight, erudition, and much common sense. The assumption of his thesis is the notion that the emergence of independent America "triggered a tectonic shift in the geopolitical foundations of Europe and the reverberations and aftershocks still continue today on a global scale." We may say, writes Mr. Maitra, "that the 'American tide' generated by its founding fathers well over two centuries back through the Declaration of 4 July, 1776, and carried by the flood of subsequent events have, so far, led it into a position of world leadership. It remains to be seen where it ultimately leads America into: a permanent world leadership or its subsequent roll back into its own hemisphere." Built around this core argument are layers of interesting, original, or simply challenging observations that make Mr. Maitra's book a fascinating read for both the expert and the general public.

Paul Dragos Aligica
Hudson Institute and Mercatus Center at George Mason University

TABLE OF CONTENTS

PART ONE

PART TWO

PART THREE

CHAPTER I

A people... who are possessed of the spirit of commerce, who see and who will pursue their advantages may achieve almost anything.
George Washington letter to Benjamin Harrison, October 10, 1784

Benjamin Franklin preferred the Turkey to the bald Eagle over the choice of the national emblem of the United States. After all, a bird known for its bad moral character, laziness, and cowardice could hardly qualify to make even a symbolic representation of a great and dynamic nation like the United States. However, the Congress took it as a symbol of limitless freedom, great strength, long life, supreme power, and accepted it as the national emblem of the United States on 20 June 1782. That decision of the American Congress was vindicated in future. Today's America has become the supreme ruler not only of the land and the sea but of the space also with its robust network of 'surveillance' satellites, not unlike the Eagle's eyes, yet carrying in its beak a universal message of unity: E Pluribus Unum.

Just as the eagle has its flight path, the United States, too, has its own set of values and principles, interests and goals that defines its orbit. It cannot deviate from that orbit. But the movement along such an orbit can be made more complete and frictionless by maneuvering the space or elasticity provided by these American values and objectives. The United States traverses in its orbit in ever widening concentric circles. Its center happens to be its values as enshrined in the Declaration of Independence that at the same time provide the necessary boost to travel towards the furthest points within the orbit through the constant urge to complete the still unfinished jobs of both the Declaration and the War of Independence.

The perimeters of these concentric circles happen to be those crucial stages that America attained through the successful conduct of its foreign policies at various crossroads in that nation's history since independence. However, the Eagle, after keeping to a low height for about one hundred and eighty years from its birth as an independent nation, till 1945, felt that its wings had become strong enough to reach greater heights when that bird of prey was boosted by Britain into a higher circle, not so higher, of course, where things would go out of the latter's hands. After some head on clash on the geopolitical 'space' with its twin super power, the Soviet Union, and 'killing' its prey in the process, the United States in the new millennium is well on its course to scale yet another height that would enable it to mange world affairs, ad libitum. It would, therefore, be well worth to take a tour of the US foreign policies since independence and trace the flight paths of the ever soaring eagle.

The United States happens to be an 'enigma within a riddle'. People in many other countries find America and its foreign policies somewhat difficult to comprehend, especially, after the Cold War period. Since foreign policies reveal a country's goals, priorities, interests, and above all, a country's identity (both in terms of traditional as well as political values), together they form the matrix of the political structure and constitution of that particular country as well as its 'market' value measured in terms of its support base and acceptability within the world community of nations. It is, therefore, extremely relevant to have a look at the basic ingredients that make up the American political structure and to see how they influenced that country's foreign policies and also their relevance in the contemporary era. It is the purpose of this book to unveil the secrets surrounding that great American mystery, referred at the beginning, by making an in depth analysis of its foreign policies since its independence and to present the United States and its foreign policies in a far more exoteric manner.

Those ingredients happen to be America-specific. Just as the property of a matter reveals its true character, these American ingredients demonstrate the directions, inclinations, limits, tolerances, aspirations, and above all the 'socializing' capacity of that country vis-à-vis others. Thus, a discussion of these ingredients is extremely relevant since the United States happens to be the world leader and seeks to perpetuate its global hegemony in an era characterized by greater democratization of information and politics. For the 'idealist' America, it becomes peremptory to examine those original 'political' inputs that I call 'American' Specialties, or a 'bevy of the American ideals in an American convoy', more correctly, the American *Cavalcade*. This last terminology is most appropriate because of America's messianic inclinations. America itself happens to be a great 'idea', above everything else. No wonder, its ideas and influences were destined to spread abroad. To know the 'secret' and truth behind the American foreign policies and their future directions, we need to turn the search light on these American specialties.

These ideals or values were virtually codified in the Declaration of the American Independence that replaced the one hundred and sixty nine years charter of the Crown. The discovery of America, the Declaration, the War of Independence, and the American Constitution, all were important milestones not only in the American history but also for international politics as they all contributed to the creation of the second wing of the Western Civilization. However, the fetus of that second wing of the Western Civilization that developed for over one and a half century in the womb of 'mother' England was not altogether a product of love and courtship but also one of bitterness and deprivation. Though it accounts for the difference in the European and the American mind-sets, it, nevertheless, conveys a distinct message: that the fate of the United States and Europe would forever remain intertwined, in war and in peace, in courtship and in vengeance, and in realizing the grand design of establishing the supremacy of the modern Western Civilization on a global scale. It was Europe that was responsible for ending the physical isolation of an unknown New World that lay unnoticed and uncaring at the edge of the globe's surface half a million years ago. It was Europe again that had not only served as the cradle of the modern American civilization but also was responsible for catapulting the United States to the status of its present world leadership. Since someone's increase must come at some others' expense, imperial Europe, in the process, virtually got reduced to the status of an American 'protectorate' after 1945.

Emergence of independent America triggered a tectonic shift in the geopolitical foundations of Europe and the reverberations and aftershocks still continue today on a global scale. It can attain stability either with the establishment of a 'permanent 'or even a 'quasi-permanent' American supremacy or with America's retreat within its own hemisphere. The entire drama from the days of the American independence till today contains all the elements of thrill, excitement, brilliance, creativity, and novelty that had brought international affairs to its present state. *Taking an analogy from Shakespeare, we may say that the 'American tide' generated by its founding fathers well over two centuries back through the Declaration in 4 July, 1776, and carried by the flood of subsequent events have, so far, led it into a position of world leadership. It remains to be seen where it ultimately leads America into: a permanent world leadership or its subsequent roll back into its own hemisphere.*

The United States, unlike the erstwhile European great powers, had neither any regional checks and balances nor any contiguity with any other continent than a 'friendly' and disproportionately 'weak' South American Continent to define its foreign policies. It is a historical fact that hostile neighborhoods happen to be the breeding grounds of constant warfare and diplomatic maneuverings. Even today, countries feel less security threats from a more distant power. Consequently, the starting point of the American foreign policies, rather, happen to be the Declaration based on certain 'American' (and universal values) principles instead of the traditional national and security 'interests' that motivated Europe to create an international political system based on power politics.

That paradigm of the regional origin of inter border politics was broken by a marvelous and epoch-making event: Colonialism. Overseas colonialism provided a much-needed safety valve for the warring European powers in transcending and transposing their regional security concerns, to a considerable extent, beyond their continental borders. International politics got the better of inter border politics till this cycle was again broken by the two World Wars of the last century, and, most recently by the third wave of globalization, portending the transition to a post-modern, post industrial and post Westphalian system. Since the beginning of the last century, security concerns came to be defined more and more in terms of transnational factors.

Meanwhile, five hundred years of European colonial domination had put the indelible seal of supremacy of the Western Civilization on many parts of the globe. The demise of colonialism in the wake of the Second World War ought to have signaled a return to the old regional and 'neighbor-centric' external politics. But that was not to be. By a strange twist of history and by a most bewildering mockery of international politics – hitherto used to the game of power politics – it was the most unlikely candidate on whom devolved the responsibility to dominate the post war international politics: *non colonial, non-imperial, and the idealistic United States.*

Truly, none of the common denominators, like, the scarcity of land and raw materials, the demographic pressures or the ambitions of the individual despots that led the European nations to occupy foreign territories were in place to justify the American expansionism beyond its borders. Only a 'remote' connection to the American 'expansionism' could be traced to the American founders' emphasis on 'trade'. Trade, in turn, depended on military power for the protection of trade routes and to ensure uninterrupted flow of commerce. Freedom of trade and freedom of the seas thus became two of America's principal foreign policy goals after independence. Little wonder that the commercial republic of the United States revealed its expansionist penchant beyond its border once the frontier expansion grinded to a halt towards the closing decades of the nineteenth century. More accurately, it is the same economic aspect of 'lebensraum' that motivated both the American and the European expansionism abroad but with a difference. While imperialist Europe shamelessly resorted to the occupation of foreign territories, America had one hand tied to its republican back.

As a result, the American foreign polices appeared to take on a less concrete, more 'abstract', and rather 'absolute' direction (in the absence of an imperialist political set-up) compared to those of Europe. Since independence, the American foreign policies came to depend on two perceptions: on the one hand, there was the American ambivalence about defining the 'American' identity in European terms because of the 'anti-colonial' and 'anti-monarchic' sentiments that not only led to the American independence but also drove America towards directing its efforts at undermining European colonial-imperialism in its own hemisphere; on the other hand, there remained the urge to further the causes of the Western Civilization initiated by the Anglo-Saxon republican values but rendered as much difficult and complicated by a 'historical' gap (discussed below) with Europe. Both these perceptions were neatly interwoven in a single landmark event in modern American history that still guides all the subsequent American foreign policies, directly or indirectly: the Declaration of the American Independence.

Explaining the 'historical gap'

Since the dawn of human history, groups, tribes and empires- driven by lust, ambition, power, security, and survival- indulged in acts of aggrandizement by laying their unlawful and immoral 'talons' on the lands, people, and resources of the 'weak' and the 'incompetent'. Independant America, ascending directly out of a civilized European 'base' instead of from the usual barbaric stage that these very nations themselves went through, promised to be somewhat different. This is the historical gap that had made America exceptional and shaped the course of its foreign policies. The American uniqueness lay in the fact that the United States spurned the European monarchic system yet founded a republican system based on the European political thoughts hitherto tried sparingly even in Europe, and, that too, in countries of smaller sizes. Another important aspect of the above historical gap relates to the aspect of trade and economics discussed below.

Free trade happened to be one of the cornerstones of the American Declaration. Driven by the lure of carrying out commerce independent of the Crown and responding to the call of the 'Promised Land' to the West, thirteen American colonies banded together to wage the war of liberation. Thus, capital accumulation and the Westward territorial expansion went hand in hand with 'state' assistance in the form of vast investments on the independent nation's infrastructure and education. This, in turn, aided the development of the biggest, strongest, and, therefore, the most productive capitalist companies in America with superior competitive means and reorganizing force to spread into the world market.

It is this unique development in the American history that further widened the above mentioned 'historical' gap and marked a sharp departure from the European 'territorial imperialism' to the US 'trade imperialism'. The message was clear: unless the whole of the world served as destinations for the American trade, American capitalism would lose its 'American' dynamics and may have to adjust to the European form of capitalism. That is why, the Great Depression of the 1930s saw greater US emphasis on social welfare programs.

American colonies were mostly settled by some mediocre, propertyless and 'socially' ostracized fellows, uprooted as they were from their own soils and transported into the Eastern seaboard of the Atlantic. Unlimited wealth opportunities and property rights that were inconceivable in Europe so motivated these mavericks in their new found 'heaven' that they set about creating an *'exceptional' country. If any single factor that can better explain this American uniqueness, it was the lure for constant accumulation of wealth and property on the part of those early Americans that had made the American political system sui generis.*

In a land where there was limitless scope to amass and consolidate 'property' with little concern to protect the same in the absence of 'enemies', hostile neighborhoods, taxes, and despotic rulers, it is obvious that property rights would become the defining features of that country's soul, status, dynamism, and even identity. The American life principle was generated by that drive and 'greed' for wealth and property (as Lincoln mentioned in his Lyceum address) and continued to act as a 'safety valve' for the strained American republican-federal system in the immediate decades after independence. The American creed, like individual liberty, freedom of religion, speech, and trade, all were meant to sustain and perpetuate individual property rights. Madison justified the American republicanism, mainly, in terms of these property rights. It is in this background that one feels able to explain the preponderance of various private groups, associations and corporations in the American civil and political life that had sustained its republican system by forming 'reefs' and barriers to deter the emergence of centralized despotism. America didn't need a strong center for the management of that vast land because America stood for its individual states, localities, and private associations.

These new political and economic 'experiments', taken together, created the above historical gap to which the apprehensive European powers looked with awe and concern at the same time. Europe saw the writings on the wall as the independent United States proclaimed its separateness from its trans-Atlantic brethren with much fanfare and, more ominously for them, with assurance. These European monarchies rather conspired against the newly independent country to undermine its republican system. This, in turn, led the founders of independent America to prescribe a sort of 'detachment' in world affairs for the fledgling nation. Immediate concern for them was to protect the American republican system and to avoid any contamination of its ideals through the European political and military contacts.

The United States started its independent journey from the farthest edge of that historical gap and replaced all other European powers as a world leader in less than a couple of centuries. Indeed an astounding feat! How could America achieve such a feat that the other similarly geographically placed British settlements like Australia, New Zealand, Canada, and South Africa failed to repeat? Why the great French revolution and even Napoleon failed in installing either a stable republic or a republican empire notwithstanding the fact that France, happened to be a great nation and an international power at that time? What made Tocqueville and Kippling to think of the American political system as distinct and superior to those of Europe? Why the erstwhile European powers started to show increasing deference to America ever since the last decade of the late nineteenth century and why they had to fall back upon the American help to save them from total rout, twice in the last century? Why in a complete reversal of history, the former archrivals and bitter foes of America had to forego their pride and historical glories vis-à-vis the neophyte United States and had even to seek the latter's assistance, economic as well as military, for their protection from the Soviet threats after 1945? Why the Bolshevik regime with all its progressive ideals needed the iron hand of Stalin to suppress all democratic values and even then why the mighty Soviet superpower succumbed so tamely before the relentless American pressures to 'de-idealize' its socio-political and socio-economic systems? The answer to all these questions lies in two words: the 'American Cavalcade'. But before we go to examine these American distinctive features in more detail in this chapter, it is important to spot some strokes of good luck for the United States in the absence of which the above astounding feats would never have been possible. Part II deals with all these items in detail.

'Strokes' of good luck for America

America's meteoric rise to world leadership in less than two hundred years since independence is due to a combination of factors in which luck played no mean part. America was fortunate to have some extremely enlightened, and clear-headed prodigies like Franklin, Washington, Jefferson, Madison, Paine, and many others, as their forerunners. *Educated in Europe, the Mecca of learning those days, these astute fellows did some hard reflections on the realities of their time. Their combined sagacity and burning will released tremendous energies, and triggered off a 'political' big bang that not only caused a great upheaval in the political foundations of the European monarchic powers but also made the American thoughts and ideals so powerful a 'religion' as to pervade the entire landmass of our planet for quite some time to come.* One interesting point to note in this regard is that most of these strokes of good luck fell on an aspiring power that was yet to enter the international arena with any certainty. That means, the United States was adding to its strength in an unusual manner without losing any of its resources, unlike other great powers, who, spent most of their resources on wars. So vast were these accumulated gains in America's case that the process of decline of Pax Americana will invariably be an extremely long drawn affair, should it begin to take place in the near future.

Many advantages accrue to an individual, group or a nation if an action is initiated at the right moment. Take the example of the traffic. If one starts from one's home at the 'right' moment, one is most likely to get 'green' signal at every 'crossroad'. Conversely, the chances of facing 'red' (stop) signals are far greater if one makes a 'wrong' start. The first stroke of good luck was what I just mentioned: the coming together of a band of luminaries at a most 'auspicious' moment in the American history. As history would testify, revolutions happen to be time-specific. A group of leaders and their followers (and then the general masses) aroused by the call of 'conscience' and animated by a single spirit in a specific historical epoch, commit themselves to perform some 'extraordinary' deeds with fanatical zeal. For that particular time period, they act as if they are all possessed by a burning desire to destroy the old order. Once that phase had run its course, these men often pass into oblivion. Fortunately or unfortunately, there is no barometer to gauge the threshold limit of public discontent till a small group of leaders appear, like the angels, to orchestrate the whole drama. This was what happened in the American revolutionary war of independence but with an extremely important exception: these revolutionary leaders happened to be the architects of a new republican-federal America, at the same time.

The second reason for America being lucky was the irreconcilable enmity between various European great powers that ruled the entire New World at that time. It was through a clever exploitation of those contradictions that the American revolutionaries not only won independence but found the means to preserve a 'fractured' independence earned after seven grueling years of fighting. After all, the new born republic virtually lay besieged by the hostile European powers, waiting as they were at the fringes, like a tiger ever on the lookout for the slightest pretext to pounce upon the young 'lamb' to recapture their lost colonies. On the debit side, such a tactics on the part of a still 'weak' nation lent a sort of negativism to America's foreign policies as they became more 'target-oriented' in future. Consequently, the legalistic-moralistic United States ran every risk of running out of ideas whenever the 'target' tended to disappear, as we see in the post Cold War era.

The third reason is related to the second. America, with its bountiful land and natural resources, was something of a 'gold mine' to these constantly warring European commercial powers. Since the latter happened to be very close neighbors in their continent, they were mutually deterred to use force to 'resubjugate' the independent republic of America, lest the ensuing war spilled into their homelands. Under the circumstance, the best bet for them was to extract as much commercial concession from independent America (mainly through bilateral trade agreements) as possible. By the by, recently released classified files and documents reveal the same British desire to extract as much economic concessions from the newly independent India as possible. Many North American states acted as free ports for these European nations. The American leaders knew well where America's strength lay. America could lure European countries with trade 'privileges' to quell their bullying tendencies and dim their red eyes. The American policy makers knew that so long as their country remained a paradise of 'trade' they needed to fear nothing. Washington's farewell address also highlighted this point. In fact, British trade volume with the United States registered sharp increase in the decades following the American independence, averaging $ 14.8 million per annum compared to France's $5.3 million during 1800-1812.

The fourth reason of America being lucky was the execution of some landmark policies, that I call masterstrokes, by successive American leaders at important crossroads in that country's history that helped America not only to consolidate its exclusive grip over the Western Hemisphere but also to expand its influences beyond its oceanic borders with remarkable ease. Proclamation of the Monroe Doctrine, the Manifest Destiny and the Roosevelt corollary, the dollar diplomacy, the League of Nations and the subsequent formation of the United Nations, the Truman Doctrine, Carter's revival of human rights issues, Reagan's adoption of a tough line against the Soviet Union and his implementation of neo-liberal economic policies were some of the 'sure shots' executed by the US leadership, coming, as if, from the 'hand of God'.

Some extremely wise selection of policies at least, on three occasions had brought the Unticd States to its present position of world leadership and, ironically, to the present impasse in the new millennium. The American history would have been different, (1) if someone like Alexander Hamilton and not Thomas Jefferson happened to be the US president in 1800 that could have stripped 'American' republicanism of its 'American' elements and reduced it to the level of any other ordinary republic geared to 'imperialist' motivation; (2) if the republican party did not come to power in the 1850s and if again, Abraham Lincoln was not the US President during those turbulent days to steer the ship of the American Civil War; and (3) if the American leadership lacked the initiative, realism, courage, and foresight to embrace a more assertive 'expansionist' role made available by the fin de siecle that enabled the United States to pursue some *foreign policies* worth the name.

The fifth stroke of good luck was perhaps the most important development in the American history and for its nationhood. The United States, as we know today, would have ceased to exist if the outcome of the American Civil War, the biggest crisis ever in the American national life, turned out to be otherwise. The American unification was the single most contributing factor towards the growth of its rapid industrialization and consolidation of its internal markets. Indeed, the United States felt able to focus its attention in building its defense and a strong Navy only after the unification.

The sixth stroke of luck was the US victory in the Spanish-American war in 1898. Teddy Roosevelt made no secret of his designs about America's 'imperialist' role. Annexation of Cuba and Philippines in the aftermath of the Spanish-American war of 1898 brought to the fore America's latent colonial ambitions. Roosevelt corollary came handy as Teddy Roosevelt affirmed the US need to exercise 'international police power' to save the civilized world from disintegrating. Towards the close of the nineteenth century, the United States was fast becoming a great power and forced every other European power to accede to its demands in various conflicting situations in the Western Hemisphere as we shall see in the third chapter.

The seventh stroke of good luck was offered by the two World Wars and the Cold War of the last century that completely did away with the traditional American isolationism in international affairs and, more importantly, catapulted the United States to the status of a super power. In most of these cases, it was Europe that suffered the losses and it was the United States that was the sole beneficiary. All these three 'wars' freed America from its earlier sage-like apathy, 'renunciation', and isolationism, for good. Twentieth century was fast becoming an American century. All these are discussed in detail in part II.

Eighthly, the United States was lucky to have a precedent in Germany about how to exert a nation's influence from a position of geographical disadvantage through use of superior technology. Germany happened to be a landlocked country with hostile neighbors all along its borders in which movement in any direction was impossible except through force or 'Bismarckian' diplomacy. Like America, it too was the hunting ground of traditional European powers for about two centuries. Yet Germany overcame those geographical disadvantages through the power of its technology and brilliant strategic planning. Immediately after the end of WWII, the United States lost no time in 'hijacking' the best of brains from Nazi Germany to settle in the United States and, even, in putting many ex Nazi personnel to positions of eminence in the occupied German territory. The American academicians and scholars mostly overlook this 'German' factor in boosting the US confidence and capability as the United States prepared itself for its post war global engagements.

Ninthly, unprecedented developments in science and technology helped compress time and space so much that they largely neutralized the geographical and cultural disadvantage of the far-flung United States vis-à-vis the rest of the world. Rather, they made the United States look like a 'mini cosmos'. Taking advantages of improved transport and communications networks and the global spread of bipolar rivalry, the United States made up for the 'lost' time (because it was a late-comer in international affairs) by rapidly sending its various government and cultural organizations to the remote corners of the earth while encouraging massive migrations from various parts of the world, at the same time. Exchange of ideas, technological know-how, goods and services, evened out, though not completely, the American disadvantages in the area of culture and geography and further prevented a possibility of reversion to the days of isolationism, if any. The 'Anglo-Saxon' United States eventually embraced multiculturalism. More importantly, the United States replaced the geographically better positioned Europe as the focal point of world activity, perhaps, for good.

These strokes of good luck rather helped the United States to reduce its 'exceptional' image and transformed it into a more involved nation in international affairs. All said and done, it is undeniable that such strokes of good luck would have been in vain absent the American enterprise and brilliance to use them as stepping-stones in slowly building a Pax Americana through the elasticity of the 'American' specialties mentioned above and discussed a little later.

The 'Unique' United States and the real implications of the Declaration

Blessed with geography (because of its vast land, abundant natural resources, and the strong natural fortification by the two oceans) and cursed by history (because it happened to be under European colonial domination that threatened to deprive the nation of its creativity and freedom), independent America faced some unique challenges and guidelines, handed down to it by the Declaration of Independence, that continues till today. *It is in and through the messages of the Declaration and the American War of Independence that the entire trajectory of the American desires and ambitions, values and ideals, policies and perceptions, goals and the American uniqueness gets fully revealed.*

American Declaration and the War of Independence needed some compelling logic to convince its own people about the rational and need to sever all ties with the 'same' group of people, the Britishers. But that was not enough to explain away the full import of the Declaration. The American Declaration was not a mere spatial-temporal litany of justifying the American independence, but, like the Ten Commandments, it transcended the mundane aspirations and ambitions of the nation through its emphasis on 'natural' and 'universal' human rights and liberties. The Declaration had a global and universal message to help all other oppressed nations through the force of the American republican 'example'.

In the introduction to the Declaration of Independence – A History, (National Archives and Records Administrations) – we find:

"Nations come into being in many ways. Military rebellion, civil strife, acts of terrorism, acts of treachery, a thousand greater and lesser clashes between defenders of the old order and supporters of the new – all these occurrences and more have marked the emergence of new nations, large and small. The birth of our nation included them all. The birth was unique, not only in the immensity of the later impact on the course of world history and the growth of democracy, but also because"... so many of the threads in our national history run back through time to come together in one place, in one time, and in one document – the Declaration of Independence."

Successive American policies strove, incrementally, to complete the unfinished jobs of the Declaration. It is on a successful completion of these tasks that America's dream of its future world domination and the prospect for a stable and peaceful international order depends. It would, therefore, be crucial to briefly list the conditions and assumptions that had rendered the American War of Independence a partial success pending the fulfillment of its broader objectives, in addition to securing freedom.

First, as I have already mentioned, the American independence was premised on the crucial assumption of severing all ties with Britain, as a first and primary step towards independence. This severing of ties with the same group of people was the most difficult choice without any historical precedence. Consequently, the revolutionaries had to look 'elsewhere' to justify their war for independence. Lofty political and universal ideals, like, individual rights and liberty, free trade and equality, in short, what Margaret Mead called 'American Creed' or my American Cavalcade, were projected as possible alternative to the political system of its trans-Atlantic 'kindred'. In that respect the War of Independence had a double responsibility: attaining liberation and establishment of an alternative order.

The last condition is unusual in international history as independence struggles are usually focused on securing freedom at all costs. The United States, through its Declaration, not only envisioned an independent future for America but also felt able to manage its own affairs all by itself, for example, non-involvement in European conflicts. What is more, the American intellectuals who framed such a declaration of independence obviously lacked the administrative experience to translate its salient messages into practice at that time.

Secondly, the War of Independence was carried on the basis of a 'patched up' unity of thirteen disparate and independent colonies and there was virtually no hope that they wound band together in a common cause in ousting Britain. Way back in the mid-eighteenth century, Franklin was extremely pessimistic about any such unity amongst various American colonies. So the alliance seemed temporary and a matter of convenience that portended all the symptoms of further fragmentation of an already loose type of confederation. George Washington was concerned about the future of the American territorial unity and the same concern haunted the successive American presidents till the end of the Civil War. The issue of state-center relations plagued the United States for a long time since its independence. The role of government and the post revolutionary political organization of the United States of America remained extremely fluid and undefined till 1789 when a written Constitution and the subsequent amendments, the Bill of Rights, were adopted.

Thirdly, the treaty of Paris in 1783 rendered independence a 'partial' one for several reasons. First, it was far from being an economic one: European colonial powers like Spain and England controlled many of the North American territories and waterways, thereby, restricting free commercial activities of the new born nation. Secondly, Europe's grip over the Latin American countries in the Western Hemisphere made the American isolation more pronounced and the American independence more insecure. Thirdly, 'nationhood' took a definite shape much later, especially, after the unification, thereby, delaying and further complicating one of the major tasks of the Declaration that continues till today: the American *uncertainty and ambivalence towards traditional nationalistic values;* and last of all, America of the immediate post independent era was in an incomplete political shape that led Marx to call it a 'defiled' democracy. Besides slavery, the Indians retained their own government and nation. Various sub governments and thousands of sub-entities other than individual states remained in place. All these made the American job of giving a concrete and complete shape to its political structure extremely arduous and transcended history. Both federalism and republicanism were yet to come out of their experimental phases.

All the above conditions meant that the United States had its hands full with the jobs of realizing those unattainable objectives not only on a national but also on an international scale. After all, the initial trickle of water from the hitherto 'untried' (hitherto, not tried in a large country) republican fountain ran every risk of being dried up soon, absent some kind of 'messianic' mission for the new-born republic, desperately in need of pushing the hostile European powers on the defensive. The Monroe Doctrine and the Manifest Destiny marked the beginnings in that direction. In a word, this long list of unfinished jobs of the American independence meant that the road to the realization of the American ideals would be either long or may not be quite attainable.

Let me now discuss below some of the key 'American' specialties in the American Cavalcade, referred above. The American foreign policies, past, present, and future, can be best understood with a proper knowledge of these 'American' specialties consisting of: the American identity and nationhood, the American Creed (political ideals like liberty, democracy, equality, civil rights and justice), and such other related issues as the undefined role of the government in economic matters. They have not only made America 'exceptional' but also imbued the children of 'Israel' with a Manifest Destiny to recast the world in the American image. No doubt, the United States now exerts an irresistible magnetic pull over a large section of people in various parts of the world.

Paradoxically, none of these specialties were made in America. They were, rather, borrowed from Europe and simply planted on the 'American' soil by some disgruntled early European settlers. Let me, in the first place, discuss the intriguing issue of the American identity and its importance for the contemporary United States as a world leader.

Issue of the American identity

Modern American history starts with the European settlement of that vast landmass around the sixteenth century. Since then, it is the descendants of the dominant Anglo-Saxon group that had so far controlled the destiny of North America despite significant dilutions in the racial and cultural composition, over time. Huntington in his book *Who Are We* writes that in the late eighteenth century, around the time of independence, America was:

> Overwhelmingly white (thanks to the exclusion of blacks and Indians from citizenship), British, and Protestant, broadly sharing a common culture...By the end of the twentieth century, the number of Americans have multiplied almost one hundred times. America had become multiracial (roughly 69 per cent white, 12 per cent Hispanic, 12 per cent black, 4 per cent Asian and Pacific Islanders, per cent other), multi ethnic (with no majority ethnic group) and 63 per cent Protestant, 23 per cent Catholic, 8 per cent other religions and 6 per cent no religion.
>
> —*Huntington, 2004, p.11*

Interestingly, it was the Algonquians and the Iroquois who were the dominant nations of North America among eight other existing groups when the Europeans first came to settle there. It is said that the entire North America would have come under the domination of the powerful Iroquois group of nations had Columbus arrived a century later. The first Pilgrims found the Iroquois nations developed ones and even called them the Romans of the New World. It was not until late eighteenth century that British settlers on the Atlantic coast began to identify themselves with the Americans. Even the American Constitution is not free from the Iroquois influence.

Modern American ancestry thus dates back to the days of European settlement of that continent. Its 'core population' group belonged to the English Protestant parent stock. New England happened to be that nucleus of the 'first effective settlement' of a small band of original settlers from which emanated the messages of Anglo-Saxon Protestantism that gripped most of the North American continent in the subsequent years. This baptism by Britain determined America's national identity for successive generations. Misconception associated with America's 'rootlessness' is due to 'young' America's 'insufficient' historical development compared to the older European nations that had grown into mighty nation-states well before America attained independence.

The United States, after independence, ignored history (only to find itself on the 'right side of history' after the end of the Cold War) and rather remained busy with creating its own history since cultural issues like racism, ethnicity, nationhood, language, and religion dominated the whole of the nineteenth and the first half of the twentieth century. However, what worked for a nineteenth century 'isolationist' and 'weak' America proved increasingly anachronistic for a more involved and a strong United States in the twentieth and now in the twenty first century. For example, if the United States still prefers to express its identity in terms of its 'core' population group, as was the case during the whole of nineteenth century and the first half of the twentieth century, there is every possibility that either it would be branded as a 'racist' nation by modern human rights standards or more importantly, it would lose 'justification' for its war of independence from its kindred group. By that logic, independent America could well have stayed as a British 'dependency'. *The issue of America identity still remains an important and unfinished job of the Declaration and is inseparable from the American foreign policies.* Huntington affirms, "National interests derive from national identity. We have to know who we are before we can know what our interests are." (ibid, p.10)

On the other hand, the American political ideals (through which the US policy-makers seek to define the American identity and with which Huntington disagrees) rather acted as hindrances for America's expansion abroad and led the subsequent policy-makers to circumvent the constitutional limitations on territorial annexations through such indirect measures as 'export of democracy' and 'regime change'. Curiously enough, the American drive for its greatest expansionism (mostly internal) took place during the nineteenth century when the American identity was defined by traditional cultural values.

American leaders of the post 1945 era, on their part, realized that they couldn't continue with their earlier policy of 'assimilation' to deepen its (America's) Anglo-Saxon base, easy, as they might have been for the Magyars of Hungary in the 1770s or even of those of the Malays and the Turks in the latter days to follow. Economic factors, like, increased trade may be partially responsible for this multiethnic shift from 'melting pot' and 'assimilationist' views, but they fail to fully explain why even in an interdependent world, driven by the market forces, other countries, including Europe and Japan, have restrictive immigration policies.

The United States thought it right to adopt far more liberal immigration policies during the 1960s to create a multiethnic and multicultural society that would spawn a 'group' or 'class' of 'Americanized' people within these immigrant communities. Today, multiculturalism has become all but an acceptable official policy in America. The United States hopes that such groups and Diasporas would act as magnets for other people in their respective countries and would entice them to embrace the American culture and ways of life. *Another implication of adopting multiethnic course may be the deliberate and 'surreptitious' attempt to dilute the core population group that had built and sustained the 'American' republican system so long. Such dilution would simply remove the*

'American' element from the American republicanism. That way, it won't be difficult to justify the American expansionism abroad and even 'imperialism' in the coming decades. Indeed, this may be an ingenious way to rectify the 'forced error' committed by its founding fathers and to do away with the ideological component that hinders the proper discharge of the American foreign policies in the new millennium. After all, the mighty Soviet Union had to unwind its empire because of 'cultural-ideological' fetters. The US policy makers, since the beginning of the 1960s, have hit upon an ingenious policy to remove the republican wrap from its original political system!

In an international political arena defined by traditional cultural issues there is greater possibility of the US becoming a 'target' given its 'exceptionalism' and given the prevalence of anti-American resentments in many parts of the world. The United States can hardly afford to ignore the issue of 'culture' any longer since it happens to be the world leader now. The United States has got two options in this regard: either encourage multiculturalism to undermine the traditional conservatism of most other nations in respect of culture or to redefine its identity in terms of its core population group to bring it more in line with other 'culture-sensitive' nations. Interestingly, *both these options are equally applicable and open to the contemporary United States. A super power wielding its leadership in an increasingly interdependent world needs to present a more cosmopolitan face or it may go the way of cultural assertion because its superpower status would be void and useless if the United States fail to implant Americanzation on a global scale.*

The United States may have to contend with this intriguing and unresolved issue on the identity angle on two counts in future: if it remains strong yet expansionist or if it grows weaker. So long as it remains powerful, as it now is, others would dare not raise any voice regarding its age-old apathy to traditional values or require that America define its identity in terms of traditional values. Yet, if it encroaches on the sovereignties and cultures of other nations, that is, if the United States becomes aggressive and brazenly imperialist, these nations would try to point toward all sorts of 'meaningless' questions on its (America's) identity angle: Who are the Americans? What are their missions and designs? If they are truly republican in the 'exceptional' and 'American' sense that they claim to be and if the American Constitution never supported imperialism, why these Americans are behaving 'differently' now? Conversely, America may have to face the same problem if it becomes weak. No wonder in the 1980s, Japan emboldened by its economic supremacy, failed to resist its temptation to call America its 'dependency'.

There are several courses open to the United States in this respect: (1) the United States may remain strong yet moderate in its behavior and not force the pace of the Americanization while resolving the question of nationhood and identity, on a global scale, in the meantime. It would, however, take quite some time if the United States prefers to exercise this course. Every other great civilization took centuries to make their imprints on other cultures. That way, the United States need at least a few more decades, since, years can now be virtually counted in days, thanks to the unprecedented developments in information and technology; (2) the United States may ally with other Western countries to further the cause of the Western Civilization and engage in some sort of power sharing arrangements with its trans-Atlantic allies to control world affairs. Huntington writes, " If the United States is primarily defined by its European cultural heritage as Western country then it should direct its attention to strengthening its ties with Western Europe." (ibid, p.10) In that case the United States have to be more dependent on Europe in managing world affairs. This would narrow its 'freedom of action' and the United States would have to pay by sacrificing its hitherto privileged status of being a carefree 'individualistic', 'history – averse' nation possessed with a constant desire to 'create' the future; (3) the United States may prefer to go it alone and assert itself unilaterally, uncaring of what others think and feel. This last option is not without merits. *After all, history has presented a unique opportunity for the United States to transcend the limitations imposed by its 'disadvantaged' geographic location (to expand abroad) and its cultural ambiguity (America's time-to-time shift from 'assimilationism' to 'melting pot' to multiculturalism has enhanced this vagueness) in the new millennium.*

For the American civilization to have a lasting influence, as I have said a few lines earlier, it has got to stay as a world leader, at least, for another few decades or so. Otherwise, like its Soviet counterpart, it will go down in history as a mere meteor that burnt itself out within a brief period, but with a far more disastrous effect on its cultural and ethnic composition. While Russia had a long nationalist history, the United States don't enjoy that advantage. Despite being a multiethnic society, Russia has its own separate 'national' identity. But the already undefined history and culture of the United States, accentuated more by its recent liberal immigration policies, makes the American task on the identity angle more difficult. Unlike Japan, which owes its civilization in large measure to the Chinese, the United States doesn't enjoy Japan's history stretching over two millennia. America's best bet, under the circumstance is to ally more and more with its trans-Atlantic partners if the United States hopes to avert another period of isolation that may or may not be self imposed. At best, it can be the leader of the Western Civilization.

An examination of major American policies would reveal that it is the twin problem of geographical remoteness and its unorthodox concept about nationhood that underlay the security concerns of that country and that still guides the future American foreign policies. While the United States has little control over geography, it can't escape without addressing those unfinished jobs of the Declaration that was conceived and proclaimed with the sole objective of giving a concrete shape to some political 'experiments' and 'ideals' of which the issue of identity happened to be a primary one.

The new millennium demands the best out of the American genius. The United States must prove equal to the occasion. For the first time in history, the geographically remote and culturally ambivalent United States stands on the ash heaps of older civilizations and interacts directly with the rest of the world, all by itself. *Who knows we may see a 'second wave' of imperial domination now that the first stage of imperial era spanning about three millennia from the days of Persia, Greece, and Rome have come a full circle with the collapse of monarchy and colonialism.*

The crux is that the United States wants to identify 'Americanization' with its lofty ideals, which are, themselves, changeable and something on which other civilizations were not based, while hoping that other nations embrace the American ways of life. Evaluating civilizations solely on the basis of ever changing political values without reference to their ethnic and geographical background doesn't make much sense. When we talk of civilizations of the Babylonians or the Sumerians, we recall their cultural achievements and not so much their 'political' identities. Huntington rightly remarks, "The decisions as to who the people may be the result of long-standing tradition, war and conquest, plebiscite or referendum, constitutional provision, or other causes, but it cannot be avoided." (ibid, p.16). It is the ingenuity of the American founders that they solved this riddle of identity through resort to value based ideals instead of ascriptive factors. They knew, like wives, values may be changed but not the consanguinity and kinship. This left a small window for the future policy-makers to make the necessary adjustments in the identity angle.

Yet there is enough logic and justification on the part of the American academicians and policy-makers to claim that there remain very few unmixed races based on pure blood relations and unique languages, at present. Miscegenation and assimilation have irreversibly diluted these primary human values. Modern civilization is evolving towards a global civilization based on political values. If the people from other parts of the world rush to the United States to secure the American citizenship and if the American people themselves take pride in being the Americans, if the American money and goods dominate the world trade and consumption patterns, if the American technology and arms are in high demand in other parts of the world, does not the supremacy of the American values sound real? Why then the rest of the world is loath to unconditionally accept the Americanization and conspire against it?

The problem is that international politics is too complicated to allow any such sweeping generalizations. Nations don't behave on the basis of rational choice theories. *There is a large body of nations with different mind-sets that exist outside of the United States and with whom the United States has to interact.* Thus any attempt at 'homogenization' of cultures may mean an infringement on their sovereignties. At present, the United States can't desist from exerting its influence in that direction because it is too strong now. The harder it pushes other countries to accept the Americanization, the more exposed the United States would be to that odd question: who are the American people to assert their superiority over other cultures? Cultural fault lines are such that nations judge each other not so much by political motives as by intrinsic cultural values. This would result in bringing the restless gene out of the bottle, thereby, intensifying cultural clashes on a broader scale.

Admittedly, great power hegemony hardly remains confined to political, diplomatic or economic domains. As the French Premiere Ferry said long before that the assertion of cultural and civilizational superiority is one among the three primary goals of great power domination; the other two being 'political patriotic' and 'commerce'. Of what good is a great power if it fails to dominate the culture of others? In that sense the spread of Americanization is but a logical corollary to the US supremacy in world affairs. Physical domination of one country by another can attain significance only through cultural domination *since a country happens to be the bearer of a distinct identity.* This may be ethnicity, religion, ideal, or language. Otherwise, a great power would have little motivation to perpetuate its reign. *It would be important to note that the United States might be a on a slope if it fails to assert its cultural superiority over others. This is because it has already lost its principal motivation by winning over its superpower rival. It is axiomatic that the United States should find another common security threat or be culturally more assertive.*

American Republicanism

All the above mentioned unresolved issues find their glaring manifestations in a single political concept: the American republicanism. It was the 'nucleus' of the Declaration of Independence and it set the tone for all successive American foreign policies till today. The adoption of the American version of republicanism was a great political experiment and, interestingly, has a great implication for contemporary international politics now that the United States happen to be the undisputed world leader. It is on a correct perception of this single 'concept' that it would be possible to determine the direction of the future course of the American policies. Just as the fruits and growth of a tree has to be judged from its seeds, so also America's conduct of foreign policies, past, present, and future, flows from the American *republicanism*.

Republics are not new to human and political history. Republics existed in ancient city-states of Greece and Italy, in Rome, and in many other European countries at varying points of times. France alternated between monarchy and republicanism several times in the last two centuries while Germany, like the United States, had been composed of several republican states. It is the smaller states that had, rather, proved to be the nurseries of republicanism. America happens to be the only exception in which so vast a nation embraced, and even preserved an uninterrupted constitutional republicanism! That is why the Louisiana Purchase of 1803 from France that, by a single stroke, increased the American territory and the number of states several fold, was believed by many to pose a real problem for its republican system. Likewise, during another crisis moment of the American independent history, its territorial vastness created Constitutional complications in which several South American states opted for secession from the Union in the 1860s.

Republics may or may not be democratic. Republic of South Korea during the Cold War era had been under prolonged dictatorial rule. Monarchic republics had been neither new nor rare. Democracy, on the other hand, is the rule by majority and may be pure or representative in form. In both this form, democracy often degenerates into autocracy, despotism or dictatorship. Most of the countries in the world, barring, the United States, underwent this kind of political swap from democracy to different versions of republicanism and vice-versa on a number of occasions. The American republicanism, one main item in the American cavalcade mentioned above, was rather born on the premise of protecting minority rights be it property, religion, or ethnic.

Neither is it true that republics can't have empires. Imperial Rome had about five hundred years of republican experience. Classical Greek empire was no exception to this. Republican France had overseas colonies in the nineteenth and the twentieth centuries. But all these republics were different from the 'American' form of republicanism. All these republics made 'war' a principal vehicle of spreading their political and cultural influences elsewhere. As a result, it was easy for these republics to produce dictators, like Alexander the Great, Caesar or Napoleon because force happened to be the bedrock of their political existences. The American republicanism, on the other hand, is entirely different from this classical form of republicanism. Independent America was born in reaction to European political systems and the latter's war 'hysteria'.

The United States not only denounced the European monarchic systems but also disapproved the 'militaristic' foundations of the European nations. Newly independent America preferred to keep its armed forces at a minimum level lest a large military establishment necessitated an enhanced role for the federal government, generated imperialistic ambitions, and adversely affected the individual and local rights and liberties. That means, while other European republics were flexible enough in changing their political forms and aspirations, the United States was bound by certain lofty political ideals that still guides its polices and that often creates 'real' complications in its new role even in a changing international scenario!

Republican and anti-monarchic America was created on a mysteriously 'creative' principle, like, the life forces, that simply generated its own momentum through constant recreation of its own 'species'. No doubt, this particular American dynamic breathes a new life into 'other' political systems. It is as if the United States, thanks to its Declaration, discovered an 'indestructible' golden seed – its 'creative' principle – that made the American system 'superior' to all other systems because the latter lacked the 'innocence' and 'transparency' of the former.

This creative principle had sprung both from the fervent desire for political freedom from oppressive colonial rules (and hence had universal appeal for all other colonies spread the world over) and from the innate human desire for individual liberty. In a word, this creative principle has its origin in the irrepressible urge for liberty. Liberty and equality had been the two cornerstones of this American creative 'principle' and both these ideas pertain mainly to the domain of politics. The American founding fathers touched a raw nerve in the European colonial practices by making individual liberty, rights, and equality the linchpin of the American identity. More generally, the American republicanism based on the American 'principle' threatened to tear loose that invisible thread of 'imperialist' exploitation that had so long shaped the human history and the international political order.

The seed of this enlightened American 'principle, as I have said, was impregnated with some 'mysterious' and 'extra-terrestrial' energy that were, however, attributed to such mundane factors as, America's vast size, its energetic racial group, the role of the Puritans and the New Englanders, a weak central government, absence of hostile neighborhoods, federalism, preponderance of various private associations, individual initiatives, and corporations, and all such other concepts for which Tocqueville racked his brains in writing his masterpiece on the American democracy. Early American New Englanders were perhaps the children of Israel who were endowed by divinity with some indestructible and messianic 'spirit'.

The United States, now, as ever, hopes to change the established international order while keeping its domestic political structure intact. The American policy makers believe that others can repeat the American feat by limiting the role of governments, encouraging free trade and expanding the frontiers of individual rights and liberty in their respective countries and that it is they (other nations), and not the United States, that *must* change in order to prosper peacefully.

For over a century till the mid-1880s the United States somewhat managed to maintain its non-entanglement (not without occasional and deliberate deviations) in world affairs and kept the role of the federal government and its military at a minimum level. Vast unexplored lands to the West offered a 'safety valve' for the continuation of the American federal republic. What went unnoticed in the process was that the American republicanism thrived on its internal westward colonization by not only laying claim to Indian lands but also by resorting to a sort of 'ethnic' cleansing in which the Indians were systematically annihilated and pushed deep into the interior 'reservations'. This concealed 'colonialism' was justified on the ground that the United States was, after all, grabbing no man's lands and even compensated the displaced Indians by offering them 'inferior' and 'used up' lands, as the latter were incapable of developing the technique and the mind-set to cultivate fertile lands. Self-government might be the 'established fact in the United States', but "for other peoples a reward to be obtained after a long and painful process of education." Obviously 'civilizing' the barbarians became a routine vocal tonic for the United States in declaring war against Mexico and in occupying the far off Philippines in the Far East in the latter decades. The American republicanism, invariably, contained seeds of expansionism

The American republicanism was established for the maintenance of civil rights and smooth 'center-state' relations within its own territory. The American successive policy-makers realized the 'unsuitability' of the 'American' republican system to act a model for the rest of the world. Orestes A. Brownson in his American Republic felt that the American republicanism must not be construed as converting other nations to its own type. Nor should America force others to accept its republican model, which is always country-specific. According to him the defining feature of the American republicanism was 'territorial' democracy.

Yet, successive generations of the American policy-makers were not willing to repeat the same forced 'error' made under compelling circumstances of the war for American independence. Every remnants of its colonial past, like slavery, deprivation and decimation of the Indians, invocation of Monroe Doctrine and The Manifest Destiny were allowed to have full interplay in the American republican system as the United States sought to justify its expansionism by pointing to the 'odds of security and survival' in hostile surroundings.

After all, a country must first of all feel safe and secured before it can project its lofty principles beyond its borders. However, nobody knows the exact nature of such 'security needs' and what are its limits. Logically, such a perception may lead one to either conclude that the republican system can't continue in a single country or that a country must grow strong by any means to defend its republican system. In both the cases, this means that one has got to expand 'outward'. The Soviet Union, after its birth, faced the same problem and resorted to expansionism. *Republican America was destined to expand outside its national geographical borders and for a capitalist republican America it was a fait accompli.* I have made a theoretical analysis of this factor of 'expansionism' in the next chapter.

It is not that the American founding fathers committed any mistake at a particular historical epoch but they, obviously, left much for posterity to navigate that 'Noah's Ark' through the turbulent waters of international 'maelstrom' to its chosen destination. What led their founders to take such enormous risks in declaring the war for independence, against so many odds, was America's unique geographical location. They reasoned that no political system or state was a permanent affair but that a vast country like America, insulated by two vast oceans, stands least vulnerable to security threats from outside forces, provided their successors behaved in a diplomatic manner.

The United States enjoyed another great advantage, thanks to the establishment of the republican system on its continent. From the very planting on the soil of independent America, its republican seed contained several features that served several American interests, in the later decades. As a result, growth in any direction was justified as an offshoot of the 'republican' values. *In short, the United States has always found a golden mine in its 'messianic' republicanism, whether this meant justifying its entry into the two world wars in the name of delivering freedom, or waging the Cold War in the name of doing the same, or in leading the current globalization movement, in the name of ensuring peace and prosperity for every nation on the earth.* This binary constitution of a half-religious (Anglo-Protestantism influenced the independent American development for well over a century since 1776) and half-political (relying on its own lofty republican ideas instead of traditional values of the old world) seed of republicanism have so far given the United States an unique advantage in world politics. For example, if anything went wrong with the international order prior to 1989, the United States could point to the shortcomings in the European and the Soviet political systems, which meant that only an unreserved acceptance by others of the American system, could provide the necessary alternative. But things are reversed in the new millennium in which it is the United States that finds itself to be the cynosure of the neighboring eyes, and on the defensive, while it is the rest of the world that judges the United States from a common plank of anti-American sentiment!

American federalism

State-center relations occupy an important place in the American Declaration. America earned its political freedom on the strength of unity among the thirteen colonies in which the independence and full autonomy of each colony was guaranteed. The inadequacy of the Articles of Confederation framed during the War of Independence and the suspicion of the states to vest powers in the national government led to the Philadelphia Convention in 1787 to frame the US Constitution with a view to form a 'more perfect Union'.

The framers of the Constitution and the participating states arrived at a compromise and reserved separate roles for both the federal and the state governments. The United States Constitution shunned both the confederated and a centralized type of government and embraced 'federalism' in which the people retained their sovereignties and vested some powers to both the national and the state governments while themselves belonging to both the national and the respective state governments. The Federalist Papers constantly kept on emphasizing the need for more power to the federal government to ensure the republic's security in managing foreign commerce and a common currency so vital to run the country's economy. The enhancement of the power of the federal government generated its own momentum in which the center itself developed its own separate identity, sometimes, even at the expense of the state powers and resources.

Externally, the United States extended its global influence at the expense of the existing European powers, while, internally, the federal government went on to consolidate its power, in tandem with, and sometimes, even at the expense of the states. The entire debate about the state–center relations the views expressed by the American think tanks like Madison, Jefferson and Hamilton in the Federalist Papers clearly revealed that the American Revolution had a definite purpose. This purpose was to transform the United States from rags to riches and from insignificance to world prominence in which the role of the national government would be extremely crucial. It is this very state-center issue that still stands in the way of the United States' pursuing a clear foreign policy commensurate with its present status, particularly, in the absence of a 'common' enemy in contemporary international politics.

American federalism, however, has undergone vast changes since independence and reveals two opposing trends, now. While the influences of the state and the federal governments have increased with the passage of time, the American global engagement now leaves more room for external factors to influence its domestic political set up. Take NAFTA and globalization, for example. More integrated and interdependent trade relations between the United States, Mexico, and Canada may require more international trade agreements than the national government can alone conduct. Conversely, national government may be more amenable to the pressures from the multinational corporations than being sympathetic to the local and the state sentiments, as is evident in various instances of the off shore business activities, by remaining oblivious to local unemployment problems. On the other hand, the influence of ethnic communities and Diasporas in the contemporary American politics is on the rise. There has been an increase in the power of each individual state as these states are given a consultative role in these trade issues. More global interaction on a state-to-state level would rather augment the influence of each individual state vis-à-vis the national government.

The power and influence of the federal government vis-à-vis the state governments shot up steadily as an outgrowth of the New Deal of the 1930s and the 'cooperative federalism' of the 1950s and 1960s in which the center through its grants-in-aid system required the states to undertake projects in selected areas. This power and reach of the national government grew exponentially during Johnson's Great Society Program that penetrated most other areas under the state jurisdictions. The US Congress, in the latter decades used its Constitutional powers to regulate the interstate commerce, imposed many conditions on the states and required them to undertake certain projects without providing any financial assistance under the 'unmandated' projects. Such an assault on state 'sovereignties' continued till the Supreme Court gave a verdict in the US-Lopez case in 1995 to the effect that the Congress had overstretched its jurisdiction and that the national government must not intrude into the jurisdiction of the states.

Two contradictory currents run through the center-state relations in the contemporary United States. On the one hand, during the decade of the 1990s, President Clinton and his Deputy Al Gore favored more devolution of power on the state and the local authorities and urged the need to solve problems on a local basis that would entail least cost. On the other hand, the enhanced role of the Supreme Court in interpreting the Constitution has given rise to a sort 'legal realism' in which the court appears to be sole lawmaker, thereby, putting the liberty of common people, as enshrined in the Declaration, in jeopardy. The net result is that the federal and the central government would always try to create a situation of 'security' threat, imagined or real, to enhance their powers amidst such confusions.

Earlier, the United States had used force to assert the right of the center over the states, as in the case of the great Civil War. Seen that way, a roll back to the pre-independence era of separate colonies and hence separate republics may not be ruled out, at least, in theory. The American *leaders know that such a theoretical possibility could become a reality only if the present American 'empire' collapses. The lesson of the dissolution of the Soviet empire and its subsequent disintegration into separate republics can't be underestimated. Thus, one of the compelling needs of the United States is to retain its world influence in order to avert such domestic crises at home. Foreign policy for the United States happens to be its live wire to keep both its federalist system and the federal government intact, just as Westward expansion offered a unique opportunity to deflect Center-State tensions.*

Conclusion

It is simply impossible for the present day United States to turn inward and to direct all its attention to domestic issues as suggested by some diplomats, statesmen, and writers, especially, after the end of the Cold War. In this connection, one must take note of the racial controversy that swept the whole of the United States in the early years of the 1990s on the 'affirmative' issue. The fact is that the 'interests' of states can be subdued in national interest so long as the country faces a common external security threat. However, these pent up grievances may blow up a country's unity once that 'common' glue is gone, as happened in post-communist Yugoslavia. *The United States still has two foots, one each on the boat of its republican-federalist ideals and another on its 'imperial ambition' to sustain its domestic harmony and territorial integrity. This means that the impact would be double in the case of the United States if any 'disaster' befalls that country. The United States must either find a way to calibrate its world hegemonic role through a step-by-step reduction of its republicanism and gradual empowerment of the center even if those halcyon days of realism of the Cold War era may not return so soon, or vice-versa, that is, gradual reduction of its global 'overstretch' without harming its domestic political structure.*

The United States grew from insignificance to a super power in a matter of less than two hundred years. But the 'incompleteness' connected with the birth of independent America, discussed above, started to unravel as the United States assumed a more assertive role in the world politics. The crux of American successive foreign policies lay on this very fact that the federal-republican America was born out of a compulsive need to attain liberation but was 'ill conceived' to carry its ideals beyond its borders. The job of resolving the crucial contradiction between the American republicanism and its 'appropriate' international role rested on the successive American presidents.

The time has arrived for the American leaders to redesign the state-center relations on a more concrete footing if the United States hopes to perpetuate its world hegemony. Since many American states were formed through the use of force, (the Mexican War, for example) and since the American unity itself was ensured through armed campaigns, as in the Civil War, there are efforts at redressing some past wrongs, in recent years. The American overtures towards Mexico in the recent decades (through the NAFTA and its soft immigration policies towards that country) clearly reveal that the United States is in the earnest to solve the long drawn Mexican grievances against America's annexation of a large chunk of that country during the Mexican war. The United States simply doesn't want to leave any lacuna as a result of its past actions in order to allow another Napoleon III of France or the Wilhelm's Germany or even a communist turned capitalist China to fish in the troubled waters of the Caribbean or Latin American lakes.

Yet the crux lies elsewhere. Had the United States been weakened by, say, the Cold War, it would never have been in a position to act so brazenly and unilaterally. Conversely, the absence of a strong leader might have precipitated unprecedented international anarchy. That way, might is still the right and the future of the US world hegemony depends very much on this force component. Successive chapters in this book would show how the United States relied more on force and less on its creed to rise to world prominence. Another factor, good or bad, is that the United States is too powerful in most areas and hence like a wealthy man enjoys the luxury of several options simultaneously. All these contribute towards the American indecision in the new millennium in pursuing a definite course.

Imperialism, by its very nature, had been exclusive and had to depend on some supreme authority for its political conduct. Republicanism, on the other hand, happens to be inclusive with a greater breadth and pluralism. That way, the United States had always an extra option that allowed the Eagle to soar into unknown heights while keeping its eyes fixed on its republican goals. Should an eventuality befall the American republic, the nation could still recover by ceding some rights to the federal government to stem the rot, without any friction, for example, the era of the New Deal. But the reverse can't happen in the case of the imperial powers without revolution, overthrow, or insurrections. This 'undefined' political space happens to be America's real advantage. The United States, because of the above 'space' factor, can continue with its present course till a new threshold is reached. Seen that way, it is the federal government that holds the key to the success of past, present and future direction of the American political and economic system.

On top of all these, the twenty first century belongs to the information and the communications age. This factor alone would lead the United States to divine ways and means to perpetuate its world hegemony, irrespective of that country's political and constitutional set-up. Nearly half a century ago, the economic historian Harold Innis pointed out that the geographical limits of empires were determined by communications and that, historically, advances in the technologies of transport and communications have enabled empires to grow.

References and readings

Gegen Standpunkt, the American *Power and its use, B.7. The domestic foundations for America's worldwide success: land and people under capitalistic management,* http//www.gegestandpunkt.com/English/us_pow_b.html#note1.

John M. Owen, *Liberal Peace, Liberal Democracy, the American Politics and International Security,* Cornell University Press, Ithaca, NY.

Theodore Roosevelt: *Corollary to the Monroe Doctrine*, December 6, 1904, http//www.u-s-history.com/pagesh1449.htm

Introduction to the Declaration of Independence – A History, (National Archives and Records Administrations).

Samuel P. Huntington, *Who We Are? The Challenges to America's National Identity*, NY, Simon & Schuster, 2004.

Samuel P. Huntington, *The Clash of Civilizations and the Remaking of the World Order*, Simon & Schuster, NY, London, Toronto, Sydney, 1996.

Niall Smith, the American *Empire, Roosevelt's Geographer and the Prelude to Globalization*, University of California Press, Berkeley & Los Angeles, London, 2004.

Frederick Jackson Turner, *The Frontier in the American History*, NY, 1920.

Hans Kohn, the American *Nationalism: An Interpretive Essay*, NY, 1957.

Rogers M. Smith, *The 'American Creed' and the American Identity: The Limits of Liberal Citizenship in the United States*, "Western Political Quarterly, 41" (June 1988)

Judith Goldstein and Robert O. Keohane eds., *Ideas and Foreign Policy: Beliefs, Institutions, and Political Change*, Ithaca, 1993.

Edward W. Said, *Orientalism*, NY, 1978.

Oswald Spengler, *Decline of the West*, NY, 1926.

Arnold Toynbee, *A Study of History*, London, 1934, 12 vols.

Orestes A. Brownson, the American *Republic*, Lanham, 1972.

Charles A. Beard and Mary A. *Beard, The Rise of the American Civilizations*, NY, 1927, 2 vols.

Louis Hartz, *The Founding of New Societies: Studies in the History of the United States* , Latin America, South Africa, Canada, and Australia, NY, 1964.

Headley Bull, *The Anarchical Society: A Study of Order in World Politics*, NY, 1977.

William H. MacNeill, *Rise of the West: A History of the Human Community*, Chicago, 1963.

Carroll Quigley, *The Evolution of Civilizations: An Introduction to Historical Analysis*, NY, 1961.

Samuel P. Huntington, *Political Order in Changing Societies*, New Haven, 1968.

Alexis de Tocqueville, *Democracy in America*, NY, 1954

Seymour Martin Lipset, *The First New Nation, The United States in Historical and Comparative Perspective*, NY, 1973.

Robert O. Keohane and Joseph S. Nye Jr., *Power and Interdependence*, NY, 2000.

Richard Rosecrance, *The Rise of the Trading State: commerce and Conquest in Modern World*, NY, 1986.

Snyder, Jack L., *Myths of Empire: Domestic Politics and International Ambition, Ithaca*, NY, Cornell, 1991.

Stanley Hoffmann, *More Perfect Union: Nation and Nationalism in America*, Harvard International Review, MA, 1997/1998.

Federalist Papers, The Avlon Project at Yale Law School, http//www.yale.edu/lawweb/avlon/federal/fed.htm.

Louis Hacker, *Major documents in the American Economic History*, NY, 1961.

An Online history of the United States, Age of the American Imperialism, the US Intervention in Latin America., http//www.smplanet.com/imperialism/teddy.html

Daqing Yang, *Technology of Empire, Telecommunications and Japanese Imperialism,1930-1945*, MA, 2003.

M. Burns, ed., *The American Idea of Mission, Concepts of national purpose*, NJ, 1967

Cecil V.Crabbb, Jr., *The Doctrines of the American Foreign Policy, Their Meaning, Role and Future*, Barton, Rouge and London, 1982.

CHAPTER II

POLITICS OF DOMINATION

"The world only goes round by misunderstanding"
— Charles Baudelaire

The urge for 'appreciation' and 'recognition' happens to be the innermost craving of every individual and nation. Such a desire for recognition may take many forms and may entail various means, fair or foul. These forms and means, in turn, depend on time, place, interest, outlook, and capability of the concerned actor to properly manifest. One individual or a nation may think at a given time and under a given condition that a cooperative and a friendly image would be more conducive towards influencing others, while under a different circumstance, the same individual or nation may feel that it has got to be more assertive. Both these approaches contain a least common denominator – the 'spirit of domination'.

Domination by itself happens to be a relative concept because it presumes the existence of the 'subjugator' and the 'subjugated', the superior and the inferior, and the strong and the weak. Power, supremacy, and domination, in turn, are all dependent on both the subjective and the objective conditions. Human mind always needs something against which to engage itself amidst doubts and trusts, hopes and fears. Human mind simply can't act otherwise. The bottom line is that if a nation is weak, others will dare to harass it while if that nation happens to be strong, others will defer to it. That means the domination level of any nation is proportional to the amount of power it can project to the outsiders. More specifically, this domination spirit is intertwined with human 'ego'.

Power, freedom, justice, and the 'spirit of domination'

Indeed man is a political animal. Political concepts arose out of some fundamental human needs, like, man's desire for freedom, power, right, and recognition. While economic improvements go a long way towards liberating human beings from the chain of poverty by creating many new channels of activities and wants, thereby, providing more means for their satisfactions, it can neither ensure complete equality nor true liberty. Yet, economic independence always happens to be the first and primary step in that direction. Political freedom is meaningless without economic emancipation. It took the United States another war (the US-Britain war of 1812) after the Revolution to attain complete economic independence. Economic equality (no matter how it was practiced), rather, led to the repression over the minority and rampant corruption in the former communist countries. On the other hand, philosophy, religion, and ethics have their own standardized and 'impersonal' set of ideas but they more often than not impede the flowering of the real personality. Freedom and the flowering of true personality can take place in a proper environment that further realizes and reinforces the inner craving for freedom. Freedom can be fully enjoyed as a social concept only and ensured only by constantly overcoming challenge. After all, eternal vigilance is the price of freedom. That means, power and more power

Power is needed to change things and conditions, but there ought to be an inherent motivation and justification to do so. That motivation is provided by the desire for 'freedom', 'right', and 'recognition' whether in the shape of the 1776 American Revolution or the 1917 Bolshevik revolution. An objective and external change or, more specifically, a speedy 'material' change in the external environment instead of a gradual or evolutionary process, can fulfill the desire for freedom and recognition more fully for 'human beings' at a given time. When I talk of 'human beings, I also presume the role of instinctive forces in shaping society, at the same time.

'Power' (used to effect external changes both as a means to liberation and subjugation), and 'morality' (whether arising out of Freudian 'guilt feeling' or a deep inner craving of the human mind) are the two essential tools that can ensure *human* freedom, in the fullest measure, since they relate to both the inner and outer realms of human beings. A person or a nation may crave for a more desirable surrounding that would give it more freedom of action and hence recognition, yet things may remain at the same level for decades, nay, even centuries, if no real efforts are applied to *change* that surrounding. African underdevelopment for centuries is one such example. On the other hand, too much effort may invite disaster and rather subjugation. For over several centuries, the European powers fought endless wars amongst themselves that brought them to the brink of destruction after WWII.

On the instinctive level, too, there is no denying the fact that emotions and ideas residing in the deep recesses of the unconscious or the 'id' need to be constantly drawn above the surface and transduced into more concrete emotional energies capable of shaping external reality and, in the process, freeing human beings from both the fetters of ignorance as well as pessimism, indolence, inertia, and subjugation. The truth is that only a judicious and conscious use of power, reasoning, and intelligence can effect such a change and that judiciousness also requires a proper mix of emotion, spirit, imagination, morality, a sense of universal well-being and brotherhood, and initiative. The next stage is to maintain and augment the sphere of that freedom and 'recognition' and that means the need for more change in external and 'material' conditions. This process goes on endlessly. A constant desire to recreate and change the status quo had been the defining characteristics of the Graeco-Roman and the Anglo-Protestant cultures of the West.

According to Morgenthau, power may "comprise anything that establishes and maintains the control of man over man. This power covers all social relations which serve that end, from violence to the most subtle psychological ties by which one mind controls another." In other words, it is the spirit of domination in human beings that regulates human social conducts through the interplay of force and inducement, sticks and carrots. One characteristic feature of human beings and nations is their desire to prove indispensable to others in order to make the latter dependent on the former. This is as true of a superpower like the United States as that of a tiny nation like Bangladesh. The entire edifice of the balance of power politics stands on this rationale, ranging from the use of 'sticks to carrots', and from 'coercion' to 'cooperation'. *But the underlying instinct behind this desire to engage others is the spirit of 'domination' that could be explained by the famous psychological law that in order to convince others one has first to allow oneself to be convinced by the former. And only then can one have full power over ones 'target'.* This is the inducement factor referred above. It is not possible in this book to deal with the full range of ideas connected with 'domination' spirit but it would be sufficient to take note of the fact that not much attention has been paid by the scholars in this angle, so far.

It is the presence of rationality in human minds that leads individuals, groups, and nations to look for common areas of interest and compromise because without cooperation no human group, society, or nation would endure. While the means to gain more power and domination may range from war to outright revolution to mutual treatise and agreements, pragmatism demands greater reliance on cooperation and agreements. Both Kant and Locke favored peace and cooperation instead of force and violence to create a sound political society. These writers, unlike Hobbes, believed in the innate 'good' nature of human beings for better human social conduct. For Hobbes, human society is, nasty, brutish, and short, while the international arena is an anarchic and a 'free for all' situation. It is, therefore, relevant, first of all, to have a psychoanalytical glimpse into human behaviors that generates the spirit of domination in human mind. But before that, let me discuss a few lines about the role of justice in human society.

Justice, one of the chief components of human political activity (because trust, faith, and security can be best ensured by convincing others through proper codes and observances), may mean many things to many people depending again on respective needs, interests, perceptions, convictions, time, and place. A drug baron's idea of justice is quite different from that of a person engaged in humanitarian activities. Conflicts and wars may arise out of clash of various interests but basically the conflicting parties would go to the extreme only when they feel that they have been wronged and pushed to the point of no return. Such a perception of the right or the wrong arises out of the need to get the other party to accept the latter's 'faults', through either force or persuasion – a relative issue again. The eradication of the 'wrong' per se is not the issue because what is wrong for one may appear justified to one's adversary and even to the same person at a different time. Incidentally, it is quite likely that the 'wronged' party in question would hardly desist from dominating others even 'unlawfully', *if it develops the capability* to do so. Remember, even a lean pig rages; even a hare would kick a dead lion.

It is the sudden 'paroxysm' of justice in human minds that spurs one nation or a group within a nation to carry out 'just' wars in the name of 'redressing' wrong and establishing 'justice'. Since nothing is wrong in love and war, the latter hardly remains a 'just' war. Even the holiest of wars were the bloodiest and most protracted in human history. This leads us to conclude that in the absence of the above spirit of 'domination', justice has little relevance. As soon as we talk of justice, a relative concept, the need to establish it arises because if justice can't be established, there is no use propagating that concept. Underlying this issue of establishing justice is the 'domination' spirit that leads one nation to fabricate 'just' causes to invade another, as was done by Hitler.

Underlying psychology behind the Spirit of domination

Scholars are divided regarding the role of objective forces and human instincts in shaping the external environment. Freud laid far greater stress on human instinctive forces in governing human actions. For Freud, consciousness expresses itself only in response to instinctual energies that lie in the "id" and on how these 'irrational' energies guide human behavior at a given time. According to Freudian psychoanalysis, it is 'largely' through the matrix of these subjective and irrational instincts that we interact with and even conceive of reality and the objective world.

Freud stressed that ego consciousness happened to be an expression of the inner urges and he defined human instincts as " a measure of the great demand made upon the mind for work in consequence of its connection with the body." It may be assumed that when he talks of 'its connection' with the body' he might have in mind the storehouse of the racial memory in the brain resulting from endless previous experiences. The reader must remember that without a social context, such instinctive behaviors are of no value. Even when we discuss a kid's behavior, we have the social factor in the back of our mind. This materialistic conception of instincts marked a watershed in delinking human behaviors from the realms of earlier theological mysticism and established the fact that nature and the outside world, as a separate entity, can also influence our 'consciousness'. Dress, food habits, cultural interactions are few such examples.

This means, human consciousness and human action are conditioned both by the instinctive, that is, subjective, as well as the objective world. *But there can be no denying the fact that the outside world or nature would have little value to human beings absent our instinct-driven consciousness.* Sheer reliance on mechanical sense perceptions could hardly elevate human beings from the level of their animal counterparts. Outside world would hardly impact human beings in any different way than the animals if the instinctive world of the human mind had no connection with that 'mysterious' factor called 'intelligence' and 'reason'. Human brain is the seat of that intelligence. The indubitable fact is that brain resides within the confines of human body. Brain cannot exist independently of the human body. As a result, brain and consciousness are bound intricately to the 'whims' of even the wildest of our bodily instincts be it sexual or any other fantasy. Animal world is deprived of this marvelous gift of human intelligence, instinct, and reason.

Human beings are rational despite those irrational and uncontrollable 'instincts'. This can be explained by the existence of a curious mechanism in human metabolic system: the adaptability factor without which human species ran the risk of getting "selected against" by nature. During the prolonged evolutionary process, human mind, like human body, discarded some of the previous attributes and traits and embraced newer ones through the process of 'natural' mental selection. Darwin, in his Descent of Man, thought that if moral and intellectual faculties were formerly of high importance to the primeval man and to his ape-like progenitors, they would have been perfected or advanced through natural selection. Now this process of mental selection at a higher and advanced stage (once the physical developments ceased) in human society helped crystallize some core or basic 'ideas' in the human consciousness because a well developed society simply can't stand on an ever-changing foundation. These ideas, in turn, became ideologies of a given socio-political system at a given time.

Interestingly, once these ideas get transferred from the ego to the super ego, they create a sort of 'superiority' complex from which it is extremely difficult, if not 'catastrophic', for an individual or even a nation to extricate and to adapt to a new system. At least, the task of further adaptation becomes extremely difficult and painful, as happened when the communist ideology literally blew off in the early 1990s or in the case of revolutionary changes in the existing socio-economic system of any country, say, under the impact of globalization and neo-liberalism. Habits die hard. The crux is whether to relinquish those ideas altogether or to modify them substantially to avert a 'psychological' catastrophe. Russian President Putin, in a recent interview to BBC News channel referred to the trauma suffered by the Soviet citizens through the loss of their country's super power status. Such a kind of shock resulted from both the loss of status in the external world as well as a shock to the belief on 70 years of ideological indoctrination.

The importance of the above discussion on the foreign policy of nations can't be underestimated. For example, the United States now finds itself in some sort of an impasse in the new millennium because of some radical changes in the 'external', 'objective', international situation following the collapse of communism. The uncertainty in the objective world impacts its inner core of republican ideals, too. Such crisis situations, however, were not new to that country's history. While the United States could regroup its inner reserves in all previous occasions as described in the next part, the present impasse is the result of some fundamental alteration in the international order or due to a systemic change that requires nothing short of an 'internal' cleansing or substantial modification of older ideals and even the adoption of newer ones. How the United States can do this is discussed below, but the fact remains that in this case both the national psyche and objective international situation impact the American 'cognition' in almost equal measure. The result is that there is a conflict between the American 'psychological' constitution developed through the centuries-old adherence to its lofty political ideals and the need to adapt to the perceptions and interests of the outside world in the changing international political milieu. The United States has got to incorporate these changes to modify its political ideals and it is the degree of modification (some sort of plastic surgery as discussed in Part III) that ought to be the focus of the US foreign policy concerns in the new millennium.

However, there is hope and promise for the United States. The unfinished jobs of the Declaration, referred in the earlier chapter, take into account both these factors since the Declaration happened to be a 'dialectical' charter in which the future was supposed to be the 'recreation' of the past but without the 'undesirable' elements of the past. 'American specialties' discussed in the first chapter constitutes the Freudian 'super ego' both to arrest as well as to expedite such transitions. That is why, post 1945 foreign policies of the United States took full account of the above 'functions' of the super ego and vested it with a kind of parallel approach to install 'liberal democratic capitalism' alongside its main policy of the Soviet containment so that the loss of that superpower could not destabilize the United States in any way.

American 'absolute' mind-set and the 'spirit of domination'

America's increasing reliance on some 'absolutist' and axiological approaches in respect of certain international issues is a clear manifestation of the 'spirit of domination' referred above. Although Kant held that 'principles' ought not to be sacrificed under any circumstance, the United States is facing some problems in its moralistic angles for quite some time. Morgenthau was critical of such American exceptionalism and cautioned, "Political realism refuses to identify the moral aspiration of a particular nation with the moral laws that govern the universe."

According to Leo Strauss, the chief function of a political society is 'self-preservation' and 'self-improvement'. The classical political philosophers held that the "survival and independence of one's own political community" ought to be that community's chief foreign policy goal. Strauss goes on, "Hence classical political philosophy is not guided by questions concerning the external relations of the political community. It is concerned primarily with the inner structure of political community." For Socrates, it is the 'city's material needs', that is, another way of saying the 'survival of one's political community', that may justify foreign territorial occupation. Since justice or the way of reasoning may be manipulated, depending on circumstances, for the post independent and the nineteenth century America it was 'The Manifest Destiny' that justified that country's internal and 'material needs' (although it is hard to justify this reasoning given the fact that the United States had never any dearth of land or resource) that justified expansionism and the Socretian 'noble' lie was that the savages ought to be trained in order to qualify for the self-governance of their territories. Coincidentally, 'higher purpose' or the Manifest Destiny served the logic of expansionism to justify the protection of one's citizens and the survival of the state as well. As a result, in the said American case, the line between realism and moralism is extremely thin.

Take the case of oil. If oil happened to be the overriding American concern to save the nation and its citizens, in short, the nation's 'material needs' to justify America's Gulf campaigns, the issue of the 'domination' principle becomes central to the US policies. The United States hoped to curb the domination instinct of Saddam (by disgorging Iraq out of Kwait) to ensure greater freedom for its regional and other allies in the 1992 Gulf War, not to speak of ensuring smooth supplies of oil. Conversely, in the second war against Iraq in 2003, the United States rather revealed its *own* domination instinct more blatantly by its flagrant violation of the sentiments even of its allies even though Iraq had not invaded any of its neighbors, at that time. So, the United States needed to resort to a 'noble lie' -Iraq's possession of the Weapons of Mass Destruction and also the issue of freedom of the Iraqi people from Saddam's atrocities. But the allies and the rest of the world were not convinced. But undergirding this US policy was the deep desire to control the energy resources of the Gulf region with a view to securing its 'material needs'. America's success in the early Iraqi campaign in 1991 rather enhanced and emboldened its own domination instinct to the extent of defying logic and the real situation.

To sum up, the United States thus revealed its domination spirit in two different circumstances: in the first case it was to decrease Saddam's domination instincts and in the second case, emboldened by its previous success, the United States acted on its own domination instinct so much so that it hardly desisted from acting on a shadowy pretext of Saddam's efforts towards acquisition of Weapons of Mass Destruction (WMDs). In both the cases, however, the overriding American concern was the 'material needs' for its cities: oil. The noble lie was Iraq's possession of WMDs because there are many other countries with such weapons already at their disposal to which the United States almost turned a blind eye, venting only occasional displeasures. Such a 'spirit of domination' found its glaring expression during the last decade of the nineteenth century when social Darwinism, international Manifest Destiny and racial supremacy dominated the American foreign policy perceptions at that time. It was just because the United States happened to be a strong and dominant power compared to its weak neighbors that the former was tempted to reveal its domination spirit. This spirit of domination was exacerbated by racism and Yellow Journalism in the 1890s, the Bankers group during WWI and the 'greed and cronyism' of the American corporate world in the post Cold War decades. For domination spirit to sustain, it must be fed continuously by the subterranean forces of interest, greed, lust, and power, like, fire that needs the fuel to keep burning. Had the United States been weak at that time it would have curbed its domination spirit and resorted to diplomacy instead of force.

One important offshoot of the above discussion is that the underlying spirit of domination must be regulated accordingly in order to avert crisis both at home and abroad. The desire for domination directed outward for a certain period, if allowed free rein, may spread like fire to consume the very nation and its own people in a reverse realization that one ought to dominate one's own house and domestic surroundings because that would be the only 'alien' territory left once foreign occupation is complete. This has been most appropriately described by Thucydides in his Peloponnesian War, " it is in the long run impossible to encourage the city's desire for 'having more' at the expense of other cities without encouraging the desire of the individual for 'having more' at the expense of his fellow citizens." Or take Marx or Engels when they commented on the perverse 'bourgeois' passion to ultimately turn to seek sexual pleasure within its own circles once the outward 'female' hunt had run its course. It is in the nature of domination spirit to indulge in all sorts of 'fantasy' if not regulated properly. The most glaring example of domination could be found in the master-slave relations. Nevertheless, it must be borne in mind that like electricity and other natural forces, domination principle may be good or bad depending on our approach to it and the degree and purpose of its application. Thus constant refinement and modification of domination instinct is an essential instrument of a sound political system, domestic or international.

Domination theory elaborated further

In his End of the History, Francis Fukuyama made a brief discussion of the classical political philosophers' views on the recognition factor referred at the beginning of this chapter. Such a discussion helps in framing a theory of domination in a far more comprehensive manner. For Plato and Aristotle, there is more to what we call 'animalistic' instincts in human beings. Plato, in his Republic thought that human beings need more than mere claim to right and recognition. There is a spiritual dimension in every human being that Plato called the 'thymos'. Plato's concept of the thymos arose out of the deep human need for justice, worth and self esteem instead of 'right' earned through 'battle'. Aristotle, like Plato stuck to 'justice' and 'lawfulness' to even guide one nation's attitude towards another. Human society can't simply stand on plunder, violence, coercion, and the law of the strongest. It needs some ethical and higher values as distinct from animalistic instincts. Incidentally, the American Declaration embraces both Plato and Aristotle's political philosophy.

However, political concepts and political thoughts, according to Hegel, arose, in the first place, from the desire for recognition by human beings without concern about economic factors. Hegel thought that desire for recognition could be realized by scoring victory over one's opponent and he, therefore, kept the option of violence, war, and force open to settle and define such issues as 'master-slave' or 'lordship-bondage' relation. For Hegel it was a question of 'rights'. Marx, on the other hand, reversed this Hegelian concept and made economics the base that sustained the political superstructure of a society. For Marx, it is the feudalist and the capitalist classes that have totally done away with the Hegelian concept of right and recognition that prevailed in the primitive world and that under the modern feudalist-capitalist mode of production, freedom must be earned through class struggle since class differentiation arises out of concentration of property, wealth, and means of productions in the hands of a minority class that is responsible for all human deprivations and miseries.

Anglo-Saxon logic is based on the application of constant activity, imagination, and innovation and of the survival of the fittest that may entail pain and patience. According to this logic, there is much room for settlement of the 'prestige' or 'recognition' issue through the use of intellect, reasoning, efforts, and acquisition of material prosperity that can modify and refine the

Hegelian concept of crude 'right' and obviate the need of the class in favor of individualism.

But I would like to base my assumption with reference to the domination instinct in human beings that can not only fully explain the issues like, power, prestige, and recognition, but also link the domination spirit with justice and freedom. Such a theoretical construct goes a long way towards a proper understanding of some important political questions of the contemporary era. Apart from desire, recognition, and the thymus, there is another element: the spirit for 'domination' arising out of pride, fear, anxiety, shame (inferiority complex), suspicion, survival, superiority 'complex' and whims. In his Peloponnesian War, Thucydides revealed that there was an inexorable and immutable 'general and necessary law of nature to rule wherever one can' irrespective of time and space and that law can neither be transcended nor be ignored. This is another way of saying that the spirit of domination is natural to living beings and is as old as the first life on earth.

However, the reader must note that spirit of domination, though an instinctual force in human beings and hence of nations, can be refined and modified by the outside world, be it through the mutual 'deterrence' factor or nuclear arms limitation talks or voluntary agreements like lowering of trade barriers. Property system, in contrast to what Marx thought, happens to be another modifying factor in respect of domination. Take the case of America. It is the American craze for property rights that had acted and still acts as checks for the 'excessive' domination spirit of the state or the government machinery. That is why Aristotle thought of property as a positive force in that it contributes further towards ensuring greater freedom for human beings. Erstwhile Soviet Union could consolidate and concentrate so much political authority in the party and the government because of the absence of property system and, in turn, became so repressive a regime.

As the human society came to be dominated by exchange activities, the initial and primary concern of a man was to acquire food, shelter, and cloth. Once that was achieved, he would try for something extra: more leisure, art, and entertainment, comforts and riches. But all these could be achieved if he has adequate power and money that could be acquired either through 'cheating' his neighbors or through his own hard and honest labor. Once he was assured of his bread, butter, home, and leisure time, he became freer. This process goes on and on.

Once a person or a group of persons cross that threshold of poverty and exploitation through means, fair or foul, they have more resources that need to be protected besides enhancing them because unless his resources are enhanced it doesn't make much sense to protect them and unless his wealth is protected they can't be enhanced. With increase in power comes the need to maintain and augment that power. This can be done only at the expense of others because power by its very nature is relative and needs a 'weaker' subject over which to exercise that domination. So long, because of 'circumstance' and lack of power, desire for domination remained latent within the same individual or the group. With more and more accumulation of power, the oppressed turns out to be an oppressor. History is full examples in which the ruler and the ruled changed places. Once this is accepted, it is not difficult to perceive that the desire or instinct for domination is ab initio ad infinitum and is one of chief driving forces of human society. However, the 'spirit of domination', as mentioned a little earlier, if left unchecked, may result into widespread use of 'immoral' and 'unethical' means and no political system can remain immune from its corrupt influence.

It is this latent desire for power and domination that drives an individual to get out of his immediate circle or to manipulate his own surroundings. In the ultimate analysis, both his 'outreach' and 'manipulation' means domination because he must, first of all, make himself appear strong, capable, and intelligent. The weak can hardly dominate. Oddly enough, the underlying factor behind this desire for 'domination' on the part of an individual is the craving for more freedom. The greater the power and the social status a person enjoys, the greater is the freedom, he feels. If allowed free rein, this may lead to what the classical liberal like Mill held that all restraints happened to be evil.

It is here that the crux lies. Freedom for one may eventually become fetter for others since freedom happens to be a relative concept when applied to society. The weak and the subjugated are forced to accept the domination by the strong, albeit temporarily, in the hope of 'deliverance' in some future and eventually to become 'oppressors', themselves. Paradoxically, domination can thus be construed both as a vehicle to ensure freedom as well as repression. Real freedom could be attained through a series of experimental processes, (through force or cooperation?), till the spirit of domination in human beings is overcome, to a considerable extent. It is this paradox that the post Cold War America faces in its foreign policy conduct: unilateral assertion or unmixed cooperation to create a viable and freer international order.

The importance of the 'relativity' factor in America's foreign policies

The relativity of the concept of freedom described above is one of the chief components of the 'dominating' spirit. Even, absolute liberty that is linked to the soul has always a tendency to 'degenerate' into its 'relative' kind. The degenerative life-styles of many Catholic Bishops and the Clergy in medieval Europe happened to be one such instance that gave birth to Reformation and Protestantism. European Protestant culture, in its turn, provided the moral impetus for subsequent colonial exploration and colonial domination. Based on some absolute values of 'Christianity', like, individual liberty and inviolable natural rights derived from the Creator, the American Declaration reduced it into a relative concept by trying to realize those truths on the American soil, in the first place. America's messianic role in spreading the message of freedom and liberty to other parts of the world was meant to replace either the prevalent colonial 'ideals' or the native beliefs, which is another way of proving the relativity of the 'spirit of domination'.

The very term 'missionary' loses significance in the absence of 'other regions'. The Declaration and the War of Independence, though based on some absolute values were actually a struggle for the establishment of some 'relative' truths and values. The very fact that the United States had imperial Britain as its adversary in its freedom struggle and had to rest content with whatever was attainable at that time (an uncertain and incomplete republicanism, a humiliating Paris treaty, and a defiled democracy that tolerated slavery and racial discrimination) was enough proof that the United States was waging a battle to attain a relative and truncated form of liberty. All the future American expansionism in the West or in the Pacific and in Latin America were motivated by this relative concept of liberty. Absolute truth and its perception by mortal human beings can't simply fit into human social concepts. What is 'fixed' and 'determined' for a generation may appear changeable and mutable for the next generation.

In a specific historical condition, the American founding fathers had to embrace some universal ideals rooted in Christianity, which were, however, realizable in relative form, viz., in a particular territory and by a particular citizenry at a particular time period. It is this 'relative' approach that obviously guided all the future American policies. It is because of their reliance on this 'relative' element that the Christianity, the Western Civilization and even the Pax Americana, the three engines of modern civilization, still thrive. Lord Buddha emphasized this relative nature of truth when he told his disciples that truth was what one saw every moment. Referring to this American eternal dynamics, president Clinton stressed in one of his inaugural addresses the need for America to change. " Not change for change's sake, but change to preserve the American ideals-life, liberty, the pursuit of happiness. Though we march to the music of time, our mission is timeless. Each generation of the Americans must define what it means to be an American ."

Water, for example, needs a certain boundary to be more effective. Oceans, too, have their limits. Otherwise, they would become destructive. Likewise, rivers and lakes provide great internal waterways nationally as well as internationally. Infinite space had little significance to the primitive men until astronomy mapped the galaxies and the universe. Likewise, the relative concept or a certain limiting of absolute truth is extremely useful in practical terms. It was the separation of the concept of 'particular' from 'general' that gave concrete shape to time and space and created both history and geography. To the primitive aborigine, time and space were so vast that he remained rather overwhelmed by the enormity of the forces of nature. Human civilization first sprang up in small quarters and in some defined territorial pockets. It is in the nature of vast empires to disintegrate into small nations. Likewise, no single civilization embracing the entire mankind has emerged and even if it so happens it would be a transitory phenomenon. Huntington rightly says that one can justify ones power and supremacy in comparison to enemies only, that is, in relative terms. The very adoption of the American Constitution was an act of recognizing this 'relative' truth.

What transpires from the above analysis is that the United States need not relinquish its republican ideals and creed but must tone down and limit the absolute 'connotation' of its values. In short, the United States ought to reduce deliberate attempts at universalization of its ideals for the better conduct of its foreign policies in the new millennium. That also means greater flexibility on America's part. This has several advantages. First, this would preserve the American republican system because the American republicanism happens to be an evolving concept and hence relative. So long as the United States remains open to new ideas it can carry out the necessary reforms to make the US republican system going. Secondly, this would reduce the gap (stemming from the historical gap referred in the previous chapter) in the perception of political and cultural values between the United States on the one hand and, Europe and the rest of the world, on the other. That would allow the United States more time to readjust its policies so that the rest of the world might not find the American policies too aggressive or assertive, but rather innovative and progressive. Thirdly, it would provide greater room for the American foreign policy makers to reveal their intentions in a more consistent and generalized manner.

Many dualities and inconsistencies engulf the present American foreign policies because of their biased approach in regard to certain 'universal' values like the human rights and democracy. The American perception that those who are with America would receive their blessings while darkness and benightedness will be cast on those who are against the United States enhances its 'spirit of domination' further. Consequently, the United States finds itself at odds in striking a balance between its ideals and national interests. Support for undemocratic regimes stand in direct contrast to the American lofty ideals of freedom, human rights, and democracy. If the United States adheres to a more flexible and relative approach by basing its policies on the relative implications of its values, it may be spared much of the present mistrusts and misconceptions that many nations harbor against it. For example, the United States may declare that so long as its 'allies' (with even autocratic leanings or governments) don't transcend the threshold of domination level, well and good. That means, the United

States must keep a safe distance from getting too demanding and entangling in the affairs of other nations. On the other hand, those 'problem' – cum 'intransigent' states that sponsor terrorism and are intent on acquiring nuclear weapons and WMDs must be branded as 'dangerous'. The United States must, above all, mean business. The United States can't face the 'scorching heat of international politics if its head is made of 'sentimental' hard 'wax'. Greater flexibility must be accompanied by hardheaded calculations along with occasional use of force. After all, values and principles are a soft, positive, and useful part of the spirit of domination (conducive to freedom) referred above. So it is better to go by the parameter of 'domination threshold' than mere branding of states on the basis of subjective feelings and perceptions.

The proper course would be to get every other actor adhere to some commonly agreed rules in which the spirit of domination would serve as the threshold beyond which things won't be permitted to go along. The Helsinki Agreement on human rights issues happened to be one such important milestone in international politics. The American post Cold War policies in promoting democracy and liberal capitalism happen to be steps in that direction. Since the spirit of domination regulates the behavior of both the strong and the weak, it would be possible to reach at some sort of a universal consensus in making this concept a useful yardstick for regulating 'behaviors' of nations despite the fact that such a spirit of domination can't be quantified. But things would be easier to spot after some time, once a beginning is made in the direction. Interestingly, the American Declaration seeks to attain the same objective by defining human freedom – the opposite of domination, in universal terms. The American Declaration does not deny such a spirit of domination altogether in so far as it seeks to respect the sovereignty of every other nation and the right of people to overthrow oppressive regimes. The Declaration's underlying message was the attainment of freedom on a broader scale, that I call perpetual freedom.

The American foreign policies since independence have always some inbuilt or spontaneous tolerance limits beyond which actions of other states were viewed as 'barbaric, 'autocratic' and excessively dominating. This inbuilt response pattern was formed on the solid foundation of the American values, political ideas, in short, the American specialties. Freedom and liberty on a global scale have been the message of the Declaration. Ruggie quotes from Senator William Borah to show how that inbuilt mechanism got automatically activated when a certain threshold of domination spirit was crossed. At the internationalist Council on Foreign Relations, Borah pointed out, "in all matters political, in all commitments of any nature or kind, which encroach in the slightest upon the free and unembarrassed action of our people, or which circumscribe their discretion and judgment, we have been free, we have been independent, we have been isolationist." Ruggie refers to another American foreign policy component in dealing with the American isolationism: " The second was a very high threshold for agreeing when it would be appropriate for the United States to involve itself in some world crisis."

One of the major emphases on the post Cold War American foreign policies is to spread and justify such political measures as regime change, promotion of democracy etc., to minimize the above domination instincts in the political conducts of every nation. For this, the United States has determined certain indices like, terrorism and Islamic fundamentalism, 'rougish' attitude of some states and their designs to rely more on weapons of mass destruction, a visceral anti-American sentiment and its frequent outburst,

The American absolutist 'lean to one side' approach rendered that country to interpret any action or policy by any other power or a group of nations, or even the United Nations, not serving the US interests, as directed against the American interests, ideals, and even its security. Such efforts at linking the American fate with every action of the outside world not only erode America's belief in its own values but also make its center of gravity dependent on others. The United States may become a bundle of 'emotions' and 'whimsicalities' – a sort of 'sentimental wax' referred just above, and any other nation may be tempted to take advantage of the American plasticity. 9/11 didn't come about as a result of a single act on a single day. It resulted from a deep resentment against the US conduct of foreign policies in the Middle East and the Gulf. The September 11 incident was one of the legacies of over four decades of the Cold War rivalry and the failure to address the issue of the 'domination spirit', properly.

Absolute mind-set renders a foreign policy more rigid. Since the United States had already some 'preconceived' and innate set of ideals well before it reached out for the outside world, a sort of super ego was already entrenched in the American mind-set. This made the United States not only somewhat impervious to accepting foreign ideas but also left a huge gap in the American perception vis-à-vis the rest of the world. The United States rather started to think in terms of the superiority of its values over any other system. This is best explained by my theory of domination.

Let me take an example of a country A, say, the United States having a greater power potential than another country, B (which in this case stands either for a single country or a group of countries). An important consideration is that the United States happen always to be the stronger and freer nation because it had developed without the help of other countries while country B has invariably prospered through contact with other countries be it war or cooperation and hence less freedom of action compared to the United States. That means, the case of the United States is sui generis and like a 'conqueror' the United States feels that it has got to offer and not to accept anything from country B – a clear example of harboring an absolute attitude. The latter, on its part, thinks of the neophyte country A as an immature power who needs to be accustomed to the perceptions and practices of other nations, particularly, country B. Both country A and country B would act, following Ricardo, on their own relative comparative advantages and both would hope to influence and 'dominate ' the other through overt or covert means.

Nevertheless, one can't take America for granted simply because it has an absolute mind-set compared to its 'rival'. This would rather overlook the absolute mind-set 'portion' of country B that remained so far latent because of lack of capability to carry out its ends. Secondly, it is not that the American absolute mind-set don't have any relative part and more importantly that the American approach even if it appears 'absolute' is wrong in a specific situation. However, the ultimate goal of both country A and country B is the establishment of superiority of the one above the other. Needless to say, history of Europe and of the world would have been different had the Axis Power or the Soviet communism won their rounds against the liberal democratic capitalist West. Did not the United States become a great power and does not the same the United States find it imperative in recent years to accommodate the enhanced role of the EU in international affairs?

If country **B** had accepted the superiority of country **A** for good, there would have been no further need to discuss the issue. But the desire for domination would hardly allow any country to rest content with a status quo position. Depending on time and place such blow hot blow cold diplomacy (assertion and pacifism) would go on forever, may be, with occasional pause. By that logic the prospect of any permanent resolution of conflicts is near zero. The international political system is like a sea saw balance mechanism that rarely attains equilibrium. Whenever a country grows stronger in economic or military terms, it would try to settle any previous unsolved issue in its favor. Such a desire for retribution highlights the presence of absolute mind-set in every country. The real issue is to get hold of and channelize the above-mentioned 'thin absolute thread' in the minds of individuals and nations into one of increasing cooperation. Economic globalization happens to be one example among many to ensure the reduction in domination spirit by making contending parties dependent on each other. Globalization goes further by obliterating the geographical separation of the nation-states. To put it bluntly, absolute approach is dictatorial while the relative approach is open and democratic. After sometime, this would bring various countries to the same platform. In the case of the United States this has some advantages. It would bring the United States closer to Europe that, in turn, is more familiar to the non-Western world, thereby, helping the United States to erase the American exceptional image that makes the latter appear incomprehensible to many backward and traditional regions. For example, if the

United States ceases to view things from an absolute angle, others will comprehend that the United States has a 'point' to establish and not the assertion of a fait accompli on others and that the United States cares for the sentiments and values of others instead of relying solely on whims. Professor Wendell Bell, the eminent futurologist of the Yale University highlights this point in his article on How has the American Life Changed Since September 11? and emphasized the need for more restraint, moderation and being understanding of others' viewpoints. People feel most oppressed whenever a particular policy is sodden with a zero-sum choice in the name of enforcing justice. People may even bear with poverty and exploitation for the simple reason that they are not presented with a fait accompli but have ample scope to improve their lots through diligence and wit. On the other hand, if there is lack of space for people to maneuver so that they feel pushed to the wall, tensions arise.

The United States may issue stern warnings against those investing huge sums on producing nuclear, biological, or chemical weapons. It may be done to bring the deviant group or the state to the path of law followed by sanctions and other approaches short of force. If such repeated cautions don't impact the wrongdoer then one may assume that above threshold limit has been crossed and actions may be taken accordingly. It is highly unlikely that unless pushed to the extreme, a democratic country like the United States would violate international norms and sentiments. The United States had many such rhetoric during the Eisenhower and the Reagan era but they hardly got translated into conflicts. That way, the United States would hardly look like a global leviathan to others.

Perpetual freedom

Perpetual freedom is based on a relative rather than an absolute concept. While freedom in the absolute sense is our God-given and natural right, it is necessary to concretize and protect this freedom in the social context. For example, freedom for one may cause problems for another fellow. Being a public good, while freedom or the utility derived from enjoyment of freedom can't be quantified or even evaluated, except when it is lost, it can be made more concretized through a perpetual effort so that would make freedom a much more livelier and shared concept. To the extent that spirit of domination in individuals and nations are refined and curbed, efforts towards attainment of a state of perpetual freedom, as an alternative, becomes easier. A drug-addict needs some alternative and constructive course to get over his addiction because human mind can't remain vacant. The only concern is to avoid the pollution of freedom by not allowing it to go unbridled and to quarantine that spirit of domination at the same time. In a word, administering a proper mix of domination and freedom happen to be an important stepping stone to arrive at that perpetual state of freedom, in a concrete manner.

But if freedom is linked to value elements, with which it is indirectly related, then it is liable to be interpreted differently because values are changeable and fungible (in the sense that it can be manipulated to suit one's aims) at the same time, as we have seen in analyzing the issue of 'justice' above. On the other hand, if freedom is viewed as the opposite of 'domination', which it is in the true and ultimate sense, there is no 'mysticism' attached to that concept and we clearly know what is to be done to attain that state. Moreover, such linking of freedom with domination takes into account the subjective and objective factors.

Transposed to international politics, this concept of freedom ought to be more open-ended, dynamic, and concrete. The above concept of perpetual freedom must take into account the relative factor of time, place, and other conditions. Every nation, including the United States must realize that a diversity of ideals and interests shape the foreign policies of nations. Esther A. Bacon and Colleen M. Harmann (The Global Century, Globalization and National Security, ed. By Kugler and Frost) list ten such variations that they have divided into two categories: values and beliefs on the one hand and ideologies on the other. These ten variations are nothing new to international politics. These are: democracy, national interests, geopolitical assertiveness, nationalism, outlaw aggressiveness, strategic preservatism, authoritarianism, traditionalism, religion and state survival. It is not possible to define any nation's foreign policy in an unambiguous and clear manner given a plethora of such diversities.

But there is one thread common to all these forms and ideas: spirit of domination. It is possible to set a limit on how far a country may pursue those ideas without jeopardizing those of others. Nations or groups or individuals can't indulge in whimsicalities if there is a voluntary consensus on thier part limit their 'domination' and 'intrusive' impulses on a continuous and perpetual basis, as can be found in various SALT and START treaties. On the other hand, there must be a sort of an authority to look after the observance of these consensus and agreements so that no other country can flout with such commonly agreed norms. Such an approach is in accordance with the UN Human Rights Declarations. A strong arbiter like the United States is ideally placed to carry out this role because of its inbuilt value-based political system. Regimes and supervisions are essential tools for attaining 'perpetual' freedom. Needless to say, perpetual freedom may not mean permanent freedom but a continuous effort towards maintaining and augmenting human freedom.

Even if the domination instinct can't be so easily quantified, there are other tests that may help. One such test may be to gauge the spirit of the rogue state or the aberrant party. To the degree that the said country appears totally impervious to advises, persuasions, and even sanctions, that country may be placed in a high-alert category of the domination table. Similarly, there may be medium and low alert countries. Another important criteria or a test case may consist in observing the inclination level and the seriousness of the said party to implement some commonly agreed programs. Yet another test may be to observe the fanaticism of the said country in respect of ethno-religious and nationalist issues, the type and volume of assistance it receives from other neutral or even semi-rival powers and the mass support base for a particular belief or movement that would harm the interests of other peace loving countries. Another extremely important test is to observe how the said country makes a case to forge anti-American alliance driven by a passionate hatred against that country merely on the basis of superficial charges. Saddam Hussein's bid to exploit the Pan-Arabic sentiments during the first Gulf War by provoking the neighboring state is one example. It may be argued that deliberate attempts at maintaining a low level of domination instinct would have little effect. But then again, how can one explain the influence of democratic and liberal ideals in the West European countries to hold these divisive forces on tight leash?

Conclusion

American adherence to absolute values and principles were based on the assumption that others would accept the American values because such absolute values resonate with the 'natural' and 'divine' in every human being and nation through the working of the principle of justice. It is these 'stoic' American perceptions regarding its political values that must be somewhat reduced to fit into its changing role in international affairs. This is not difficult for America since its republican concept of liberty, unlike those held by classical liberals, is open-ended. The American republicanism has more room for the rule of law to ensure freedom. Kant believed that preventing a rights' violation was not a hindrance to freedom. Locke maintained that the end of the law was to 'preserve and enlarge freedom'.

But there remains an anomaly in the above approach. How can use of force be reconciled with the more flexible and tolerant policies at the same time? However, there is no contradiction involved here. It would depend on the American adroitness to use the concept of 'perpetual freedom' to properly address various issues connected with domination spirit, just as the United States did with its 'Neutrality' policies some two centuries back. Neutrality for the United States did not mean absence of force as discussed in the next chapter. Moreover, the United States has the capability to use its hard and soft powers to fulfill this responsibility in a better way than any other great power in history. The American hard and soft powers could be used more effectively if the United States bases its policies towards realization of 'perpetual freedom' on a global basis.

To deny the presence of this spirit of domination and the lust for power in human mind and society is to deny the existence of the 'natural' man and the laws like the 'struggle for existence' and 'survival of the fittest'. Rather the acceptance of such principles enables human beings and nations to formulate appropriate means and policies to negotiate them in a far more practicable manner.

Once we accept the universality of the desire for domination, our major concern as human beings becomes either to enhance or curb these 'domination' instincts through war, violence, and hatred or through mutual cooperation and adjustment. The whole dynamics of human history, and international politics is guided by this one factor only: domination. *It is the change in time, place, and the actors having different priorities and interests and their interactions contingent on 'domination' factor that lends direction, richness, and variety to the course of international politics and history.* Presence of domination instinct in men was well admitted by Anthony Lake, the NSC advisor to Clinton when he commented, "Until human nature changes, power and force will remain at the heart of international relations". Leo Strauss aired a similar view in The City and Man, "no bloody or unbloody change of society can eradicate the evil in man; as long as there will be men, there will be malice, envy and hatred, and hence there cannot be a society which does not have to employ coercive restraint." The Machiavellian man having selfish, ungrateful, and fickle human nature needs the coercive rule of law to ensure human liberty.

Yet these instincts can be for good or bad depending on the purpose. Lincoln in his Lyceum speech in 1837, told that the 'American Revolution and its aftermath had directed enmity 'outward.' Referring to the outlet that these "deep-rooted principles of the hate, and the powerful motive of revenge, ... " directed "exclusively against the British nation", Lincoln felt that such a condition was temporary and the United States got to be prepared accordingly.

Since no concept is perfect, there always remains some 'space' (in the sense that the 'incomplete', the 'untried' and the 'untested' factors may surface again and again), through which the roots from the fallen seed of 'opposition' sprouts again and again. Former Soviet Union had its own sense of justice and political ideology based on egalitarianism and equality. Soviet demise hardly meant absolute supremacy for its arch rival, the United States, now beset with all the legacies of the just bygone era. The legacies of communism still haunt the American post Cold War foreign policies. Likewise, the recent cooling of relationship between Europe and the United States is rooted in the same differences of interests and perceptions that emanate from the spirit of 'domination'. Europe is skeptical of America's enhanced power, and wants to regain its past glories (its own 'domination', too) while the United States feels that it is justified in completing the unfinished job of its independence to fully realize its republican goals.

Political history is all about increasing democratization and gradual limiting of the powers of kings and monarchs that began with the days of the Magna Carta. The growing failure of and corruption within the ranks of religious and feudalistic rulers, the growth of industrialization, the Reformation, and the Renaissance, overseas colonialism with its successes and failures, and growth in scientific discoveries in the subsequent periods had all led contemporary political and economic thinkers like Adam Smith, Ricardo, and the Physiocrats to seek a more viable political and economic order on the basis of private property and free market forces. So profound were the changes brought about by the above developments that capitalism put its indelible stamp of dominance on modern societies.

Now, in the third millennium marked by post modernism, post industrialism, post communism and post Westphalianism, we are in a better position to judge all these theories and dogmas. History that started with the domination of the strongest still remains in place as money and capital, mostly, supplanted brute physical force. The combination of these three elements in a single political power still works, as the age old political concepts like freedom, recognition and rights veer round a single factor: domination. History has not changed, least of all ending, so far as the issue of the 'spirit' of domination was not addressed properly despite Fukuyama's claim: "The triumph of the West, of the Western idea, is evident first of all in the total exhaustion of viable systematic alternatives to Western liberalism." A single hegemon can't dictate for long the course of history because it would only be a matter of time before the tree of opposition from the past seed grows ever bigger to pose a challenge to the incumbent hegemon.

Moreover, all those above-mentioned liberal and socialist thoughts and revolutionary movements were the products of the eighteenth and the nineteenth century Europe. The world has come a long way from becoming Euro-centric. As industrialization, commerce, and democracy have spread to the far corners of the earth, no nation now enjoys an absolute advantage over the others just because some of them possess enormous wealth and power to force the issue in international affairs. The just bygone era of the Cold War had shown that in an interdependent world even the insignificant states could 'blackmail' the strongest. So, it is time to look beyond those age-old concepts of domination by the 'few'. While these are prerequisites to attain a position of dominance in world affairs, they fail to explain the reality that nations, strong or weak, are guided by 'spirit of domination' and are not civilization-specific.

In a way, realism itself can be better understood in the light of 'domination' instinct. While the realists proceed from the fact of the mere existence and interplay of national interests, 'domination' theory goes deeper in explaining the very roots of such 'interests' and thus affords better scope to resolve disputes. Since it is not possible for any modern power to completely 'dominate' others, the power in question can still maintain its leadership and advantage over others by manipulating the desire for domination in itself as well as in others as the neo-liberalists aim to do. That way, theory of domination is all inclusive and happens to be the mother of all political theories.

Much of the American problems in negotiating the post Cold War issues arise out of the fact that the United States hopes that its Anglo-Saxon philosophy could be the answer to that age-old problem of 'recognition' factor through the medium of material prosperity and free trade. It may be largely true but if it ignores the fourth factor of 'domination' it might make a fatal mistake now that it wants to create a 'different' kind of world order. The age-old instinctive factors like 'prestige' and 'recognition' were and are still important but once the world has become more interdependent and freer, and now that every nation *recognizes* every other sovereign nation, it is time to think beyond. This is more so in an era of interdependence in which most nations possess the economic (for example, oil for the Middle East countries) and military means (Weapons of Mass Destruction or the WMDs for rogue states and various terrorist organizations) to secure the recognition of other countries easily.

The 'domination' factor assumes more significance in a changing international perspective where nations and its people are politically more conscious and socially more interconnected. An open and flexible approach on America's part would enable it to deal with revisionist powers and aspiring individuals in far better ways than one based on the absolute mind-set. It was only when (much later in the Cold War days) the United States accepted the reality of the existence of a different socio-economic system that it felt free to pursue a more matured and flexible foreign policy. It was only when the United States, in a rare demonstration of refining its domination instinct, shook off its post war China 'allergy' and played the China card that the end of the dark Cold War tunnel could be seen. Since control or domination of others happens to be ultimate goal of every nation (there is no other way in which relative power can be demonstrated), there are many ways and means to effect such domination. Domination is a complex mechanism.

Nevertheless, the only realistic answer to resolving the riddle of the domination factor lies in a prolonged continuation of the United States as a benign hegemon in the capacity of the single global leader.

References and readings

Charles Darwin, *The Descent of Man*, John Murray, London, 1871.

John Gerrard Ruggie, Winning the Peace, *America and the World order in the New Era*, Columbia University Press, NY, 1996.

Wendell Bell, *How haste American Life Changed since September 11?* Journal of

Future Studies, August, 2003 8(1) 73-80.

The Global Century, Globalization and National Security, Ed. By Richard L. Kugler and Ellen E. Frost, vol II, National Defense University, 2002.

Hans Morgenthau, Politics among Nations, the struggle for Power, 3rd Edition, NY, 1952.

Thucydides, Peloponnesian War, tr. By Hobbes, ed. By David Greene, Michigan, 1959.

Lewis Mumford, Technics and Civilization, NY, London, 1934.

Kenneth Waltz, *A Theory of International Politics*, NY, 1979.

Robert A. Keohane, *International Institutions and State Power, Essays in International Relations Theory*, Boulder, 1989.

Samuel Huntington, The Erosion of the American National Interests, Foreign Affairs, vol.76, no.5, September-October, 1997.

Helen Milner, *International Theories of cooperation among nations: strengths and weakness*, World Politics, vol. 44, no.3, April ,1992.

James Der Derian & Michael Shapiro, eds., *International/Intertextual Relations, Postmodern Readings of World Politics*, Lexington,1989.

John Rawls, *A Theory of Justice*, MA, 1971.

Francis Fukuyama, The End of History And The Last man, London, 1992.

Robert Nozick, *Anarchy, State, Utopia*, NY, 1974.

Abraham Lincoln's Lyceum Speech, ed. By Roy P. Basler, Collected Works of Abraham Lincoln, the Abraham Lincoln Association.

Steven Cahn, *Classics of Modern Political Theory*, NY, 2002.

Rousseau, *The Social Contract, London*, 3rd ed., 1948.

Thomas Hobbes, *Leviathan*, reprinted from the ed. of 1651, Oxford, 1952.

Sigmund Freud, The Ego and the Id, London, 1927; The Standard Edition of the Complete Psychological Works of Sigmund Freud, London, 1955.

Handbook of Political Theory, ed., by Gerald F. Gaus, Chandran Kukathas, pt1, London, 2004.

Adrian Oldfield, Ordered Cities, Ordered Souls: Introduction to Greek Political Thought, London, 1995.

Leo Strauss, the City and Man, Chicago, Rand McNally, 1st edition, 1964.

CHAPTER III

EARLY AMERICAN FOREIGN POLICIES

The War of Independence and the following decades

The primary task before the American revolutionaries was to justify the secession and the War of Independence, According to Niall Ferguson, independence was not what the colonists originally had in mind, divided, as they were, in their loyalties to the Crown. According to the Wikipedia free encyclopedia source, about 40 to 45 per cent of the population supported the struggle for independence and the Loyalists comprised about 15 to 20 per cent. Niall Ferguson felt that the cause celebre 'no taxation without representation' rather implied the American desire to identify themselves with their trans-Atlantic brethren. "What the colonists said they were doing was demanding the same liberty enjoyed by their fellow subjects on the other side of the Atlantic". (Ferguson, p.91-92) Even the Declaration read,

> Nor have we been wanting in attentions to our British Brethren. We have warned them from Time to Time of the Attempts by their Legislature to extend an unwarrantable Jurisdiction over us. We have reminded them of the Circumstances of our Immigration and Settlement here. We have appealed to their native justice and Magnanimity, and we have conjured them by the Ties of our kindred to disavow these Usurpations, which, would inevitably interrupt our Connections and Correspondence. They too have been Deaf to the Voice of Justice and of Consanguinity.

Apart from the issue of taxation and the Crown's high handedness, the real bone of contention was over the right of the Parliament to impose taxes on the colonies as highlighted in The First Continental Congress.

One major hurdle in the way of waging the war was to ensure the unity of thirteen disparate colonies in a common struggle against Britain. Charles Townsend thought that jealousy and divergence of interests among the various colonies were so great that it seemed extremely improbable that they should ever be able to resolve upon a plan of 'mutual security and reciprocal expense.' Benjamin Franklin felt frustrated once the 1754 Albany Plan of

Union was rejected by the colonies. The primary task before the revolutionaries was to mobilize the various state militias to raise a regular Continental army needed to wage and carry out the war. Besides, the inexperienced and the irregular US forces hardly seemed to be any match for the organized and the far better equipped armed forces of England, not to speak of the enormous finances that would be needed to sustain the war. There was virtually no hope for independence without outside help.

For the other European powers to be enticed to range against Britain, the revolutionaries needed some a fortiori logic. The latter felt that principles must be clearly defined. So long as a country wages a just war and so long as it sticks to the path of 'right', even the enemy finds it difficult to justify its invasion or occupation of that country. America fighting for its own cause in its own land was better placed to carry out the armed struggle against England. Rather it was the British army that suffered from a sort of guilt feeling and, sometimes, fumbled to crush the 'rebels'. British Commander-in-chief William Howe in one such moment of deliberation let George Washington off the hook when he had a chance to annihilate the latter's army in the Long Islands. Ferguson remarked, "In short, London lacked the stomach to impose British rule on white colonists who were determined to resist it. It was one thing to fight the Native Americans or munitions slaves, but it was another to fight what amounted to your own people." (ibid, p.97) Nevertheless, the lofty values enshrined in the Declaration of the American Independence allowed some space for other European states to help America in its war against Britain. After all, America was fighting their arch rival for a just cause.

It was obvious from the beginning that the averment of America's 'distinctiveness' from Europe would have some far reaching consequences after the War. The founders accepted the fact that under the prevailing conditions they did not have much room of maneuver, either. Thus, independent America's future had to rest on many "ifs" and "buts". As stated above, objective conditions were not altogether helpful to wage the war with Britain. But the rebels felt that it was a 'now or never' issue even if it meant a 'fractured' and a far from complete liberation, and this, notwithstanding the apperception that the future course for them might be bumpy and would entail many sacrifices – a situation that every revolution faces when it tries to break away from the establishment. The chief concern of the founding fathers was that the United States must return to the mainstream of international politics as early as possible and how the fledging nation would get there remained the new-born nation's principal foreign policy goal in the immediate post independence era. Since the bedrock of the American independence happened to be the establishment of America's 'political' distinctiveness from Europe, no wonder, all the successive American foreign policies remained sensitive to the issue of this American 'uniqueness' and guided accordingly.

With faith in Annuit Coeptis and with Novus Ordo Seclorum as its flambeau, the newly independent America started its journey to find its separate and equal station amongst the powers of the earth which the "Laws of Nature and Nature's God" entitled them. Yet this was half of the story. *Behind every major American foreign policy decisions in the succeeding decades lay the genuine concern about the country's relative cultural and geographical remoteness from the rest of the world.* This became more so after the war, since America not only lost the motherly 'protection' of the all-powerful and the 'omnipresent' Royal Navy but also it had now to deal with a 'step mother' as the Royal Navy remained entrenched all along its Atlantic shores.

The American leaders, on their part, felt that such geographic and cultural uniqueness must be turned to America's advantages. Washington in his farewell address admitted this in the following words, "Our detached and distant situation invites and enables us to pursue a different course. If we remain one people, under an efficient government, the period is not far off, when we may defy material injury from external annoyance;...", and again, "why forego the advantages of so peculiar a situation? Why quit our own to stand upon foreign ground? Why, by interweaving our destiny with that of any part of Europe, entangle our peace and prosperity in the toils of European ambition, rivalship, interest, humor, or caprice?" Paradoxically, it is the same American 'uniqueness' that had made America more dependent on the rest of the world, as I shall discuss, later.

Apart from the daunting job of framing a written Constitution for maintaining the country's integrity and defining the state-center relations, another major task after independence was to formulate appropriate foreign policies to make the 'American' position clear to outsiders, mainly, the European powers. Too much reliance on any particular ally, say, France, would not only annoy Britain – already humiliated by the loss of its American colonies-but also would make America more dependent on a particular country and to the latter's policy changes contingent on every change of government in that country. The situation in France during the tumultuous years of the French revolution and after, led Jefferson to plead for abrogating the wartime alliances between America and France to avoid the 'French trap'. Moreover, continuance of such an alliance after the war would deprive America of the very justification of their freedom struggle against Britain. Washington, too, made it clear in his farewell address that too much reliance on hatred or fascination for a particular country meant 'slavery', either way. It was only by assuring them of continued and equal trade opportunities in America that the latter could blunt the sharp edges of those European powers that encircled the newly independent country on all sides.

For all these reasons, the founding fathers found ' Neutrality' a very potent weapon to gain time and to attend to the process of nation building, silently. They knew that only a strong America could be the most befitting answer to constant European threats and to their unjustified demands and, most importantly, to bring the United States into the mainstream of international politics from the isolation forced on it by those very hostile European powers. George Washington went a step ahead and even conceived America as a new and rising empire. "However unimportant America may be considered at present......there would assuredly come a day, when this country would have some weight in the scale of empires." The first step towards the United States growing strong was to ensure internal stability and the frontier expansion that couldn't be achieved until the Americans had done with the Indians.

So the skirmishes arising out of America's territorial encroachments continued after independence in which the Indians got marginalized further deep into their relocated 'reservations'. The next two decades of battles with the Indians were bitter, protracted, and one of survival as the European powers often incited and aided the Indians. Savagery, betrayal, and cruelty of the Indians made the white Americans even more ruthless. Victory over the Indians, like the latter day victory over the South in the Civil War, had been the two most important developments in the independent American history. On both these occasions America fought for the survival of its nationhood.

For the colonists, the stakes in the war of independence were extremely high, as they had to fight with both the British and the Indian forces at the same time. For the independent country, the war had hardly ended with the signing of the peace treaty of 1783 in Paris. The need to complete one of the many unfinished parts of the war of independence – the war against the Indians – helped the United States to endure the stress of strained state-center relations for another few decades. The states needed the help of the federal militia to defeat, assimilate, decimate and marginalize the Indians into their reservations.

Thus, one of the rationales behind the Westward expansion had been to defeat and destroy the Indians. If the Americans stopped at their stipulated wartime boundaries after securing independence, the United States would have remained a divided nation. In that case, it would have to share its lands with the Indians. This double dimension of the war of independence also underlined the fact that the American nationhood and the American identity ought to be defined in non-traditional terms. While the white Americans happened to be the agnates of early British settlers, it would be an absurdity to express their identity through the same British ancestry, particularly, after independence. On the other hand and concurrently, the original inhabitants, that is, the Indians happened to be the principal enemies of the Americans. The answer to this intriguing question must be found elsewhere. It couldn't have been otherwise for a 'settler's nation' that had cut its umbilical cord with its progenitors.

Interestingly, while the Americans were single-minded in suppressing and decimating the Indians, the federal government continued to support rebel groups, elsewhere, in its own hemisphere. America's support for revolutionary movements in the Latin American countries made the formers' intentions clear: to drive away the European powers from the New World, to grab the trade opportunities all by itself and to realize the latent desire to be a regional and even global hegemon. The United States, since its early days sent several expeditions abroad not only to chastise the 'Barbary' forces in Africa but also elsewhere in Latin America, Japan, and Korea to draw the limits of its projected imperial contours. This paradigm of 'negation', that is, elimination of enemies, first, the Indians and then the European powers, fostered 'exclusivity' and even intolerance, more euphemistically, an 'absolute' mind-set, in the conduct of the successive American foreign policies, e.g., the American tirade against Soviet communism after 1945. Little wonder that Neutrality, a negative approach, would fit well into the post independent American foreign policies.

The Neutrality

The United States proclaimed its Neutrality policy in 1793 (that became really effective after Washington's farewell address in 1796) to keep itself out of the great and the protracted war then raging in Europe as an aftermath of the great French Revolution. The United States hoped to keep its Atlantic trade routes safe, ensure uninterrupted movement of its merchant vessels, and keep the flow of trade going with all the parties involved in the conflict. In the process, the United States exploited the Franco-British rivalries to fill up the vacuum created by the reduced number of merchandise vessels of both these countries in the Atlantic. Washington in his Farewell address clarified that the United States should "steer clear of permanent alliances with any portion of the foreign world; so far I mean, as we are now at liberty to do it ..." and again, " Harmony, liberal intercourse with all nations, are recommended by policy, humanity, and interest. But even our commercial policy should hold an equal and impartial hand; neither seeking nor granting exclusive favors or preferences;..." Thomas Jefferson stated clearly:

> I have ever deemed it fundamental for the United States never to take active part in the quarrels of Europe. Their political interests are entirely different from ours. The mutual jealousies, their balance of power, their complicated alliances, their forms and principles of government, are all foreign to us. They are nations of eternal war. All their energies are expended in the destruction of the labor, property and their people.
>
> —*Jefferson to Monroe, 1823*

However, a few years later Jefferson used the 'elastic clause' to circumvent constitutional problems in acquiring Alaska from France *in national interest*. Madison went to war with Britain in 1812 over Canada to gain economic advantages. Louis M. Hacker commented that the virgin lands of the St.. Lawrence valley led America to proceed towards Canada. He thought that it was greed, not the Indian threats or neutral rights, that had led America to the 1812 war. John Quincy Adams in the capacity of Secretary of State to James Monroe bought Florida from Spain for a paltry five million dollars. Andrew Jackson led military campaigns in 1818 into Florida that America considered belonged to it. It was rather the fertile lands of Florida that impelled the people and the planter class to start settling there. That the propounders of republican values harbored a subterranean desire within their hearts to prepare America for the fulfillment of its imperial destiny gradually came to light in the subsequent years as the full import of neutrality unraveled.

American neutrality was heavily tested during the whole of that Great European War. America went out of its 'defensive' neutrality, that is, from passive and half-hearted response, to 'offensive' neutrality, by requiring its newly created small Navy to patrol the high seas and to redress any wrong done to the American vessels even if it involved armed skirmishes with the European powers. Many times during this period, the United States came to the brink with both France and Britain. Over time, as the United States grew stronger, successive policy-makers made every effort to break that shell and shackle of neutrality. After all, the American policy of neutrality was rather forced upon it and, whenever the country got the slightest opening to free itself from that yoke, the American policy makers never deliberated. Interestingly, it took the United States about two centuries to shift its foreign policy stand from neutrality to intervention on a global scale. Things were, however, different in its own backyard in the Western Hemisphere , especially, after the promulgation of the Monroe Doctrine as far back as in 1823. My theory of domination in the previous chapter fully explains the American situation and its policies.

The Greek Insurgency

The controversy over the issue of getting involved in European affairs surfaced once again during the Greek nationalist insurrection against the Ottoman Turks in the 1820s in which most of the European states lent active help to Greece. In a speech given before the House of Representatives on July 4, 1821, John Quincy Adams stated his country's neutral stand in the following lines,

> Wherever the standard of freedom and independence has been or shall be unfurled, there will her heart, her benedictions, and her prayers be. But she goes not abroad in search of monsters to destroy. She is the

> well-wisher of the freedom and independence of all. She is the champion and vindicator only of her own... She well knows that by once enlisting under other banners than her own, were they even the banners of foreign independence, she would involve herself beyond the power of extrication, in all the wars of interest and intrigue, of individual avarice, envy, and ambition, which assume the colors and usurp the standard of freedom...She might become the dictatress of the world. She would no longer be the ruler of her own spirit.

Yet the real reason for not supporting the Greek insurgents had not much to do with the ideals and policies of non-interference, elsewhere. The Greek revolution of the 1820s, drew its inspirations from the French Revolution. But it lacked a mass base and it was basically the handiwork of few personalities who dreamt of 'reviving the classical empire.' It relied on Russia for support. European powers like France, Britain, and Spain were, however, reluctant to see a more powerful Russia that had already registered significant territorial and strategic gains following Napoleon's defeat.

While the formation of a ring of Christian states around the Mediterranean basin was to the liking of the European powers, threat of Russia loomed larger in their minds. These European powers wanted to destabilize and weaken the Turkish Empire but not its disintegration for fear that the Turkish Straits and the Mediterranean trade routes would fall to Russia who had always looked avidly to control them. Moreover, the European nations calculated that a Greek victory would be a temporary affair and would finally benefit the Eastern colossus because of religious commonness.

The same considerations influenced the American policy-makers. They would not like to see Russia emerge as the strongest power at the crossroads of three continents at a time when that Holy Alliance partner had shown 'territorial' interest in the North Pacific impinging on the American territory. So, by not supporting the Greeks, the United States once again had shown that it was national interest that mattered above everything else. Neutrality in this case rather implied observance of the rules of real politics – another expression of the spirit of domination-for attaining a more 'desirable' situation in future.

John C. Calhoun in his balance of power doctrine made it clear that while the principle of Neutrality meant non-aggrandizement and non-intervention in the affairs of other countries, this didn't mean 'passivity and dull headedness' by remaining oblivious of the surroundings. The American neutrality rather required 'skilful' perceptions of others' concerns and priorities and judging their impact on the American interests while maintaining the rights and interests of America at the same time. Neutrality, according to him was rather greater involvement and awareness of what was going around and to take actions accordingly even if it meant resort to arms.

Neutrality underwent changes with time. Earlier, these Neutrality provisions pertained only to war between countries and did not cover civil war within a country. The new 1937 Neutrality Act covered civil wars. As a result, the United States was unable to provide assistance to the loyalist government in Spain during the Spanish Civil War of the 1930s while Hitler's Germany kept on helping Franco's rebel forces. However, the Roosevelt administration modified its Neutrality policy further from 'thoughts to deeds' as Germany invaded Poland on September 1939. The US Congress, at Roosevelt's urgings, allowed arms supplies to both France and Britain by requiring all export deals to be settled within that country before the goods left America. May 1940 destroyer-for-bases agreement between the UK and the USA was the final straw that broke the back of the neutrality once and for all. After that, the United States never looked back to its days of isolationism.

The Westward Expansion

For the whole of the nineteenth century, America remained busy in its own hemisphere in a cleaning up operation of the Indians and the European powers and in eking out its territorial boundaries through its frontiers expansion. The defining features of the American foreign policies during the first half of the nineteenth century were outright purchases, decimation of the Indians, overtures ranging from financial deals to the threat of using force in Latin America, and intermittent campaigns against the European powers in and around the North American continent. In that sense America had already become an expansive and 'imperial' power because of its unquenchable thirst for territories rich in natural resources. Jefferson Pressurized Napoleon I to sell Louisiana to America lest he would 'annihilate the French fleet' and 'fight any French troops who landed at New Orleans'. The United States pre-empted the French design in Louisiana through America's support for the black revolutionaries led by Toussaint L' Overture in Haiti.

The only justification for America's westward 'colonization' came from the belief that the United States had been annexing 'empty' lands. Where it involved evicting Indians from their rightful native lands, the white Americans justified that they were doing so on behalf of the 'civilized' race, as the Indians were incapable of making good use of lands in their possessions. Moreover, the latter were compensated with lands, albeit unproductive and used lands, elsewhere. Yet the underlying American concern was also one of security and survival. First, it became necessary to reduce the number of Indians as much as possible to strike at the European design to secure a foothold in the Continent. Secondly, by expanding its continental frontiers, the United States hoped to be in a position to put a counter pressure on the European powers to leave the New World. Most of all, such a situation would enable the United States to observe its policy of neutrality from a position of strength.

The spirit and rational behind America's Westward expansion could be best captured in the visions of two scholars, Jefferson and Fisk. Jefferson, as far back as 1780's remarked, "Our Confederacy must be viewed as the nest from which all America, North or South, is to be peopled." President Jefferson yearned for people 'speaking the same language, governed in similar forms and by similar laws'. John Fisk wrote,

> The work which the English race began when it colonized North America is destined to go on until every land on the earth's surface that is not already the seat of an old civilization shall become English in its language, in its religion, in its political habits and traditions, and to a predominant extent in the blood of its people.
>
> —*Zimmerman, 2004, p.18*

Anti-colonial and anti-imperial United States, indeed, needed its pre-colonial 'English' identity to carry out the unfinished job of the Greco-Roman civilization. The United States realized that to remain out of sight was to remain out of mind and that to influence other people, the American 'beacon' ought to be fitted on an ever moving Anglo-Saxon 'silo', (or for that matter, the American Cavalcade), heading towards these regions instead of remaining impaled within its own hemisphere.

Another contributory factor towards the Westward expansion was the massive migrations from Europe since the end of the eighteenth century and a burst of population growth during the first half of the nineteenth century in the United States. The US population grew more than five million in 1800 to more than 23 million by the mid century. An estimated 4,000,000 Americans moved westward between 1820 and 1850. This 'internal colonization' was a prelude to future American expansions far beyond its borders. Richard W. Van Alstyne believed that nationalism being a universal feature and America being a part of the world of nation states ought to build its empire with 'proper limits'. For some scholars, however, the American Westward expansion was the result of calculated motives, peasants' interests, handiwork of the political parties and individual personalities.

Still, it would be wrong to say that the American Westward expansion was the same as colonization. New states arising out of the acquisition of new territories were allowed to enjoy the same rights as the original thirteen states. The Northwest Ordinance of 1787 served as the bedrock and basis for the Westward expansion in which new territories were not allowed to be treated as colonies of 'continental American empire.' The above Ordinance also sought to ensure the rights of Indians over their landed possessions. For the American policy-makers, setting their home in order happened to be one of the top priorities after independence.

The Monroe Doctrine

During the early 1820s, the American leadership took a decision that proved to be momentous for the subsequent American foreign policies. The United States followed the line of least resistance to drive out the European powers from its peripheries through the promulgation of the Monroe Doctrine. It would have been a folly to venture straight into the Pacific or to send fleets (America had little of them prior to the 1880s) in the Atlantic where the Royal Navy had bases all along its shores. On top of it, the intriguing issue of center-state relation, frequent addition of new territories and subsequent granting of statehoods to them kept the American political structure in too fluid a state to carry on the business of war on a protracted scale. Nevertheless, as referred earlier, America made judicious use of most of the available means, e.g., limited and short wars, support for insurrections and freedom movements elsewhere, trade concessions, treaties, and outright purchases. Can one deny the similarity between a problem-ridden US with that of the Soviet Union during the Cold War days? The great lesson of international politics is that when in trouble, nations or aspiring powers tend to spread the areas of disturbances without direct involvement. The Eagle had been waiting impatiently for the take off for quite some time. The Monroe Doctrine came handy in this respect:

> With the existing colonies or dependencies of any European power we have not interfered and shall not interfere. But with the governments who have declared their independence and maintained it, and whose independence we have...acknowledged, we could not view any interposition for the purpose of oppressing them, or controlling in any other manner their destiny, by any European power in any other light than as the manifestation of an unfriendly disposition toward the United States.

By this declaration, the United States further legitimized its own War of Independence, went one step forward in defending the rights of self-determination of nations and laid a new course in international politics that further marginalized the monarchical powers and made way for the eventual emergence of many new republics, especially in Latin America. The central argument of the Monroe Doctrine followed from the Declaration that the people had the right to choose their own government and it was wrong on anybody's part to try to change a form of government chosen by the people through military interventions. According to Anne R. Pierce these two principles had their influences on both Wilson and Truman.

The Monroe Doctrine was a major step in paving the way for the American hegemony in the New World. The possibility of revival of colonial rule in Spanish America at the behest of powers like Russia, Prussia, and Austria prompted the promulgation of the Monroe Doctrine. The United States won't henceforth tolerate any intended colonial domination of Europe in the Western Hemisphere . However, one must not gloss over the fact of America's commercial interests. The United States eyed enormous trade and commercial opportunities in the entire New World. As the vast territories under the Spanish dominion were freed, the US commerce flourished and became more secured by treaties with new governments.

The Monroe Doctrine was more of a unilateral assertion of the American policy for limiting and even eliminating the European influence in the Western Hemisphere than a formal treaty. British Prime Minister Salisbury raised questions about legality of the doctrine in the 1890s while several other European powers like Spain and France violated its message in San Domingo and Mexico in the early 1860s. Even, in the initial decade after the proclamation of that doctrine, the United States remained passive to its enforcement as the Europeans powers, sometimes, defied it, e.g., France in Haiti and Britain in Malvinas in 1833.

The Latin American countries, on the other hand, were suspicious and critical of the US assertiveness in the New World. As Tyler made use of this doctrine to annex Texas, one Venezuelan newspaper displayed a cartoon depicting the wolf approaching the lambs. William Seward, later to become the US Secretary of State, sought to implement this doctrine to take away Mexico in order to avoid the impending civil war. Later, in that century, the United States made use of that doctrine to settle a boundary dispute between Venezuela and Britain much to Venezuela's annoyance. Richard Olney, the US secretary of State, made no secret of America's right as a great regional power to 'interpose' in disputes between these countries and any other European power. Germany complained that the United States hoped to convert Pacific Ocean into an American lake while Russia felt that the Monroe Doctrine was 'imbibed' into the American mind like a mother's milk into a child's mouth.

Another message of the Monroe Doctrine was America's reciprocal proposal to European powers not to intervene in the internal affairs of other nations while reserving the right to support freedom movements in the colonies in the Western Hemisphere . Warren Zimmerman writes, "Through the nineteenth century the doctrine became expansionist as well as exclusionist, a divine text for any president or secretary of state who sought to plant the flag in new lands". (Zimmerman, 2004, p.1)

Later on, the Monroe Doctrine also became a potent weapon for the US intervention on a global scale. During the Cold War, the United States tried to apply this doctrine in the case of Cuba and other Latin and Central American countries to counter and beat back communism. Even during the 1989 Panama crisis, President Bush widened the scope of the doctrine to include any threat, internal or external, to these countries as a pretext to intervene. Later on, as scholars point out, this doctrine was made global to justify interventions in various parts of the world from Afghanistan to Iraq. Likewise, even at the height of the Cold War, the United States did not object to Britain's violation of that doctrine when the latter invaded the Falklands. It is realism again and not the principles that mattered in the American foreign policy conducts.

The Monroe Doctrine completed another unfinished job of the war of independence. The promulgation of the doctrine made America free to pursue its independent foreign policy goals. With John Quincy Adams refusing to act as a 'cockboat followed by the British man-of-war', America saw through the British design of persisting on a joint declaration aimed at leashing America's interests in Cuba and Texas. Adams was not only concerned with growing assertiveness of France and Spain but also about Russian overtures close to the American border that sought to restrict the American interests in the Pacific. America was well on course to its destined role to take its place within the 'imperial' club. More than that, Monroe Doctrine paved the way for the American unilateralism.

The Manifest Destiny

The Manifest Destiny-another landmark event in the American history – proved to be invaluable both in terms of ideology and for all future American expansionism. The Manifest Destiny, according to some scholars can be viewed more as a phenomenon and idea than a doctrine for a specific historical era. The Manifest Destiny was rather an American version of colonialism based on racism, social Darwinism, cultural superiority, and the white man's burden. Like the Monroe Doctrine, the Manifest Destiny was another important plank for legitimizing the US expansionism in Latin America.

Although trade interests and new lands motivated this grand articulation, the Manifest Destiny was something more than that. The American business class had always looked upon the Westward expansion as a step towards the lucrative markets beyond the Pacific and thence into the Far East. So they needed some moral and 'spiritual' justification to convince the American people. John O' Sullivan gave expression both to the American adventurism and dynamism marked by constant mobility and to the imperial desires of the American policy-makers, at the same time. Here is an excerpt from what Sullivan wrote about his idea in 1839:

> The far-reaching, the boundless future will be the era of the American greatness. In its magnificent domain of space and time, the nation of many nations is destined to manifest to mankind the excellence of divine principles; to establish on earth the noblest temple ever dedicated to the worship of the Most High-the Sacred and the True.

> For this blessed mission to the nations of the world, which are shut out from the life-giving light of truth, has America been chosen; and her high example shall smite unto death the tyranny of kings, hierarchs, and oligarchs, and carry the glad tidings of peace and good will where myriads now endure an existence scarcely more enviable than that of beasts of the field.
>
> *—Zimmerman, 2004, p.33*

Such an amalgamation of the imperialisti penchant with value-based ideals was aimed at legitimizing America's 'divine' destiny to rule and remake the world in America's image. In a sense, The Manifest Destiny was what Communist Manifesto was for the Marxists. It sought to create a new national identity. It, too, had a global mission. That way, it was another step towards completing the unfinished job of the Declaration and the War of Independence. The Manifest Destiny gave concrete shape to some abstract ideas: how to implant the ideas of freedom and individual rights in the minds of other people. Zimmerman felt that 'much of the impetus for overseas expansion in the last third of nineteenth century was mental'. My Theory of Domination fully explains both the Monroe Doctrine and the Manifest Destiny in so far as the void created by the removal of the European powers from the Western Hemisphere was filled by the United States: replacement of one kind of domination by another. A quote from William Channing, a little later, would bear out the truth about this claim.

The Manifest Destiny enabled the United States to pursue its national interests boldly. It provided the requisite moral support to carry on the two-year US-Mexican war over the annexation of the independent republic of Texas that, in turn, added new territories in the shape of California, New Mexico, and Arizona via the treaty of Guadalupe Hidalgo to the territory of the United States. Likewise, negotiations were made in the 1850s for 'buying' off parts of Mexico, Cuba and Hawaii. In 1853, Captain Perry forced Japan to open its markets to the American traders. After the Civil War, then Secretary of State, William H. Seward took some official steps towards expanding the American political control from Alaska and Canada in the North to Mexico in the South and even beyond, into the Pacific islands of Hawaii, the Danish West Indies, Santo Domingo, Haiti, Culebra, French Guiana, Tiger Island, Cuba, Puerto Rico, and St.. Bartholomew. The Manifest Destiny quelled many of the state-center bickerings of the era and breathed a new life into the American republican-federal system. The Manifest Destiny happened to be the most potent vehicle to carry the 'Anglo-Saxon' silo referred earlier, closer to other parts of the world.

Nevertheless, The Manifest Destiny had its opponents even in its earlier days. In an 1837 letter to Henry Clay, William E. Channing wrote:

> Did this country know itself, or were it disposed to profit by self-knowledge, it would feel the necessity of laying an immediate curb on its passion for extended territory... we are a restless people, prone to encroachment, impatient of the ordinary laws.... We boast of our rapid growth, forgetting that, throughout nature, noble growths are slow. It is full time that we should lay on ourselves serious, resolute restraint................................"
>
> ... The Indians have melted before the white man, and mixed, with this vile sophistry! There is no necessity for crime. There is no fact to justify rapacious nations, any more than to justify gamblers and robbers, in plunder. We boast of the progress of society, and this progress consists in the substitution of reason and moral principle for the sway of the brute force...we talk of accomplishing our destiny. So did the late conqueror of Europe (Napoleon); and destiny consigned him to a lonely rock in the ocean, the prey of ambition which destroyed no peace but his own.
>
> —*Blum, p.276*

The Manifest Destiny was the American equivalent of the European Renaissance. It coincided with the period of the American Awakening and Romanticism. The Manifest Destiny became popular and acceptable in less than seven decades after the American independence, thanks again to the divisions amongst European powers. For example, had Napoleon not sold the vast tracts of land that we know today as Louisiana (he did so to marginalize the British further), Westward expansion would have lost its momentum. Had not Spain sold Florida to America, the United States could never claim Texas. The Manifest Destiny was destined to serve as the most 'enlightened' form of colonialism for the 'benign hegemon' in the modern era.

The Manifest Destiny, like other 'American' concepts is a constantly evolving idea. Earlier, it was aimed at consolidating the American grip in its own hemisphere. During the two world wars, the United States got a chance to fulfill its Manifest Destiny of liberating freedom-loving people from forces of oppression. During the Cold War it was America's divine duty to counter the Soviet brand of communism and to provide an alternative socio-political system for the rest of the world. The United States needed bases and support in every part of the world to counter communism and hence felt politically and morally justified in spreading the ideas of 'The Manifest Destiny', in the name of ensuring 'freedom' on a global scale. After the Cold War, it remained for the United States to fulfill its moral responsibility of completing the unfinished job of the Cold War, lest the rest of the world feels betrayed. The once 'divine' ideas behind the Manifest Destiny now worked in tandem with political and economic prescriptions like, democracy, liberal capitalism and human rights in the twentieth century and even beyond.

What we see in the post Cold War American foreign policies are the efforts at realizing a new Manifest Destiny on a global scale. If the first and older Manifest Destiny owed its principles to the transportation (railroads) and communications (the telegraph) revolutions then the new the Manifest Destiny of the new millennium owes it to the Information and the Internet revolutions. Taken together, the philosophical essence of the Manifest Destiny is that America has a right to reach out to other people of the rest of the world to spread its lofty ideals. The new Manifest Destiny of the new century is the New Bush Doctrine.

The Civil War

The American Civil War was another landmark event in the independent American history. Again the right man, Abraham Lincoln was there to take the war to a decisive end. The Civil war was the culmination of a series of developments over the conflicting issue of state-center relations that was raging throughout the United States for the most part of the nineteenth century. The North got concerned that the addition of new territories was tilting the balance in favor of the slave-holding South. Also, the ideals of individual rights and freedom as enshrined in the Declaration and the American Constitution would be a mockery so long as a large segment of population remained in eternal bondage.

Prior to independence, slavery was a common practice in every colony in America. While many states in the North abolished slavery by the end of the eighteenth century, the rural and plantation based economies of the Southern states found it profitable to continue, especially, after the cotton boom. The industrial North depended on free wage labor while the agricultural South employed slaves in huge numbers This alone created some irreconcilable differences over the future incorporation of slave holding states. Industrial North needed to modernize the less developed South with a view to secure an outlet for its accumulated capital. The annexation of the 'slave-populated' Texas from Mexico, whose government harbored anti-slavery policies, was a bone of contention between the North and the South prior to the Civil War. On top of it, Lincoln, unlike the previous American presidents, sought to stop the annexation of new territories.

However, economic compulsions made expansion a sine-qua-non. The single-cropped South had worn out its fertile lands and needed new territories for its cotton growing. The manufacturing North equally needed new territories to serve as outlets for its markets and investments. Acrimonious debates raged throughout the nation regarding the acquisition of new territories during the 1850s.

To make the matters worse for the South, Britain abolished the practice of slavery altogether in 1832. The Republican Party was already in favor of abolition of slavery even though many influential Southerners still dominated the Democratic Party. With the victory of Abraham Lincoln, a great protagonist of anti-slavery movement, some states in the South thought about outright cessation. It was on this the issue of cessation that the great American Continental War took place.

The South took advantage of the leniency of the American Constitution that reserved the right of cessation to the states. The crux was that if any Southern state seceded from the Union that would not only strike at the root of the federal republican system but also jeopardize the integrity of the nation because of 'domino' effects on other Southern states, and more ominously, a roll back effect on the Northern states. That would mean a repeat of another 'independence' struggle – a stark reminder of the fact that the American founders used the same weapon in 1776 against Britain.

The US Constitution honored the rights of states over those of the federation and based the American unity on the basis of voluntary association. Such a loose federation of 'independent' states contained seeds of secession at a later date. What is more, if secession were to be the order of the day, then the rational of the Declaration would be gainsaid.

Nevertheless, some states in the South were actually against slavery. It is this unity amongst the Northern states and disunity among those of the South that had been one of the causes for the South's defeat. It was a do-or-die battle for both the Unionists and the Confederates. The Southerners thought that they were upholding their constitutional rights of individual liberty in choosing their own governments while the North felt equally justified in trying to preserve the unity of the country.

Lincoln's proclamation of the abolition of slavery in mid-1862 was intended to destroy the economic and moral base of the South and to bring the war to a rapid conclusion. Many of the blacks volunteered to swell the ranks of fighters in the North. As a result, the North could muster an armed force of about 21 million men compared to the South's 7.5 million. The decision to abolish slavery could not have come at a better time as the Presidential election was due in a year's time and stakes for Lincoln were high. Thus both the Unionist and the Confederate armies were desperate to win important strategic locations before the elections.

In fact, stakes were much higher for Lincoln and the North. First, they happened to be the aggressors and the Southerners had merely to defend their territories on their own soil. Secondly, for the North, the battle must be carried to the extreme while the South needed some exemplary heroic acts and some gains, here and there, to force the North to come to the negotiating table. Any negotiation with the South would have justified and legitimized their demands. On top of it, Britain was closely watching the happenings in of every theater of war and Palmerstone even thought of siding with the Confederates till the reversal of the Confederate forces at Antietam led him to abandon his plans. Napoleon III's France made a dangerous overture in Mexico by installing Maximillian of Austria as the Emperor of Mexico.

Against all these odds, the North had three key advantages: its overwhelming superiority of manpower over the South, the presence of some brilliant army personnel that eventually turned the tide in the North's favor and securing Britain's support. The North also succeeded in keeping the European powers at arms length by its decision to abolish slavery. Yet another major reason for the North's win over the South was Lincoln's unflinching faith in the ultimate victory of the North in those dark days of the war when the South kept winning. The Civil War memories and its many legends became the American folklore as the average American viewed war not as a barbarous act but a noble and heroic act.

After the end of the Civil War, America showed its expansionist interest in the Pacific and Latin America, evident from William Seward's efforts to secure new territories in these regions: purchase of Virgin Islands from Denmark and Alaska from Russia in the 1860s. Only Cuba, Puerto Rico and a few smaller islands in the Pacific remained in European hands. I have already mentioned about the US overtures in Korea following the end of the war. By the end of the century, the United States achieved its principal goal of driving out the European powers from the whole of the New World.

Zimmerman interpreted the American expansion into the Pacific in terms of technological and industrial development in the aftermath of the unification. Even as late as 1880s, the US Navy was smaller compared to that of Chile. Zimmerman observed that during the Civil War economic strength passed from the planters to the industrialists, the financiers, and the businessmen. By the mid-1880s the United States led the world in the production of timber and steel, in meatpacking, and in the mining of coal, iron, gold, and silver. The United States grew to become the leading global energy consumer by 1890s and, by the turn of the century, the United States turned out more coal and steel than Britain and Germany combined. (Zimmerman, p.25)

D. The Spanish-American War, the Open Door, the Roosevelt Corollary and other policies till 1914

It remained for the Spanish-American war of 1898 to fully eject the European powers from the Western Hemisphere . Spanish-American war completed another unfinished job of the War of Independence by furnishing the

United States with a real opportunity to spread its ideals and values beyond its continental borders. The requisite mind-set for expansionism was already in place thanks to the Monroe Doctrine, The Manifest Destiny, Kippling's White Man's Burden, the Mexican War, the Civil war and the unification, the policies of the US presidents like Polk, Tyler, Buchanan, the good works done by some Secretaries of States, expansion of the American navy, inspiring works by intellectuals like Jack Turner and Brook Adams, the racial teachings and social Darwinism of that era, [Ernst Haeckel (biogenic law), John Fisk (Anglo-Saxonism) and Josiah Strong (Civilize and Christianize)], and the American growing economic might to transform America from the 'first period of the American history' to the next stage of its 'imperialist' take off.

The pressure of the newly expanded Navy Department and the interests of the business lobby proved to be the straws that broke the camel's back and led McKinley to declare the US-Spanish war in 1898. Nebraskan Senator John M. Thurston proclaimed, "War with Spain would increase the business and earnings of every the American railroad, it would increase the output of every the American factory. It would stimulate every branch of industry and domestic commerce". James Mason Callahan felt that

> Adding territory after territory to the American union, and extending her commerce and beneficent influence to distant lands and peoples, is the great central fact of the American history. Expansion, no-parasitic, vigorous and attractive, developing by affinity, contending against both restriction and secession, has been America's greatest feat.
>
> —*James Callahan, 1908, p.1*

The Spanish-American War

Two landmark developments in the US foreign policy history at about the same time heralded America's great sojourn beyond its borders: the Spanish American War and the Open Door Note. Native uplift and support for rebel movements had been the favorite catchwords of the American policy makers as a cover up for expansionism during this period. Prior to the Spanish-American war, the American media and various journals highlighted Spanish incompetence in Cuba. The American interventions in Cuba and the Philippines, however, had more to do with economic gains than the native uplift.

John Hyde remarked in the editorial in The National Geography that some justification for such intervention as in Cuba ought to be derived from the need to revive the US commercial relations with the vast and profitable market of Cuba. An editorial reprinted from Financial Review argued,

> What claim can any power advance, or by what right can they demand

> that our government evacuate these islands? None! .... this war will result in untold advantages to the United States. Our aim is to banish Spain from the Western continent and free an oppressed people. Our reward is the unexpected acquirement of territory and control of the trade of the Antilles, and a foothold in the development of the Orient.
>
> —*Hyde, NGM 9, No. 6, June 1898*

No less significant was the craving for the big Chinese market behind the acquisition of the Philippines. However, all these evoked strong reaction against the American expansionist policies. Richard Olney thought that the costs of bearing the above territories, like, Cuba, the Philippines, the Caribbean, and the Hawaii were not worth the exercise in view of the strains on the American resources. The obvious contradiction between republican values and imperialist aspirations called for fresh debates and newer interpretations in the changed circumstances.

Growing unrest in Cuba and the Spanish government's failure to quell the rebels led a reluctant American president, already under pressure from the Navy (since its initial build up, the Navy needed some 'theater' to test its power), media, academics, and the business groups, to order the American battleship USS Maine to proceed towards the Cuban capital, Havana. On February 15, 1898 that ship capsized following a 'mysterious' explosion killing 260 Americans on board. The United States seized this opportunity to foment anti-Spain sentiments by displaying the banner slogan, "Remember the Maine". Efforts by the Spanish authorities to deal with 'responsible' officers and the promise of granting autonomy instead of freedom to Cuba proved belated. McKinley, already dubbed as a weakling by the Spanish foreign Minister, De Lome, had little option other than to declare war against Spain.

The war was brief and the American victory complete in every theater of the war from the Caribbean to the Philippines. Some scholars, however, point to a $20 million US deal with Spain in bringing about such a swift American victory. Formal peace treaty was signed on 10 December the same year enabling the United States to gain domination over the Philippines, Guam, Puerto Rico and Cuba. While the European powers kept increasing their territories in the Dark Continent at about the same time, the United States added some 310,000 square kilometers, that is, 1, 20,000 square miles with 8.8 million people, only comparable with the gains of the Mexican war.

The Open Door Note

By the end of the nineteenth century, the American possessions in the Pacific consisted of a few islands like the Hawaii, Midway, Guam, and the Philippines bringing it closer to the gates of the Far East and China. Significantly, at about the same time the Chinese empire was in its last legs. The 1895 Japanese victory made China more vulnerable to outside interventions. Several great powers converged on the collapsing empire like hawks to carve out their respective spheres of influence. In the three years after 1895, Japan, Russia, Britain, Germany, and France succeeded in extracting more territorial and commercial concessions through force and persuasion.

Such ominous developments perturbed the British policy-makers, who, in early 1898 proposed free commercial access to Chinese markets. Secretary of State, John Hay took the initiative once the 1898 war ended. The United States, all by itself, declared an open door note to all the above powers (a modern version of the 'most favored nation' status) to allow every other nation free access in all the Chinese ports under their spheres of influence while urging them to preserve the sovereignty and territorial integrity of that great land, at the same time. Demands for a uniform railway and harbor charges for every trading nation were meant to serve the growing economic interests of the American tradesmen. China, in its turn, was supposed to benefit from the proceeds of tariffs and duties that would accrue to the imperial government instead of these powers.

The response to Hay's note was lukewarm as each contending power made its response conditional on the decisions of others. At one point of time, Hay felt that unless America had power to force the issue, his plans for Open Door to China wouldn't materialize. The United States didn't have sufficient military strength to do so at that time. Nevertheless, Hay's note encountered no objection either. Hay declared in March 1900 that the open door plan was "Final and Definitive".

The Open Door could be seen as a Far Eastern version of the Monroe Doctrine to caution other powers to stay away from spheres of influence politics in China and to facilitate the American entry into the vast Chinese markets. Other contending powers, however, hardly desisted from meddling in the affairs of China. The Open door was the continuation of same old American policy to force open the hitherto inaccessible markets to the American traders, so long tried in Latin America, Central America, and the Caribbean basin throughout the nineteenth century, and in Japan after 1853.

The US Open Door policy towards China at the beginning of the twentieth century was aimed at denying absolute commercial advantage to the European powers and Japan. It was an undeclared policy of America, just like the Monroe Doctrine, not to let Europe expand to areas not under the latter's control. However, the United States could do nothing to stop Europe from grabbing Africa in the last decades of the nineteenth century partly because of its geographical disadvantage and partly because of the need to justify its own interventions in various Latin American countries.

There is a definite link between the American policy of Neutrality in the late eighteenth and the early nineteenth century and the Open Door policy, a century later. Both were aimed at keeping the American trade routes and commercial markets intact. The American decision to send armies to quell the Boxer rebellion was to prove that the United States was in the race for managing affairs in China. The United States played its traditional 'value' card by advocating the observance of the Chinese territorial sovereignty to gain maximum trade concessions in the Far East.

Besides other advantages, the Open Door had a clear geo-strategic significance: to consolidate the American gains in Latin American countries and extending America's area of operation in the Far East. Time was in America's favor as Spain lost most of its New World possessions and imperial Britain, alarmed at the prospect of Germany's rise to prominence, turned less hostile to the United States while France was still recovering from its humiliating defeat in the 1870 war against Germany. A few years later Russia would be humiliated by Japan in the Far East. Growing Japanese influence in the Pacific and Japan's overtures to Hawaii in the 1890s also hastened the proclamation of the Open Door Note.

Other developments

In the closing decade of the nineteenth century, fearful of the challenges from a revisionist Germany, Britain turned friendlier to the United States by falling in line with the American demands on the Venezuelan and the Panama crisis. Britain compromised on the issue of the Alaskan – Canadian border dispute and, more importantly, lent support to America in its 1898 war against Spain by allowing America to use its Caribbean and Far Eastern ports as bases of military operation against Spain. The United States reciprocated by maintaining a low-key attitude in imperial Britain's war against the Boers.

Theodore Roosevelt sent a veiled warning to the European powers and Japan as the Great White Fleet sailed around the world on a good will mission from 16 December, 1907 to February 22, 1909. America assumed the role of a mediator in the Russo-Japanese War in 1904 and in the Moroccan crisis in 1906. The message was loud and clear: *the United States was fast becoming a great power and was poised to play a balance of power politics alongside other imperialist powers.*

Pan Americanism during the 1890s was merely an extension of the Monroe Doctrine for dominating the Latin American nations. The main issues and tools were the economic ones like the lowering of trade barriers and formation of Customs Union. These were not different from what we see in post 1945 American efforts at reducing tariffs and other trade barriers on a global scale and imposition of sanctions against countries engaged in unequal and unreasonable trade practices with the USA. Here, too, we find the continuity of the US foreign policies. Several treaties of reciprocity were forced on most of the Latin American countries barring, Columbia, Haiti and Venezuela. By the turn of the twentieth century, America became more active in Central America and even established a Central American Court of Justice, to arbitrate disputes among the Central American states.

The Roosevelt Corollary

With the annexation of the Philippines and the conversion of Cuba into an American protectorate following the end of the Spanish-American war of 1898, the US colonial ambitions could no longer be suppressed. In his State of the Union address, Theodore Roosevelt, clarified the US perceptions of the world, "The increasing interdependence and complexity of international political and economic relations, render it incumbent on all civilized and orderly powers to insist on the proper policing of the world." After the Spanish-American war, the United States found itself in a position to add another tick at its expansionist instincts through a far more assertive declaration. Roosevelt, content with engaging the European powers in the Far East, thought about consolidating America's 'exclusive' grip on the Latin American and the Central American countries through the proclamation of what could be construed as an extended version of the Monroe Doctrine.

Roosevelt was obviously concerned about the new pretexts adopted by the European powers to collect their debts from the defaulting Latin American nations and use them as grounds for intervening in Latin American affairs in defiance of the tenets of the Monroe Doctrine. Ominous developments in Venezuela and the Dominican Republic led Roosevelt to carry out the import of the Monroe Doctrine to its logical extreme by developing on an idea, first floated by the Argentine foreign Minister, Luis Drago. Drago had pleaded that the European powers ought to desist from using force to occupy various defaulting Latin American countries unless these defaulters defied any arbitration in this regard.

Roosevelt corollary, as it came to be known, stated that the United States could not remain indifferent to European bullying in an area that had grown increasingly sensitive to the security and commercial interests of the United States and that the latter rather reserved that right for intervention in the region. In doing so, he supported the right of the civilized nations to strengthen 'failed' civilizations but emphasized that such a role could be best played by a stronger regional power than the far away countries.

> Chronic wrongdoing, or an impotence which results in a general loosening of the ties of civilized society, however, may in America, as elsewhere, ultimately require intervention by some civilized nation, and in the Western Hemisphere the adherence of the United States to the

> Monroe Doctrine may force the United States, however reluctantly, in flagrant cases of such wrong-doing or impotence, to the exercise of an international police power.

There were sixty cases of the American intervention to civilize the rebel and rogue governments in Latin and Central America in just twenty-five years after the proclamation of the new version of Monroe doctrine in the form of the Roosevelt corollary. For Roosevelt, the higher must supplant the lower. As for the Philippines, he believed that the American rule in that archipelago would rather improve the conditions of the native people. However, it remained for Franklin Delano Roosevelt to moderate his uncle's high-handed approach towards Latin America through his Good Neighbor Policy.

Let me now sum up the implications of the various major developments and policies discussed above from the standpoint of the American specialties like the "American' republicanism, the 'American' federalism, the 'American' identity, etc.

Independent America was conceived with the idea of liberty but in reality, it showed all the manifestations of dominating the neighboring Central and Latin American countries. During the course of the nineteenth century, the United States subverted many revolutionary activities detrimental to its interests in Chile, Cuba, and Santo Domingo. This was in clear violation of what Jefferson meant by the right of people in every nation to determine their fate in whatever way they liked. There was, of course, occasion when the United States declined to wage war against a republican dominated Chile that turned hostile to the US interests in the last decades of the nineteenth century only to carry out its campaigns against the same country a few years later when that country ceased to be republican.

Latter generations of the American policy-makers and intellectuals realized that the principle of non entanglement in the affairs of other countries, laid down by their founders, were, rightly or wrongly, equated with the policy of isolationism by some statesmen and politicians, within and abroad. Isolationism, they felt stood in the way America's becoming a great international power. No country could dictate terms in the international affairs by staying aloof. Lippmann went so far as to say, "The interrelation of people has gone so far that to advocate international laissez-faire now is to speak a counsel of despair."

The United States, however, encountered some problems as it sought to extend its influence beyond its borders through its efforts at transposing the American political values abroad. For example, the American federalism bestowed complete sovereignty to its constituent states. Yet the American history so far was one of strained state-center relations. If the United States found it problematic to deal with issues connected with its principles in its own land, how could it hope to implement such ideas on other countries whose political systems differed significantly from those of the United States?

More specifically, the right of self-determination of nations required their people to have the right to choose their own governments. The American policy of installing democratic governments elsewhere thus ran counter to its own federal-republican principles. How can the natural rights of individuals, as enshrined in the Declaration, be reconciled with democracy, that is, rule by majority? Secondly, the promulgation of inviolable natural rights failed to abolish slavery in the newly independent states of America and to emancipate the blacks after independence. By that logic, carrying the concept of the American republicanism to other parts of the world seemed illogical. Even the Declaration admits the sovereignty of other people. The net result of all these contradictions is that the United States often had to modify its original stand regarding 'liberty and freedom'. For example, ensuring 'peace and security' for the human kind as a whole seemed more appropriate during the Roosevelt era in the 1930s. Later, various presidential doctrines and phrases like, containment, enlargement, etc., were regularly floated to justify the US foreign policies in a desperate bid to maintain its republican face. This creates tremendous confusion in the minds of other people who see only narrow national interests behind such American values.

A look at the existence of the opposites – involvement and isolationism – helps in explaining the American mind-set and its foreign policies. First, America developed an anti-colonial mind-set because of the oppressive nature of European colonial rule in the North American continent. Secondly, since America was under prolonged domination both of Spain and Britain, it assumed many of the characteristics of their cultures, peninsular or islandic, good or bad, humane as well as anti-human, entanglement and isolationism, in its thoughts and perceptions of the outside world. As a result, despite the avowed declaration of its founding fathers to stay aloof in the matters of other countries, a parallel trend towards 'colonial-imperial' approach could be found in such cases as the Louisiana Purchase; in the hidden agenda for annexation of Canada in the US-British war of 1812; in the Monroe Doctrine of 1823; in the Manifest Destiny of the 1840s; in the annexation of Texas; in the American occupation Hawaii and Samoa in the Pacific; in captain Perry's forced opening of Japan in 1853; the American interventions, diplomatic as well as military, in the Central and Latin American countries such as Nicaragua, Haiti, Mexico, the Dominican Republic, Venezuela, Chile, Brazil and the isthmus in Panama during the course of the nineteenth century. The American specialties, referred above, helped in creating a protective aura round the American body-politic and had given the United States an extra shield and advantage over any other great power in history in matters of foreign policy conduct.

Whether it was the Neutrality, the Monroe Doctrine, the Manifest

Destiny, the American Civil War, the Open Door, and the Roosevelt Corollary – all these policies went a long way towards completing some unfinished jobs of independence mentioned earlier. For example, the Civil War settled, once and for all, the intriguing question of state-center relations and paved the way for the emancipation of the black African-Americans. The Manifest Destiny carried the message of the American republican faith in the freedom and natural rights of human beings to choose their own governments beyond its borders. Roosevelt corollary acquainted other nations with the 'real' nature of the American identity and nationhood by its insistence on the acceptance of the ideals of democracy, peace, rule of law, and transparency by other nations.

The simple truth is that the American foreign policies since independence were inconceivable without those American specialties. Since the American specialties were creative principles, as mentioned in an earlier chapter, this meant that the American foreign policies ought to be continuous and consistent. The American political system would rather be rendered despotic once these American specialties is removed or changed. *It is another thing that the United States might be arriving at the same 'expansionist' destination reached by other erstwhile great powers but it has been doing so from earlier times by riding the "American' Cavalcade and by a detour with the advantage of having one or two extra options than other great powers. For other great powers foreign policies were and still are means towards enhancing their national interests through direct territorial expansion while for the United States values and national interests run parallel although national interests are sometimes couched in value terms.*

The last decade of the nineteenth century and the successive years in the next century provided a set piece situation for America's global expansionism. Yet, the United States continued to suffer from two bottlenecks during this period: its republican ideals and its isolationist hangover. How could America meaningfully justify its lone republican system when most of the world abided by the rule of imperialism? Two options lay ahead: either the United States must spread its republican ideals and its politico-economic system elsewhere or it must assume an imperial role – benign and tempered by the American specialties. America faced two conflicting choices: whether to lead the life of a 'holy' mandarin and enlightening others through moral precepts or to act out the role of a messianic 'missionary' who would go abroad not to slay monsters but to bring other peoples from darkness to light, even if it, sometimes required use of force.

The Declaration being an open charter, in the sense that its meanings need constant evaluations and adjustments to suit changing circumstances, it is congruent with my concept of perpetual freedom discussed in the last chapter. Likewise, the American specialties or the American creed-an outgrowth of the Declaration – need ever-new testing grounds to verify their relevance under changing conditions. This can be done only through the compelling need to work towards 'perpetual freedom'.

A special mention must be made of the year 1913 that propelled the United States well on the course of wielding world leadership. The creation of the FED, the Income Tax Act and President Wilson's support for democracy on a global scale changed the entire complexion of the American foreign policy from a regional to a global one.

The US and the First World War

President Woodrow Wilson, in his second inaugural address, March 1917, summed up the American position on the war raging in Europe in the following words:

> We are a composite and cosmopolitan people. We are of the blood of all the nations that are at war. The currents of our thoughts as well as the currents of our trade run quick at all seasons back and forth between us and them. The war inevitably set its mark from the first alike upon our minds, our industries, our commerce, our politics and our social action. To be indifferent to it, or independent of it, was out of the question.

Wilson emphasized that the principles upon which America was founded never pertained to a single province or to a continent but those were global. Indeed, WWI presented the first real opportunity to break America's centuries-old isolation. Interestingly, the US isolationism would have been more pronounced if the United States remained aloof in the war. Both the winners and the losers would have looked upon the United States as an extremely 'selfish', 'unsociable' and an 'alien' nation. To be honest, the First World War served a sort of fait accompli for that great nation: either socialize more deeply with the world community of nations or languish in the hemispheric isolation, forever. The United States seized the opportunity provided by the First Great War to fulfill its long cherished dream of erecting an empire, albeit, an invisible one.

By the beginning of the twentieth century, transportation and communications were already sufficiently developed. An abundance of economic opportunities thrown open by unprecedented developments in science and technology, particularly, in the giant public utility sectors, the telephone and the electricity, meant that the world had become much more interdependent than ever before. This, in turn, led to more bold and imaginative thoughts in political, philosophical, and social spheres as more and more common people got involved in politics. The orthodox, fixed and 'divine rights' of monarchs came under another round of scrutiny following the consummation of the gains from the second wave of industrial revolution as social democratic and socialist movements held sway in Europe. Colonialism as an international system was fast becoming anachronistic as wars became more frequent and lethal.

Improved communications meant that the gap between the distant and the near-by places, colonies and their mother countries, and between nations themselves, were so narrowed that happenings in one country could be known in a few hours time instead of several days they took in the preceding century. Just half a century ago, it took several days for the news of Lincoln's death to reach Europe. Once the distance factor lost its enchantment, colonialism lost its viability and value. As the repressive activities of the colonial rulers were brought to the knowledge of the people in the mother countries, they caused great embarrassment for the rulers at home.

In the motherlands, European colonialism was fancied as long as they delivered the goods to their own people. With the passage of time, many new competitors arrived on the scene and the clash of national interests more often led to armed conflicts. People in the mother countries no longer remained immune from the disturbances in the overseas colonies. Citizens in the motherland became weary and started to dislike the system that now demanded more and more financial and even physical 'sacrifices' from them. The same zeal and energy that were spent collectively in justifying the incumbent regime recoiled on it with equal hatred and intensity.

Once colonialism fell from the grace of people, it was doomed. This provided a golden opportunity for the United States to fill in the vacuum and benefit from the hitherto closed huge colonial markets. While the colonial powers simply exploited their colonies and did little to develop their economies and markets, this meant that United State would have to shoulder that responsibility of developing these underdeveloped economies, as well. As described earlier, objective conditions were already ripe for a new international order to replace the existing one. No wonder, the United States floated the idea of the formation of a community of nations, the League of Nations, to spread the American political, economic, and cultural values on a global scale.

The United States had never been in favor of a single power domination of Europe, not so much because of its own security concerns, but because of the fact that such a situation would destabilize Europe and disrupt all trading activities, as was the case during the great Napoleonic wars. The United States knew that any single power domination like that of the Habsburgs or the British, would deprive them of the vast markets in the colonies and their dependencies and would be the greatest stumbling block for free trade. Nicholas Spykeman in his book America's Strategy in World Politics was even against the formation of a single Europe via an all-European federation.

Wilson had initial problems with entering the war and choosing allies because he had won the election on the promise to keep his country out of the war. Moreover, the American population was divided on this issue. Both the Anglo-American group and the Irish-German groups exerted significant influence on the American policy-makers because of their numerical strengths. It was the latter group that opposed any American attempt to enter the war on the side of the allies. So Wilson had to wait till things deteriorated further in the European theater of war. Meantime, his efforts were limited to urging the warring parties to a peace conference formulated in 1916 by the House-Grey memorandum and to the Sunrise Proposal in assessing the willingness of Congress to support the American entry in the war. Wilson wanted a peace in Europe in which no party should either be a winner or a loser. Already, the business class was getting nervous and impatient, as they feared heavy financial losses in the case of a German victory.

However, there were other happenings that had expedited the American entry into the war. First, German U-boat campaigns against the US merchant vessels culminated in the Lusitania episode and hastened the American entry into the war. Samuel Flagg Bemise thought that it was the German submarine attacks that had compelled the United States to enter the war. Secondly, the unearthing of the German foreign Minister, Arthur Zimmerman's telegram to the German Embassy in Mexico offering Germany's support in the event of a Mexican invasion of the United States should Mexico try to retrieve its territory in Texas, New Mexico, and Arizona, lost in the Mexican war, made the United States aware of the real threat of a possible German invasion of North America. Thirdly, the US entry into the war was a foregone conclusion at a time when the Atlantic route to Britain was nearly totally cut off and the collapse of the Italian and Russian front became imminent. In an important way, World War I turned out to be a battle for supremacy between Germany and the United States.

It still is not easy to comprehend why the United States took the side of the Allied powers. More specifically, why the US chose to support Britain and not Germany? Was it due to the common bond of language and the Anglo-Saxon sentiments? Parkins in his The Great Rapprochement, commented that this Anglo-American tie had grown stronger by the turn of the twentieth century. Britain's softer attitude towards the US in regard to the Venezuelan and the Alaskan disputes and a new agreement on the control of the Isthmus Canal, referred earlier, was a pointer in that direction. The same sentiment was echoed when Mahan eloquently said, " We stand at the opening of a period when the question is to be settled decisively, though the issue may be long delayed, whether the Oriental or the Western Civilization is to dominate throughout the earth." And again, " In the unity of heart among the English-speaking races lay the best hope of humanity in the doubtful days ahead." Social Darwinism and increasing immigration from Asia and Southern Europe reinforced these Anglo-Saxonist feeling. Yet there were several real political reasons that finally determined on whose behalf the United States would enter the war.

Germany had little possession in the New World compared to Britain. So, there were less anti-German feelings in America. The state of the German economy and its development signified that Germany needed a huge market in some future and that can be obtained only in the vast Latin American countries. Even then, Germany had to share it with some other power because it was beyond Germany's capacity to meet the mass demands of a whole range of products in these regions, alone. For Germany, a power sharing either with France or Britain was out of the question simply because Germany wouldn't like to see an economically mighty neighbor. The United States fitted the bill. According to Roland G. Usher it wouldn't be threatening either to the United States or Canada. Yet there was a caveat. Once in possession of the English and the French colonies, a victorious Germany would command tremendous resources both in terms of men and material. It would then be easy for Germany to launch an attack on the United States and to overpower it.

Conversely, victory for Britain would have meant that the latter would be free from the conflicts of Europe and a significant gainer of German colonial possessions in Africa and the Pacific and to some extent in Latin America, simultaneously. Britain would be far stronger and well placed to turn its attention to regain its lost possessions not only in Latin America, (neutralizing the force of the Monroe Doctrine) but also would be tempted to 'invade' North America via the land route of Canada where it wielded more power than the US. A win for Britain would not only upset the balance of power in Europe but also would lead its navy to resort to unrestricted bullying tactics in the Atlantic so far held in check by the German sea power. Samuel Bemis pointed out how the British Navy deliberately closed the West Indies to the American ships after the American independence and how they were demanding compensation for the Loyalists who fought by their sides. If a victorious Britain could claim the Panama Canal, the lifeline of the American trade that connects both the Atlantic and the Pacific, then it could portend danger for the entire North American continent.

Despite the above reasons for supporting Germany in World War I, the United States took the side of the Allied powers. The dream of a League of Nations led Wilson to take the side of the Allies because it was Britain and France and not Germany who controlled most of the overseas colonies. The American trading interests and overseas markets could be secured and maintained through a quid pro quo arrangement for entering the war on behalf of the allies. Being a landlocked country, Germany had virtually no significant overseas colonial possessions. Above all, Wilson's personal fascination for Britain and his Anglo-American sentiments tilted the US support for the allies led by Britain.

If the Great Napoleonic war presented unbounded opportunities for the American businessmen and policy-makers (the promulgation of Monroe Doctrine helped drive away the hawkish European powers from its backyards), WWI offered the US vast scope to extend the US influences on a global scale. The American policy makers acted according to an assumption: the United States must have unbridled freedom of trading rights with all the nations of the earth freed from the bondage of colonialism – again, an unfinished job of the Declaration.

The United States in the inter war years

Lord Cecil compared the position of the United States after the First World War with that of Great Britain after the Napoleonic wars. WWI, indeed, enabled the United States to become the focal point of global trade activities as its own merchandise exports increased nearly four-fold compared to its pre-war figure of $2.5 billion and the export of manufactured goods registered significant increase.

Referring to the inter war years, Paul Kennedy observed that the United States, after the end of the war became the world's greatest financial and creditor nation with largest stock of gold, besides being the largest producer of manufactures and foodstuffs. This period of economic boom lasted throughout the 1920s till the Great Depression of 1929 set in. The US willingness to join the World Court, sign arbitration treaties and to discourage war by outlawing it were all aimed at ensuring international stability that would serve and enhance the American economic interests after the War.

But all these failed to reverse the American policy of isolationism in the post war period despite Wilson's frantic efforts to support rights of self-determination of nations and to set up the League of Nations. The American isolationism during the inter war era was also influenced among others by the mid-Western populism and the pressure from the agriculturists, who, having made enormous profits through export of their produce, needed more protection at home to offset the resulting contraction of markets following the end of the war. Wilson hoped to create a new international order in which the League of Nations would act as a 'supra-national' body to solve conflicts between nations without recourse to war. Wilson's failure to win both the political parties at home shattered his dreams about a future international order based on a world of democracies.

The Articles X, XIV, and XVI of the League covenant were unacceptable to the US Congressmen. Article X read, " The Members of the League undertake to respect and preserve as against external aggression the territorial integrity and existing political independence of all Members of the League. In case of any such aggression or in case of any threat or danger of such aggression the Council shall advise upon the means by which this obligation shall be fulfilled." The United States had reservations about article XIV's provision for a "Permanent Court of International Justice". Article XVI evoked intense opposition from the Congress as that article sought to impose commercial, financial, and economic restrictions on a covenant-breaking member and for raising necessary forces from member countries to counter the errant member. The commitment that the United States would be required to take part in any war should any League member be attacked by another country was perceived as taking away the power of Congress to declare war. Moreover article XVI concerned the issue of sovereignty of America in controlling its armed forces.

The US policies in the inter war period met with mixed response among the scholarly communities. Walter Lippman (the US Foreign Policy Shield of the Republic) observed that World War II could have been averted if the US had cooperated with its erstwhile Allies of the First World War. Instead, the whole of the inter war period was spent in aimless pursuits of subversion of the League of Nations by the Americans, the Washington Naval conference, Kellogg-Briand Pact, the Stimson Doctrine, the Neutrality Acts and the Great Depression of the 1930s.

The United States revived Germany from its dismal economic position by generous loans under the Dawes plan because the 'democratic' Weimar republic was doing America's bidding. A strong and peaceful Europe sustained by the US aid was deemed a sine-qua-non to defeat the forces of communism. Economic compulsions also led America to help European economic recovery because of the need to market American goods. Other American policies focused on the disarmament treaties of the period to limit arms race and the drive for land hunger and elimination of war from the face of the earth. These were, (1) the treaty between the United States of America, the British Empire, France, Italy and Japan signed at Washington, in the Conference on the Limitation of Armament in Washington, November 12, 1921-February 6, 1922; (2) Conference establishing a commission of jurists to consider the laws of war, February 4, 1922; and (3) the signing of the Kellog-Briand treaty to renounce war as an instrument of national policy.

Edwin Gay held America's "narrow nationalist" tariff policy the main culprit in precipitating and prolonging the Great Depression of the 1930s.

Nevertheless, the American foreign policies towards Europe during the inter war years appeared incomprehensible, half-hearted, and inconsistent. The United States supported Fascism to combat communist autocracy and even supplied Italy with oil despite the latter's occupation of Abyssinia. On top of it, Italy had violated the 1925 Geneva Protocol by deploying 300 to 500 tonnes of mustard gas during the war. Some authors even found a deliberate intention on Roosevelt's part not to ally with France and Britain even during the 1938

Sudetan crisis that could have stopped the German aggression.

All these dangers could have been avoided if Britain, Russia and the United States woke up to the dangers that seemed to threaten the entire world and acted promptly instead of indulging in calculations about their respective benefits out of power politics. Britain and the USA hoped that a stronger Germany would turn to the East or, at least, would act as a counterweight to the Soviet Union. In Stalin's calculation, German aggression must be diverted towards the Western powers to enable the USSR not only to expand in the Baltic and the Balkans but also in the Far East where it could amass its armed forces in large numbers. The result was, as Brewster C. Denny felt that with a little more commitment on the part of France, Britain and the United States, like in the first World War, at least 20 million lives could have been saved. Instead it became a story of missed opportunities from Manchuria to Munich.

By the end of the 1930s, it had become increasingly clear that the impending Armageddon could be delayed, if at all, but not prevented. The United States did not sit idle, either. It had the premonition that it might be called upon to join the war on behalf of the allies for the same reasons that had led it to do so in the previous war. To start with, Japan's ravenous bid to subjugate China led Roosevelt to normalize relationship with the 'pariah' Soviet Union. The United States recognized the USSR in 1933. The United States made it up with its 'aggrieved' regional partners (because of the bitterness generated by the US highhandedness in Central and Latin America, in the early decades of the century) through Roosevelt's Good Neighbor policy to deny the Germans any leeway in rupturing the hemispheric unity. Memories of the Zimmerman episode were still afresh. Secondly, the United States had never tired of reminding Italy, Germany, and Japan regarding its disapproval of their aggressive policies in Ethiopia, Saar, the Rhineland, and Manchuria in the 1930s. The United States tried to isolate Mussolini from Hitler by being somewhat soft on the League-mandated sanctions on Italy. However, all these proved inadequate to prevent the war.

American entry into the Second World War followed the same pattern as in the previous war: (1) initially, adopting a neutral stand; (2) subsequent tilt in favor of the allies with the tacit US support for the allied 'blockading' of German ships; (3) helping the allies with all sorts of indirect help sufficient to perpetrate serious doubts about the American neutrality in the minds of the German leaders. All these American ploys worked well during the First World War till Germany became convinced that it was better to go to war with the United States rather than allowing it any further freedom of the seas to 'help' Britain. Yet, Hitler's Germany desperately tried to avoid that earlier German mistake and exercised utmost restraints in the high seas even in the face of growing American provocations.

According to one school of thought, this might have led an impatient Roosevelt to fix his eyes on a growingly arrogant and expansionist Japan. He ordered freezing of Japanese assets and imposition of trade sanctions, thereby, precipitating severe economic and energy crisis for that country. Japan tried to make up by turning its attention on the South East Asian colonies under European domination and, thereafter, launching a surprise attack on Pearl Harbor on 7 December 1941 (a repeat of the 1904 surprise attack on Port Arthur in the Russo-Japanese war) to deactivate the American naval forces in the Pacific. America declared war on Japan. Germany made the fatal blunder of declaring war on the United States.

As in the previous war, the United States entered WWII at a late stage. On both the occasions, it waited for the warring parties to get utterly exhausted in order to make the *'American'* presence indispensable and decisive. The United States hoped to extract many diplomatic and strategic advantages by letting things to worsen further in the European theater so as to increase the odds of survival for the contending parties. After all, there was no direct and immediate threat to the American security. Roosevelt managed to extract some rights in the British Caribbean bases in lieu of a few old American destroyers. There was another reason for such initial deliberations on America's part. Besides the 'value' elements that led George Washington, Quincy Adams, and Jefferson to advocate non-entanglement in European conflicts, the United States knew that colonialism suffered from an inherent systemic defect that led to frequent wars between the European powers. Would it not be a sheer wastage of resources if the United States intervened to merely keep the existing international order going at its present form? An alternative to prevalent international order must have to be offered in order to ensure peace, stability, freedom, and prosperity for every nation. The United States believed that such a thoroughgoing change couldn't be brought about in the colonies until a more deepening crisis compels these powers to turn to America for help.

Anyway, it was once again the national interests, and not values, that played a major role in the American foreign policy decisions during and after WWII. In the initial years of the war, the United States limited its role in helping the allies with financial and material assistance to keep the war going and prevent their fall. America thought (because of the 'distance' factor) that a full-scale American commitment was unwarranted. The American logic as mentioned above was simple: the more protracted grew the war, the more would it exhaust all the warring parties and the more they would come to depend on the United States for economic help, both for meeting the mounting costs of war and for their future economic reconstructions. It was a set-piece situation for the United States to realize its imperialistic dreams on a global scale.

There were other important security considerations, too. The 1936

Berlin pact of the Axis alliance and Japanese attack on the US navy at Pearl Harbor made America wake up to the realities of the international political situation. What would happen in the likely scenario after the fall of the Soviet Union and Britain? This would not only ensure a single party domination of Europe but also lead to the emergence of a far stronger Germany controlling the resources of Europe, Asia and Africa. Secondly, this would put Germany in control of the vital trade and oil routes in the Atlantic, the Mediterranean and the Middle East. Germany would also be in a position to consolidate its grip in Latin America where it had its few colonies and control the Panama Canal and the Gulf of Mexico, thereby, cutting off the vital US trade routes and commerce with the outside world. Moreover, Japan, on the other side of the Pacific, would further constrain the American trade in the Far East. On the other hand, a Soviet victory without or with minimum American help would again mean a single power domination of Europe by another totalitarian state who would then turn its forces in the Pacific to put its imperial talons in the Far East.

The United States, thus struck at the most appropriate moment when the developments in Stalingrad made it clear that it was beyond Germany's capacity to defeat the dogged and determined Soviet army. The United States had already started providing the "lend-lease" Aid package to keep the Soviets in the war. Truman as a Senator once commented that the American policy was to support Germany if the Soviet Union were winning and vice-versa until both the Soviet and German forces spent themselves out. However, the growing US realization of Germany's pathological racial hatred and the inhuman atrocities committed by both Japan and Germany finally led the United States to enter the war on behalf of the allies.

References and readings

Niall Ferguson, Empire, *How Britain Made the Modern World*, Penguin Books, London, 2003.

The Declaration of Independence, In Congress, July 4, 1776, A declaration by the Representatives of the United States of America, In General Congress Assembled. http//www.linecamp.com/merchants/freedom_documents/declaration of Ind us_declof independence.htm

Washington's Farewell Address, 40, 42 www.usinfo.state.gov

Thomas Jefferson to James Monroe, 1823, ME: 15: 436

Warren Zimmerman, First Great Triumph, *How Five the Americans Made Their Country A World Power*, Farrar, Straus and Giroux, NY, 2004.

Walter LaFeber, the American *Age, the United States Foreign Policy at Home and Abroad since 1750*, W.W. Norton & Company, NY, London, 1994.

Frederick Merk, *The Manifest Destiny and Mission in the American History*, Vintage Books, N.Y., 1963; Richard W. Van Alstyne, *The Risingthe American Empire*, NY., W.W. Norton, 1974.

The Monroe Doctrine, President Monroe's Seventh Annual Message to Congress, December 2, 1823, Avalon Project at Yale Law School, According to LaFeber, the US exports to Latin America shot up from $6.7 million in 1816 to 1821 and the latter absorbed 13 per cent of the US exports.

Blum Schlesinger, jr.et.al. The National Experience: A History of the United States, 6th ed., NY, Harcourt Brace Hovanovich, 1985.

James Callahan, An Introduction to the American Expansion Policy, Department of History and Political Science, West Virginia University, 1908.

John Hyde, Commerce of the Philippine Islands, NGM 9, no. 6, June, 1898.

Richard Olney, *The Growth of Our Foreign Policy*, Atlantic, 85, 1900.

the Roosevelt Corollary, www.ourdocuments.gov

Woodrow Wilson, Second Inaugural Address, March,1917. http//www.bartleby.com/124/pres45.htm/

R.G. Adams, *History of The Foreign Policy of the United States*, NY, Macmillan, 1924.

Max Boot, *The Savage Wars of Peace, Small Wars and the Rise of the American Power*, NY, 2002.

H.W. Brand, What America owes to the World, Cambridge, 1998.

Robert W. Tucker and David C. Hendrickson, *The Fall of the First British Empire: Origins for the War of the American Independence*, Baltimore, 1982.

Richard D. Burns, eds., *Guide to the American Foreign Relations since 1700*, Oxford, 1983.

Arthur B. Darling, *Our Rising Empire, 1763-1803*, New Haven, CT, 1940.

North American Review, vols1-20, Ithaca, Cornell University Press, http//cdl.library.cornell.edu/moa/browse, journals/nora.html

Norman Graebner, eds., *Traditions and Values: the American Diplomacy, 1790-1865*, Washington, 1985.

Richard W. Van Alstyne, *The Rising the American Empire*, NY, 1960.

Albert Bushnel Hart, *Foundations of the American Foreign policy*, NY, 1970.

William Graham Sumner, *The Fallacy of Territorial Extension*, Forum, June, 1916.

Richard B. Morris, *The Peacemakers: The Great Powers and the American*

Independence, NY, 1965.

Jerald A. Combs, the American *Diplomatic History, Two Centuries of changing Interpretations*, Berkeley, 1986.

Tyler Dennet (John Hay: From Poetry to Politics) and the Americans in Eastern Asia: A Critical Study of the Policy of the United States with reference to China, Japan, and Korea in the 19th century , NY, 1922.

Charles Tansill, *America Goes to War*, NY, 1963.

Charles A. Beard, *Devil Theory of War*, NY, 1936.

Newton Baker, *Why We Went to War*, London, 1972.

Ernest May, *The World War and the American Isolation, 1914-1917*, MA, 1959.

Thomas Bailey, *Woodrow Wilson and the Great Betrayal*, NY, 1945.

Charles C. Tansill, *Backdoor to War: The Roosevelt Foreign policy, 1933-41*, Chicago, 1971.

Frederick Mark, *The Manifest Destiny and Mission in the American History: A Reinterpretation*, NY, 1963.

Reginald Horseman, *Race and The Manifest Destiny*, Cambridge, MA, 1981.

Foster Rhea Dulles, *Prelude to the World Power: the American Diplomatic History, 1860-1900*, NY, 1965.

James MacPherson, *Ordeal by Fire: The Civil War and Reconstruction*, NY, 1991.

David Healy, *the US Expansionism: The Imperialist Urge in the 1890s*, Wisconsin, 1970.

Alfred Thayer Mahan, *The Interest of America in Sea power, Present and Future*, Boston, 1898.

Alexander Deconde, *Ethnicity, Race and the American Foreign Policy*, Boston, 1993.

Arthur S. Link et al, eds., *Woodrow Wilson, The Public Papers of Woodrow Wilson*, Princeton University Press, NJ, 1967.

Letters of Theodore Roosevelt, MA, 1965.

Samuel Bemis , *Jay's Treaty: A Study in Commerce and Diplomacy*, NY, 1923.

Samuel Flagg Bemis, A Diplomatic History of the United States, 3rd ed., NY, 1980.

Alfred Thayer Mahan, *The US Looking Onward, 1890, in the collection of essays, The Interest of America in Sea Power, Present and Future*, London, 1970.

Major Problems in the American Foreign Policy, vols. 1&2, Edited by Thomas G. Peterson, MA, 1989.

The American Encounter, The United States and the Making of the Modern World, Essays from 75 years of Foreign Afairs, Ed. By James F. Hodge, Jr., and Fareed Zakaria, Basic Books, NY, 1997.

CHAPTER IV

THE POST WWII US FOREIGN POLICIES

Introduction

Unlike the First World War, there was no formal treaty after the Second World War. Allied powers had no intention to revive Germany, at least, in the near future. No reparations were demanded from the vanquished as it was the victors that determined the terms of reparations, compensations, division and occupation of Germany and Japan. Since the six-year war drove all the warring parties virtually to the limits of their 'patience', the Allies were desperate to end the war on all fronts once Germany surrendered in May 1945. Nothing is unfair in war. The Allied Powers fell into the same trap of brutality, hatred, and arrogance that characterized Hitler's Germany and Tojo's Japan. The American decision to end the war in the Pacific through the use of the 'ultimate' weapon fostered mutual distrust even within the allied camps and its nightmarish effects haunted mankind for the entire Cold War period. The observance of the Hiroshima day in 6 August every year is a permanent blot on the republican United States.

The Allied Powers missed another golden opportunity to ensure a long peace that reigned after the Concert of Vienna where the vanquished party was treated as equal. After all, it was just a decade into the post war era that both Japan and Germany regained their rightful places within the community of nations. By that logic, it could well have occurred in 1945 in a manner of greater goodwill. In another development, the Soviets turned intensely hostile to the capitalist West led by the United States. In a complete U-turn from the war years, former enemies and allies changed places as the war ended. Henceforth, the world would be polarized into two opposing camps and Europe divided accordingly: a communist block led by the Soviet Union and a capitalist camp (including Germany and Japan) led by the United States.

All these developments reinforce the argument that international politics is mostly defined by action-reaction patterns and driven by the ''spirit of domination' referred to earlier. Unless, a consensus amongst various nations to negotiate this 'domination' factor is reached, efforts towards international peace and understanding would result in colossal waste of human and natural resources in repetitive war cycles. Only a constructive approach towards the goal of attaining 'perpetual freedom' can break this vicious circle and create a more unified and an advanced civilization based on peace and prosperity for mankind, in general.

During and after the First Great War, England and France, though weakened, were still strong enough to retain their Asian and African colonies and the former even managed to gain some leeway in the Middle East, thanks to the League mandates. The United States, at that time deemed that it would be better to tone down its clamor for self-determination of nations to decelerate the growing popularity of Bolshevism in the colonies under the European domination. The United States, on its part, thought that discretion was the better part of valor and it would be unwise to let the genie of mass resentments out of the 'colonial' bottle that was sure to plunge the international situation in deep chaos. The American leaders made similar about face after WWII by 'supporting' the continuation of European colonial rules in Asia and Africa in the belief that an unprepared America still have problems and that many parts of the world could still be better managed by the erstwhile great colonial powers. Moreover, this would keep the colonies from falling into the Soviet arms.

However, Churchill was not sure of Britain's capabilities after WWII, though he declared himself to be the 'last person to preside over the liquidation of the British Empire'. In fact, Churchill even made a 'percentage deal' with Stalin in Moscow in October 1944 for sharing some extra territorial 'booties' in the Balkans, bypassing the United States. Yet, he wanted the United States to remain close-by in case England ran into another trouble in Europe. However, the change of government in England and the mood of the people led the British rulers to dismantle colonialism already rendered unpopular by ever rising anti-colonial movements in Asia and Africa. No less important was the growing economic crisis at home that worsened further due to the bitter winter years following the war.

The Soviet Union proved to be a threat for Britain (still a bastion of capitalism) in the absence of a balancer like Germany in Europe as the former registered significant strategic gains in the Balkans and in Central and Eastern Europe, during and after the war. Growing communist influences in the post war France and Italy bode further ill for Britain. To make the matters worse, Stalin's Russia had already set its eyes on the sensitive Eastern Mediterranean and the Middle East by stirring up communist movements in Greece and pressurizing Turkey to have joint control of its key waterways. Russian troops stayed in Iran longer than required after the war that made Britain and the United States suspicious of the Soviet design in the Gulf region.

It was precisely at this time that Britain played the American card. *Common ties of blood, culture, and language kindled hopes of 'resurrection' of an 'American' version of the British Empire and, more importantly, the activation of the second wing of the Western Civilization.* Sometime in February 1947, Britain expressed its inability to help prop up the regimes in Greece and Turkey and hoped that the United States would assume that responsibility. Such an offer presented a golden opportunity to the United States to break its hitherto geographical-cultural fetters, referred to earlier, and to realize its long standing desire of becoming a world leader, albeit, with British 'leads'.

British opinions in matters relating to international politics commanded sufficient respect from the American policy makers in Washington. Already in August 1941, Churchill and Roosevelt met in Newfoundland in Argentia Bay aboard a ship to formulate the Atlantic Charter that formed the bedrock of the post 1945 international political architecture and, more importantly, America's future role in world politics. The basic premises of the Charter were no different from those that had been enshrined in the American Constitution and the Fourteen point program of Wilson, e.g., emphasis on liberty, equality, freedom, and democracy, among other things.

This "invitations to empire", as Geir Lundestad preferred to call it, and the subsequent donning of the global 'imperial' crown by the United States, was based on a tacit mutual understanding: the United States would guarantee military protection to West European countries against possible invasion by the Soviet Union in lieu of their unreserved allegiance and acceptance of the American hegemony in Europe and elsewhere. This, of course, was not the first time that Europe sought America's help. Paradoxically, no single power, including the erstwhile Soviet Union could dominate Europe with such an authority as the United States with its post-war remote control machineries.

'Coming events cast their shadows' and this is nowhere truer than in international politics. Countries adjust their policies in anticipation of the emerging international political situations. Matured European powers were very quick to size up what lay ahead of them and what they had got to do. The next two decades after the end of WWII saw the liberation of about 100 colonies with 800 million people- nearly one-quarter of the total world population- due to both the Soviet and the American initiatives. The erstwhile European colonial powers had to bear with this ignominy that was entirely of their own making but they were matured enough to accept 'fate'. They now faced a more crucial issue: the choice of the lesser evil, the United States or the Soviet Union.

This was easy for Britain for the reasons I have already given in the previous chapter. What about France, Germany, Italy and Japan? France, especially under De Gaulle, was more or less equidistant from both these superpowers and its eyes lay centered on the future course of Germany. It never wanted a rejuvenated or a unified Germany that had been the cause of its woes since 1870. France was the most errant and disgruntled partner in the NATO alliance. Yet the attractions of the American capital and the threat of the 'Red scare' of the immediate post war era led a reluctant France to side with the United States.

Both Italy and France received special *care* from the United States during the late 1940s because of the sweeping communist influences on the masses in both these countries who were still ruminating the fond memories of the war days. Soviet heroism against the mighty Nazi forces, the Soviet anti-war campaigns and the 'progressive' image of the Soviet-backed communists in fighting the fascist Spanish dictator, Franco, continued to fascinate people in these countries. The massive American injection of capital in elections led to the victory of the Christian Democratic Party in Italy and gave a tremendous boost to anticommunist trade union movements in France that finally stalled the threatening communist advances in these countries in the late 1940's.

As for Germany and Japan, the United States proceeded according to a plan. It could see through Stalin's post war design to create an eastern bloc of socialist countries that would act as a magnate for drawing the West Germans and to keep 'unified' Germany under the Soviet domination. The United States did exactly the opposite of what the Soviets intended. The United States sought to create the state of West Germany by a merging of the trizonia under the French, British, and the American occupation that comprised three fourths of the occupied Germany. In the 1948 London Conference, the United States secured the Franco-British consent for the establishment of the West German state. The United States decided to revive West Germany by bringing it under the Marshall Aid Package and by its subsequent induction in the NATO in 1955.

The United States took complete command of Japan in the immediate post war years through the administration of Douglas McArthur who had a hand in the framing of the Japanese Constitution. Truman had already resented some of the concessions granted by Roosevelt to Stalin (in lieu of the latter's acquiescence in the unilateral US control of postwar Japan to the exclusion even of the Soviet Union) at the Yalta. While Japan had little choice, the German question remained alive because of the French and the Soviet oppositions. Nevertheless, the American 'will' prevailed. Instead of creating a 'denazified', 'pastoral', 'deindustrialized' and 'demilitarized' Germany, or agreeing to the Soviet demand for a 'four-power control and ten billion dollar compensation' at Yalta, America deemed that Germany must develop economically. Edward Pessen commented:

> In recreating a strengthened, pro-Western German state, and later incorporating West Germany within the NATO alliance, we charged that sinister Soviet actions and intentions compelled us to do it. The American diplomats on the spot, like critical scholars at home, could discern nothing more malevolent in Soviet actions than a desire for

reparations and a militarily impotent Germany that the West had earlier approved.

—*Edward Pessen, 1993, pp.66-67*

Neither Germany nor Japan had any freedom in choosing between the superpowers. For Britain, things went, more or less, according to its plans. Henceforth, it will be the United States who would have to devote much of its time, resource, and energy to counter the Eastern Colossus. With Europe giving a green signal to the United States to play an active global role in the post Second World War situation, the Eagle was about to soar into new heights.

This chapter will focus attention on major developments of the US postwar foreign policies during the entire the Cold War period, e.g., formation of the United Nations, the Truman Doctrine, NSC-68, the European Union, the US-Vietnam War, etc., not ignoring other important developments of this period, at the same time. In the next chapter, I'll deal with the Carter, Reagan and the Bush era and the decline of the Soviet empire.

The Iranian, Greece, and Turkish Crisis

Soviet diplomatic arm-twisting in Iran, Greece, and Turkey were the first salvo that marked the beginning of the undeclared Cold War era. Soviet overtures in the Eastern Mediterranean and the Persian Gulf were in response to the vacuum created by the disappearance of the British 'curtain' from Gibraltar to Singapore. The Soviet Union lost little time in filling the void created by the disappearance of several empires in Eastern and Central Europe in the aftermath of the two World Wars.

Persian Gulf had always been the zone of rivalry between the two imperial powers, Britain and Czarist Russia, over the control of Iran and India. After the breakup of the Ottoman Empire and after the installation of the Bolshevik government in Russia, imperial Britain got the League mandate to look over the affairs in Iran. Britain, in the process, initiated the extraction of the vast petroleum deposits in the region and even wielded some leverage on the Iranian government. During the course of the Second World War, both the Soviet and the British forces occupied the northern and the southern halves of Iran, respectively, to ensure uninterrupted flow of arms and other vital materials destined for the Soviet Union through the Persian Gulf. Some American forces joined the British forces in the South, later. Once the war ended, the US and the British forces withdrew from Iran within the stipulated six-month period, that is, March 2, 1946.

Soviet forces remained busy in thwarting the Iranian government's attempt to quell a separatist revolt by the communist backed Tudeh party in the northern province of the Iranian Azerbaijan, adjacent to the Soviet border. The

Soviet Union, all but secured the autonomy of Azerbaijan and oil concessions from Iran pending ratification by the Iranian parliament. However, mounting criticisms from both the United States and Great Britain forced the Soviet Red Army to withdraw from Iran. Soviet plans fell through as the Iranian parliament did not to ratify those agreements.

Czarist Russia had always avidly looked to the resource rich Caucasus region contiguous to the Iranian and the Turkish borders. Imperial Russia's great going after the Napoleonic wars were set back in the Crimean War that kept alive the enmity between Turkey and Russia for several more decades. In the 1878 Russo-Turkish war, Russia inflicted defeat on Turkey and annexed some territory in the Caucasus region. Turkey, however, recovered those territories after the First World War. Turkey and the newborn Soviet Union entered into a pact of friendship and mutual non-aggression in 1925. Once the Soviet Union managed to consolidate its grip on its Central Asian backyard, Moscow not only denounced the 1925 agreement but also demanded back the territory in Caucasus that it had lost to Turkey after WWI and a revision of the Montreux Convention of 1936 to include a joint control of the Turkish Straits that would give the Soviet Union basing rights along the Turkish shores.

The outcome of the WWII presented the USSR with a good opportunity to fulfill its grand design to control the regions bordering the Black Sea, the Caspian Sea, the Mediterranean, the Horn of Africa and the Persian Gulf and, perhaps, the eventual control of India. But to its utter dismay, the Soviets discovered that the earlier Russo-British rivalry had been replaced by the US-Soviet rivalry. Soviet dream for a unilateral domination of the resource rich regions of North Africa and the Middle East were shattered as Truman and his administration, sensing Soviet intentions in Turkey, decided in August 1946 to send an American naval contingent to the eastern Mediterranean with a view to stationing the American fleet in the region, permanently. Like in Iran, the Soviet Union had to retreat.

The United States could not help the Greek insurgents in 1822 lest it benefited Czarist Russia. That fear nearly came to pass in 1946 as the threat of the formation of another communist state close to three other communist states of Yugoslavia, Bulgaria and Albania loomed large when Greece got embroiled in a civil war between the communist and the nationalist-conservative forces following the German withdrawal in November, 1944. On 21 February 1947, the British Foreign Office in an official intimation to the State Department expressed its inability to continue its financial and military responsibilities (Britain had about forty thousand troops stationed in Greece at that time) towards Turkey and Greece beyond March 31, and asked the United States to step in as these two countries needed massive financial assistance to bolster their economies. I shall return to this Greek episode a little later.

At about the same time another important development took place in the Middle East. The Truman administration preempted the British design of settling the Palestinian and the Jewish statehood problems, by conniving with the Soviet Union to support the UN General Assembly Resolution 181, in November 29 1947. That resolution sought to divide the mandate of Palestine between the Arab and the Jewish state, with Jerusalem under the UN administration. Earlier, Britain restricted the Jewish migration to Palestine in 1939 (following massive Jewish exodus from various parts of Europe in the wake of political upheavals in Europe and Hitler's ruthless persecution of the Jews) to enlist Arab support in the Second World War.

The Arabs rejected the UN Partition Plan. Just as the British forces left Palestine, the Jews, on May 14, 1948, proclaimed the creation of the state of Israel. Truman, hoping to cash in on the Jewish votes for the impending presidential election, soon recognized the new state. Stalin's Russia followed suit. That single action by Truman alienated the Arabs from the United States and created a permanent unrest in the region and perhaps a permanent American commitment to Israel to justify its 1948 action. Syria, Iraq and Egypt invaded Israel. Israel continued to gain territories at the expense of the Arabs through every subsequent Arab-Israeli war. Arab-Israeli-Palestinian problem converted Middle East into a tinderbox region for the most of the Cold War years and even beyond.

The Truman Doctrine

The Truman administration sprang into action immediately after that British request to the United States to assume responsibilities in the Eastern Mediterranean. In his famous address before a Joint Session of Congress in March 12 1947, popularly known as the Truman Doctrine, the US president sought the Congress approval for financial aids to Greece and Turkey. These funds were needed for building their economies so that these countries could fight off the threat of communism. The Truman Doctrine, however, hardly remained limited to these two areas. Truman held that, "one of the primary objectives of foreign policy of the United States is the creation of conditions in which we and other nations will be able to work out a way of life free from coercion." By coercion he meant pressures from the totalitarian Soviet regime. He openly called upon other nations to choose between two alternate ways of life: one way of life based on democracy and the rule of majority, law, free elections, freedom of speech, and individual liberty, and the other, treading on the heart of others by imposing the will of minority over majority population and relying on reign of terror, 'controlled press and radio', 'fixed elections', and 'suppression of personal freedoms'. After fifty four years, President G.W. Bush in his address to the nation following 9/11 incident, reiterated the same Doctrine as he called upon other people to make a choice between 'good and evil', "us' and "them".

While Truman declared that the United States would abide by the principles of the UN Charter in helping free and independent nations fight off the forces of oppression, he noted that the incipient world Organization was ill equipped at that moment to discharge its responsibilities even in the Mediterranean and the Aegean. Hence it devolved on the United States to combat this emergency situation. By a stroke of pen, Truman made the UN subservient to the US policy decisions from the very beginning.

At first, Truman sought the Congress authorization to provide $400 million aid to Greece and Turkey to preserve their existing institutional structures and national integrity against 'attempted subjugation by armed minorities or by outside pressures.' This aid was both for economic and military purposes. The American personnel were sent to these countries to assist in both the civilian and military matters. Military supplies to Greece alone registered 74,000 tons in the last five months of 1947 that included artillery, dive-bombers, and stocks of napalm. Turkey was to receive $150 million worth economic and military assistance, out of the $400 million appropriated by the Congress for the above purpose. With massive military supplies from the United States, the Greek Royal army at last succeeded in driving away the northern communist rebels into the lands of their communist patrons across the border. With Tito unable to help the Greece any longer after Yugoslavia's split with the Soviet Union, the civil war ended, by 1950. Soviet intimidation in Turkey also grinded to a halt.

The Truman Doctrine would never have been so effective had it not been backed by another landmark development in the US foreign policy: Containment. The US policy makers knew that mere economic assistance to bolster 'weak' economies would not be sufficient to halt the march of the Soviet communist juggernaut. The United States must initiate direct measures, short of war. Already such policies of 'deterrence' have yielded desired results in Iran, Turkey, and Greece. George Kennan in his "Sources of Soviet Conduct" interpreted the Soviet expansion beyond its newly created borders as guided more by that country's historical nationalist instinct of expansionism than by the communist ideals. He concluded, "Soviet pressure against the free institutions of the western world is something that can be contained by adroit and vigilant application of counter-force at a series of constantly shifting geographical and political points."

Truman obviously brought friendly nations within the purview of the American assistance to fight off the threat, overt or covert, of the Soviet communism. Paradoxically, both containment and the Truman Doctrine happened to be elastic concepts because no one knew the limit of freedom. In that sense these two concepts fit well into my model of 'perpetual freedom' as a means to advance the American ideals to other parts of the world. As for the US containment policy, Alan P. Dobson and Steve Marsh commented, "Over the next forty years, containment policy underwent various permutations along a continuum which stretched from selective flexible power responses to meet whatever threats were mounted by the enemy, to a commitment to massive retaliation against whatever breach of the containment line was made. Where would the US stand on this continuum preoccupied its strategists throughout the Cold War" (Dobson and Marsh, p.22-23)

The Marshall Aid Program

The American aid to revive the economies of the Western Europe through the European Recovery Program (ERP) or the Marshall Plan was a direct offshoot of the Truman Doctrine. During most of the 1940s, Italy, France, and Belgium suffered from the relentless communist backed trade union unrests in their lands. As the communists infiltrated and even participated in the governments in these countries, the United States felt the need to improve the standards of living of the people residing in these regions. Already, reports from some quarters, notably, the US Undersecretary of State for Economic Affairs, William Clayton, regarding the dismal state of economies in Europe had the great foreboding that Europe may be drawn into deep political and social disaster without massive financial assistance from America.

Meanwhile, George Marshall, as the Secretary of State, visited Moscow and had talks with the top Soviet leaders. In one such meeting with Stalin, it dawned on Marshall that Stalin was not really interested in solving the European problems but in precipitating the European crisis further so that Europe may become an ideal breeding ground for communism. In his famous Harvard Speech in June 1947, he called upon European nations to come forward with their plans and estimated costs for the European Recovery Program to be financed by the American capital. On September 22, the same year, the sixteen participating states of Europe submitted their plans for a four-year recovery program detailing their own budgetary conditions. The Marshall Plan got the Congressional approval on April 1948 under the European Cooperation Act (ECA) and it remained operational from July 1948 to June 1951.

The United States poured in over $13 billion to the countries of Europe over a four-year period on annual installments. At the end of the aid period, industrial and agricultural production in Europe touched 35 per cent and 10 per cent above the pre war level, respectively. According to the president of the Marshall Aid Foundation, Albert J. Beveridge III, the amount of aid was not much in terms of the European requirements (it only supplied 10 per cent of Europe's capital needs and the rest was provided by the recipient countries themselves). Beveridge III felt that it was the psychological value of the ERP that went a long way towards convincing the nations of Europe that the United States had come to stay in international affairs.

The Marshall Aid had come under critical evaluation from various scholars. Most scholars agree that the enormous capital congestion in the United States had driven their businessmen into finding an immediate outlet in the European markets. They knew that without this program neither the economies of the United States nor those of Europe could survive. Some scholars rightly say that one of the key objectives of this 'prime pumping' was the industrial recovery of Germany. Some scholars feel that the objective of the Aid package failed because it had helped in creating a 'protectionist' European block. Others think that the aid package was a means to create a network of the American corporate control over the globe and, in the process, to project its political influence over the countries it aided.

The Marshall Aid was not the first of its kind in the post war period. Marshall Aid, however, differed from all other previous bilateral American largesse in a significant way, being multilateral in nature. To that extent, the Marshall Aid was a trendsetter for the creation and even consummation of the American Trade Empire. The Marshall Aid could be more appropriately termed as the capitalist manifesto of the free world. A second version of the Marshall Aid in a rather 'hard' form reappeared during the 1980s following the infamous debt crisis of that period. While the Marshall Aid imposed no political or humanitarian conditions, during the 1980s the IMF-World Bank combine demanded structural reforms in the recipient countries that included humanitarian and political reforms also. The third version of the Marshall Aid could be found in operation in the 1990s in the case of assistance to the erstwhile second world following the Soviet collapse. Interestingly, history repeated as Russia failed to develop its economy along democratic capitalist line even with the American financial assistance.

The Soviets, though invited to join the Marshall Aid Club, decried the ERP as an infringement on the sovereignty of Europe. It may be remembered that Nazi Germany, in the 1930s, repudiated free trade on the same ground that such practices led to bondage and loss of sovereignty. However, the Soviets had their own reasons to refuse the proposal, as the package required greater transparency and the American supervision on the internal affairs of that country. They felt that Marshall Aid was an American design to wean away the East European countries from the Soviet fold and they even threatened Czechoslovakia not to join. Underlying this Soviet objection was their unflinching belief in the demise of capitalism through inherent contradictions in that system.

After the end of the Marshall Aid Program in 1952 most of these aids were shifted to non-communist dictatorial regimes in various parts of the world with a view to secure military bases for the US troops there. Of the $50 billion in aid granted by the United States to ninety countries, in the next ten years, only

$5 billion was for nonmilitary economic development. Already by the end of the 1950s, the State Department sought to club military aid with economic aid to include them in a single bill on the presumption that the Congress would care more for security issues than for purely economic ones. One State Department memo concluded: "The distinction between aid in support of foreign military effort and aid for economic recovery is largely artificial." (Fred block, p.176)

The American efforts at granting aids to a large number of non-Western developing countries on ideological lines (that is, on the basis of anti-communism), though not under the heading of Marshall Aid, added a new dimension to international politics so far used to multi polar power politics. The United States knew that its 'aid' programs had double advantages. Besides serving as markets for the American goods, these recipient countries would become the bulwarks against communism. Secondly, by accepting such aid, these countries would come to depend more and more on the United States for their export markets and on 'dollars' for their oil and other trade transactions. Already, Dean Acheson in a Congressional testimony laid bare the US priority to create such an US-centric international financial order for the 'survival' of the American system.'

> We cannot go through another ten years like the ten years at the end of the Twenties and the beginning of the thirties, without having the most far-reaching consequences upon our economic and social system.... When we look at that problem we may say it is a problem of markets. You don't have a problem of production. The United States has unlimited creative energy. The important thing is markets. We have to see that what the country produces is used and sold under financial arrangements which makes its production possible. ...You must look to foreign markets.
>
> —*Ikenberry, 2002, p.170*

The Berlin Blockade of 1948 and the Berlin Crisis of the Early 1960s

One of the key objectives of the Marshall Plan was to resuscitate the German economy. Since the Soviet-led Eastern block of nations had already declined to participate in the Aid Program, this had further reinforced the division of Europe and of Germany along ideological lines. East Germans in Berlin could, by the post war arrangements, still move freely to the western part of the city and had the opportunity to have a glimpse at the opulence of the people living there. This was something that worried the Soviet leaders. West German economic revival resulted in a mass exodus of skilled manpower from the East. Matters came to a head when a new currency system Deutschmark was created for the state of West Germany in mid-June, 1948. The Soviets retaliated by hitting at the soft belly that further precipitated the 1948 Berlin crisis. The Soviet Union closed the only ground access of the West to East Berlin to end the West's 'magic' run in drawing vast numbers of Germans from the East. Recent documents from the former East German archives also point to the Soviet frustration over the glitches in reparations issue, its desperate need for capital and other resources to rebuild its own sagging economy, and Stalin's fear of West Germany's revival as additional causes for the Berlin blockade.

Thus the Soviet Union paid back the United States in its own coin by its 'Berlin' version of the Monroe Doctrine. Since the Soviets didn't harm the western part of the city, physically, western powers could not think of using force. Another reason for not using the option of force may be the overwhelming military presence of the Soviet ground forces and tanks. Instead, the US and it's allies retaliated by resorting to airlift programs for supply of food and other materials. Over 550,000 sorties during the whole year from June 1948 to May 1949 were conducted by the Berlin airlift operation that carried 500,000 tons of food and 1.5 million tons of coal. The Soviet Union balked in the face of the American determination to carry out the airlift against all odds and lifted the blockade in May 1949 amidst international condemnation. Not the least, the Soviet intelligence apprehended that the United States might use nuclear bombs to break the stalemate.

In contrast, the Berlin Wall episode was a long drawn and heart-renting affair for the German citizens on both sides of the divide for about 28 years. Over 260 Germans died in trying to scale the wall. Prior to the erection of the wall, as per wartime arrangements, Berlin remained divided into four zones under the occupation of the Soviet Union, the United States, Britain, and France. The people inhabiting the city could move freely to any part of the city. As a result, Berlin remained the only exit point for the East German exodus to West Germany following the closure of the borders between the East and the West in 1952. East German leaders, fearful of the flight of over 1000 people, per day, including professionals, insisted on the Soviet leaders to declare East Germany a sovereign state so that it could manage the 'exodus' problem, probably, by taking control of the long check posts leading to the West Berlin borders.

In 1958, Nikita Khrushchev served an ultimatum to the western powers to make a final settlement on the German question, failing which, Moscow would sign a separate peace treaty with the GDR, thereby, threatening the western access to Berlin. The Soviets felt that the occupation of West Berlin by the western powers had no other purpose than to subvert the stability of the Communist East and so they must leave. The Soviet leaders were deeply concerned that West Germany was growing militarily strong following the American efforts at German rearmament since the middle of the 1950s. The installation of tactical nuclear weapons in West Germany alarmed the Soviets, further. Khrushchev renewed his demands to the West to declare Berlin a free city and set a six-month deadline. The United States feared that this was a Soviet move to unify Germany under Soviet communist control. America pledged its intention to defend the status of Berlin.

Finally on August 13, 1961, East Germany, in collusion with the Soviet Union erected a barbed wire fence along the East-West border. After some show of force on the part of both sides, things cooled down a bit, when Kennedy, through his September 1961 correspondence, conveyed to Khrushchev the American decision not to pursue the unification issue. This allowed the Soviet Union to lift the 'deadline'. This arrangement thus made it easier for both the superpowers to postpone the issue of German unification, and continue with their status quo arrangement in Germany.

North Atlantic Treaty Organization (NATO)

The formation of NATO was another milestone in the history of the American foreign policies. According to the First Secretary General of NATO, Lord Ismay, NATO was created to keep the Germans down, the Russians out and the Americans in. By assuming the task of guaranteeing the European security, the United States, again, following the British lead, launched NATO that was to serve as the fulcrum of stability in Europe during and after the Cold War. *The formation of military alliance between the states of North Atlantic nations at America's behest was also a novel development in the post war peace period* whose full import was unclear to every other member of that organization except, perhaps, the United States.

West European countries had little option than to accede to the proposal of the formation of NATO in the late 1940s, since they required the American aid for their economic recovery and they faced considerable security threats from the Soviet army. Signed as the North Atlantic Treaty on April 4, 1949 by twelve signatories from amongst nations on both sides of the Atlantic, the United States, Canada, Belgium, Luxembourg, Denmark, Norway, France, Britain, Italy, Iceland, the Netherlands, and Portugal (to be extended to Turkey and Greece in 1952) the Organization formally came into being in July, 1949 and came into effect on August, 1949. The treaty made little justice to its geographical name, as Italy-a distant nation from the Atlantic shore was inducted. Turkey and Greece had to wait for three more years. Secondly, another important country Spain in Southern Europe had a late membership of the organization in 1982 because of Franco's sin. I have already mentioned of Germany's inclusion in the organization in 1955 till a unified Germany replaced West Germany in 1990 as a NATO member. Hungary, Poland, and the Czech Republics further swelled the number of NATO membership to 19 by 1999. Today, there are twenty-six members with the inclusion of Bulgaria, Estonia, Latvia, Lithuania, Romania, Slovakia, and Slovenia in March 2004.

Originally conceived as a collective security mechanism to defend any of its members in case of attack from other nations, the member countries had little obligation or compulsion to do so and the treaty remained only in paper in the initial months after its signing. The preamble sought to promote common values of its members and "unite them in their efforts for collective defense." Article 5 provided for the availability of the armed forces of the member nations for the same purpose. Yet, the key issue of guaranteeing the European security against the formidable Soviet armed forces roved round America's nuclear monopoly that was considered adequate to deter any Soviet aggression. But several disturbing events, viz., the discovery of the Soviet atom bomb within a few months of the formation of NATO, the Berlin blockade, and the outbreak of the Korean War, led the United States to take real initiative in giving a concrete shape to the organizational and military structure of NATO.

The North Atlantic Council consisting of permanent delegates from all the member nations happen to be the decision making body of NATO, headed by a Secretary General. Besides, the Council attends to the administrative, budgetary and general policy matters. The military committee comprising of the chiefs of staff of the various armed forces has to submit its reports to the North Atlantic Council. Below the military committee are the various geographical commands like the Allied Command Europe, Allied Command Atlantic, and the Canada- US regional Group that deploy armed forces in their zones.

Since the main purpose of NATO has been to 'enhance the stability, well-being, and freedom of its members through a system of collective security' and since article 2 of the Treaty deals with economic and political cooperation of the parties, it was obvious from the beginning that NATO would have a dual purpose – defense and ensuring peace. It is this latter function that has been the main focus of NATO activities in the form of peacekeeping, peace enforcement, humanitarian interventions, alongside the UN forces, in the post Cold War period. Throughout the entire the Cold War period, NATO remained the main military bulwark against the Soviet designs in Europe. While the 1960s saw such unpleasant developments like the French withdrawal and the shifting of NATO headquarters from Paris to Brussels and the 1970s experienced some limited breakthrough in arms limitation talks, NATO failed to arrest the growing Soviet military build–up during these decades. However, the Soviet deployment of intermediate range ballistic missiles close to the European borders and the reciprocal installation of the Pershing missile close to the Soviet borders made the Soviets more vulnerable and willing to sign the Intermediate Nuclear Forces Treaty (INF) in 1987. This signaled a clear-cut victory of NATO over the Warsaw group.

We, generally, judge a thing by its action. By this logic, once Europe attained its desired level of economic growth and felt able to deal with the Soviet Union on its own, NATO ought to have lost its significance as early as the 1960s, because most of the post war international crisis situations except those involving Berlin, took place in various other parts of the world: the Korean war in 1950, the 1956 Middle-East crisis, the Cuban missile crisis in 1962, unrest in Central and Latin American countries, and in Indo-China in the 1960s. But that was not to be. NATO continued to stay, implying that the United States, too, lacked both the confidence and the courage to manage international affairs without the help- moral and otherwise- of its European allies.

This reality became more pronounced after the end of the Cold War. With two primary conditions for the formation and even sustenance of NATO gone, viz., the dissolution of the Soviet Union and loosening of the American pressure on the veto power nations in the UN on major international issues, it may appear that there was little justification for the continuation of an additional collective security body other than the UN. To that extent present efforts at redefining NATO's role may be viewed as the silent battle for its supremacy with the United Nations. Underlying this rivalry is the American factor. Just remove the United States from the NATO alliance, and the Organization would soon vamoose into the blue because Europe never had any real interest in sustaining such an organization in the absence of the super powers.

The post Cold War Russia remained the only hope and justification for NATO's 'survival', once its precursor communist 'empire', by its sudden withdrawal, took the rag out of NATO's feet. Josse Joffe once remarked, that since the Christmas Day, 1991, the Atlantic alliance was experiencing a slow death as the alliance lost its central purpose once the Cold War ended. He compared it with a bridge decaying slowly through disuse. Yet Nato survived with some modifications to meet the challenges of the post Cold War era. Many new strategic concepts were formulated in various meets and conferences in various Western capitals during the whole of the 1990s. NATO in its new role was supposed to serve as a "force multiplier" and "toolbox" for the American interventions beyond the European borders.

After the collapse of the Soviet Union, the main purpose for which the alliance was formed was gone. NATO groped to find its appropriate role in the post Cold War era. But it did not have to wait long, as ethnic and religious clashes engulfed the Balkans for several years. The unwillingness of Europe to employ its forces – a sort of apathy fostered by the four decades of Atlanticism – to tackle such ominous developments even in their own continent made things worse in the Balkan theater. NATO had to intervene and prove that it was the only viable option to guarantee peace and freedom in various parts of the world. NATO's success in quelling the situations in erstwhile Yugoslavian provinces and in Kosovo underlined the fact that United Nations may not be the ideal choice in such conflicts.

NATO's post Cold War objectives or its New Security Agenda were laid bare by the Secretary General Javier Solana in the 50th anniversary of NATO: to monitor the transformation of Europe, Russia and the transatlantic link. Traditional security concerns like territorial defense has now been replaced by a broader definition of security that takes into account various other factors like political, economic, social, and environmental factors as well as unorthodox threats, like, terrorist attacks and indiscriminate use of biological, and chemical weapons (NBC) by rogue states and the terrorists. Another major goal of NATO in the new millennium is to develop sufficient and diversified military capabilities in deterring security threats in all dimensions. To be more specific, the future role of NATO can be summed up as efforts towards safeguarding of the freedom and security of the countries of the Western Civilization.

One interesting offshoot of the post Cold War development was efforts at enlisting the communist states of the erstwhile Eastern block in the organization, as NATO, much to Russia's mortification, made a peaceful march, eastward. NATO members proceeded with a purpose and caution in inducting the former Warsaw Pact countries to its own fold in a phased manner viz., through the formation of the North Atlantic Cooperation Council in 1991 – a consultative forum for NATO members and countries of East Europe and the former Soviet republics. This was followed by the Partnership for Peace (PFP) in which non-members could take part in 'information sharing, joint-exercises, and peacekeeping operations'. Russia was granted a special privilege in NATO under Clinton. Just as the EC was created to bind 'wild' Germany to Europe, similar efforts are on to democratize the Polar bear and to include it in NATO in order to tie it up militarily with its European compatriots that would eliminate East-West tensions. As per the 1996 London Conference, NATO membership was open to any European state that would further the principles of the treaty and contribute to the security of the North Atlantic area. Unlike the EU, there are no eligibility criteria for entering NATO. NATO would rather help these nations to upgrade them to their desired level after incorporating them into the Organization.

Interestingly, NATO may become a crucial lever for the United States to maintain balance in Europe even in the new millennium. For example, if the EU is usurped, someday, by Germany, who may be tempted to dissolve NATO (Schroeder's Germany grew, somewhat, disinterested in that organization), the United States along with Britain and other smaller European states, notably the new entrants, may isolate Germany. So long as the United States manages to exert its influence in the European affairs, Germany could be effectively contained.

NSC-68

National Security Council (NSC), like the creation of the Central Intelligence Agency (CIA), was the outcome of the 1947 National security Act that had led to the creation of the Department of Defense through the merging of the War and the Navy Departments. All these were prelude to the creation of an industrial-military set-up in a country that had so far shunned large military establishments. But the Cold War made it imperative on the Truman administration to go to the extreme. National Security Council 68 Resolution was, therefore, another landmark in post war American foreign policies. To repeat, it was Kennan's Long Telegram and the "Sources of Soviet Conduct" in 1946 and 1947, respectively, that had led to the proclamation of the Truman Doctrine to counter the growing Soviet threat, first in Europe, and then on a global scale. Nevertheless, the American policies towards the Soviet Union, initially remained largely confined to economic and diplomatic arms twisting, for a number of reasons. First, all these policies related directly to the European and not to the American security itself; secondly, European nations, by themselves, were too weak to defend against the overwhelming military might of the Soviet Union; thirdly the United States had the ultimate advantage over its rival of having the monopoly of the nuclear bomb; and lastly, but most importantly, the United States, as a non-European country could hardly transpose its military and political control over the industrialized democracies of Western Europe at a speed and scale required to counter another Eurasian power. These four considerations kept the United States from taking full proof measures to effectively counter the Soviet threat in Europe, in the immediate post-war period. Nevertheless, Kennan's prescriptions to apply economic and political pressures began to lose its bite following the crises in the Eastern Mediterranean, Berlin, and the communist take-over of Czechoslovakia.

Two major developments in 1949 altered the nature of the US perception of the post war situation: Soviet possession of nuclear bomb and the emergence of communist China. Truman asked for a comprehensive probe into the relative capabilities of the two super powers and the need for the United States to develop thermo-nuclear bomb. Paul Nitze of the US State Department was entrusted with the job of that investigation and to submit his reports to the President on an emergency basis which he did within two months. Nitze prepared a lengthy and detailed document regarding the relative military strengths of the two rivals and his report suggested massive rearmament needs and funding of armed forces of both the United States and its West European allies. Furthermore, NSC-68 recommended the development of the Hydrogen bomb.

Prior to the recommendations of NSC-68, the American defense expenditures amounted to about $15 billion a year. The United States needed a solid boost and an equally plausible pretext for greater militarization of its foreign policies. The framers of NSC-68 recommended a defense spending around $40 billion per year. The resulting document explored the capabilities of both the super powers in respect of their military, economic, political, and psychological standings. President Truman asked for further details and thus delayed its submission before the Congress for its eventual ratification. The outbreak of the Korean War gave the United States a unique opportunity to get the NSC resolution accepted by the Congress.

For about six more grueling months, the United States stood on the edge of the 'known-unknown' divide in its foreign policy execution, torn as it was between the centripetal force of an age-old 'isolationism' and the centrifugal force of expansionism. Interestingly, this phase in the American foreign policy may be likened to the atom-splitting phenomenon within 'matter' (notably, both the super powers developed atom bombs during this decade) with all the promise of releasing a second wave of energy (the first pertaining to the days just prior and after the American War of Independence), this time, to not only blast off another Eurasian power but also to take concrete steps to permeate the entire post war international situation with the 'ether' of 'American specialties'.

NSC-68 marked a radical shift from the earlier American perception of the anarchic nature of international politics, hitherto, defined by a system of sovereign and independent states over which no state was supposed to secure hegemony. The NSC document described the Soviet behavior as "animated by a new fanatic faith, antithetical to our own, and seeks to impose its absolute authority over the rest of the world." One important assumption of the Resolution was based on a crucial premise that can be applied in a reverse way to the present day United States. According to NSC-68 document "...any substantial further extension of the area under the domination of Kremlin would raise the possibility that no coalition adequate to confront the Kremlin with greater strength could be assembled." Ironically, immediately after the end of the Cold War, Paul Wolfowitz as Assistant Secretary of Defense laid out his plans in a Pentagon memorandum (46-page classified document) that would enable the United States to perpetuate its single-power domination of the world. Wolfowitz felt that the United States "must sufficiently account for the interests of the advanced industrial nations to discourage them from challenging our leadership to seeking to overturn the established political and economic order", while maintaining the American military capability at such a high level as to "deter potential competitors from even aspiring to a larger regional or global role."

NSC-68 was, in one respect, a historical inevitability. With the collapse of colonialism, the search for a viable and alternative international order became imperative. In 1941, Henry Luce had already claimed in the Life magazine that 'American century' had begun. Historically, great powers, more often than not, emulated their immediate precursors. It was, therefore, obvious that the United

States would not only try to tread on imperial Britain's shoes but would also surpass the latter. Pax the Americana was fast coming of age with the spread and consolidation of 'base' empires.

NSC-68's recommendation for massive rearmament and defense funding was primarily aimed to serve the industrial-military complex in the United States – an altogether new development in republican American history. The federal government's 'militarization' policies rather replaced the job of the creation of wealth and employment opportunities by individual Americans. Large defense industries would henceforth provide vast employment opportunities for the American citizens. The warnings of the founding fathers to avoid militarization of the American society fell into deaf ears in the post 1945 international political situation. I have already mentioned that being a latecomer in international politics and with the 'space' provided by the American specialties (discussed in the first chapter), the United States had the unique advantage of some 'extra' options over other erstwhile great powers. For example, while other imperial powers, from the beginning, relied on the size and strength of their armies, the United States reserved them as the second line of defense behind the American cavalcade.

The United Nations Organization (the UNO)

The emergence of the United Nations out of the relic of the League of Nations was another landmark development in international politics. The two wars in the last century virtually destroyed the prevalent world order based on colonialism. Both the United States and the Soviet Union supported decolonization after the First World War and upheld the rights of self-determination of nations. Strangely, both these powers stayed away from the League because of political and domestic compulsions. The outbreak of another war made the establishment of a true world body a reality.

Both the United States and the Soviet Union calculated the benefits to be gained through establishment of such a world body as the UN. The United States felt that it had more leverage in terms of summoning a majority as it counted on the support of various European and Latin American countries while the Soviets pinned their hopes on their East European 'satellite' states and the rising number of newly liberated countries out of the colonies that would manipulate the General Assembly proceedings.

Already, as early as November 1944, referring to the possibility of any future German attack, Stalin emphasized the creation of a special organization to tackle that problem.

> "There is only one means to this end, in addition to the complete disarmament of the aggressive nations: that is to establish a special organization made up of representatives of the peace-loving nations to uphold

> peace and safe guard security; to put the necessary minimum of armed forces required for the averting of aggression at the disposal of the directing body of this organization, and to obligate this organization to employ those armed forces without delay if it becomes necessary to avert or stop aggression and punish the culprits.
>
> —*Hunt, Crises in the US Foreign Policy, pp.132-133*

Obviously, Stalin was referring to some kind of a world body like the United Nations. Roosevelt and Churchill in their Atlantic Charter agreement in August 1941, stressed the need for a world body to manage international affairs in the post war scenario. Roosevelt coined the name United Nations and the name was used for the first time in 1 January 1942, in the "Declaration by United Nations". He, on his part, did everything to revive the Wilsonian dream of the League. He sent a couple of republican senators to the San Francisco Conference in 1945, represented by 50 countries, thereby ensuring the Congressional support. The United Nations came into being in October 1945.

From the very beginning, the United Nations was based on a hierarchic structure in the form of Security Council, General Assembly and six other wings. Only the Security Council has the sole authority to sanction and conduct war. Issues and agendas may be framed in the General Assembly, the most democratic part of that organization, pending ratification and approval of the Security Council to become effective. The five permanent members, the United States, the Soviet Union, Great Britain, France and China have veto powers to negate any resolution not to their liking. Originally consisting of 11 members—5 permanent members and 6 nonpermanent members elected by the General Assembly for two-year terms, Security Council membership has now been increased to 15 in which the number of non-permanent members increased to 10. Recently efforts are on to include four other countries, India, Brazil, Germany, and Japan as permanent members with no veto power. But the asymmetry in the voting system and the provision of veto power crippled the UN from its very birth.

During the rest of 1940s, the United Nations became a forum for assertion of superiority through random exercise of Veto by the superpowers. The Soviet Union cast their first Veto in the Security Council over disputes regarding the presence of Russian troops in the Iranian Azerbaijan. The Soviet Union boycotted that Organization in 1950 in protest against permanent sitting of Nationalist China. The United States had no difficulty in getting the UN resolution authorizing the use of force against North Korea. There remained the all-important question: how far the superpowers were going to sacrifice their sovereignty to make a viable and efficient UN? In other words, would the superpowers abide by the rules of democracy in international politics and desist from playing the game of power politics or spheres of influence, and most importantly, treat the world body as their equal?

As the recipient of five Nobel Peace prizes, the UN and its various organizations are engaged in a vast array of international activities that are beyond the reach and capability of any single power. According to the UN website, apart from recent peace-keeping and peace making operations, its activities include child survival and development, environmental protection, human rights, health and medical research, alleviation of poverty and economic development, agricultural development and fisheries, education, family planning, emergency and disaster relief, air and sea travel, peaceful uses of atomic energy, labor and workers' rights, promotion of democracy, strengthening of international laws, ending of apartheid in South Africa, ensuring the Soviet withdrawal from Afghanistan, ending the eight-year Iran-Iraq conflict, and arranging for free and fair elections in Cambodia, Namibia, El Salvador, Eritrea, Mozambique, Nicaragua and South Africa. The list of the UN achievements may go on.

However, failures offset its achievements. The United Nations failed to contain the genocide in Rwanda and exercise its authority in the second Congo war, 1998-2002, that claimed about five million lives there. The UN had failed to effectively intervene in the Bosnian crisis and could not stop the killings in Srebrenica. Its efforts at delivering food and other humanitarian relief in Somalia and Congo and its role in matters of national sovereignty in Katanga (where it acted assertively to establish national sovereignty) contrasts sharply with its reluctance to follow through its resolutions that underlines its powerlessness to rein in some members violating the UN resolutions. To make the matters worse, the Organization had inducted many countries with poor human rights records, like Sudan, Cuba, and Libya in the United Nations Commission on Human Rights (the UNCHR) while ejecting the US out of the same organization.

There were two occasions when the UN membership made quantum jumps. During the late 1950s and the early 1960s quite a number of nations in Africa, Asia, and the Middle East attained independence and were admitted to the UN, raising its membership to 125. But the nuclear monopoly of the superpowers and the escalation of their intense rivalries offered little space for the world body to impact world affairs significantly. Another surge in the number of membership came in the early 1990s after the dissolution of the Soviet led Eastern block of communist states, this time, swelling the UN membership figure to over 190. For a time, during the 1990s, it seemed that the United States had come to rely more on the United Nations to manage world affairs. The UN endorsement of the 1991 Gulf war against Iraq to liberate Kuwait and President Clinton's cooperative approaches led Butros Butros Ghali, the new UN Secretary General, to prepare the UN for more dynamic and innovative roles in the coming years.

It may be a shrewd move on the part of the United States to uphold the UN in the last decade of the last century in the wake of the collapse of an empire that triggered off vast ethnic and religious conflicts in various parts of the world. With NATO struggling to survive in the post Cold War period, the United States reckoned that its capacity was limited and that its domestic priorities precluded involvement in too many conflict-prone zones and that a multilateral body was better placed to tackle such nationalistic issues. However, growing influence of the United Nations conflicted with those of the US interests. From the American viewpoint, the UN could be allowed to quell regional and other ethno-religious disturbances but it would be a trespassing if it interferes in matters that concern 'vital' American interests.

Still, there are other reasons for such American attitude towards the UN. In the first place, the United States, through its globalization programs in the 1990s, hoped not only to limit roles of national governments but also to considerably dilute the concept of nation-states, itself being a nation state, though. Obviously, the interests of the UN (which is rather composed of nation-states) and the US were bound to clash over the prioritizing of international issues. One such example was the situation in the Gulf. While the UN endorsed armed action against Iraq in 1991 because of the latter's occupation of another sovereign state, the Organization opposed the use of force twelve years later when it found no evidence of Iraq possessing weapons of mass destruction (WMD). The United States had a hard time in convincing other members of the world body about Iraq's complicity in such programs.

Secondly, the United States had borne the brunt of financial costs during the initial decades of the formation of the UN. Yet, by the end of the last century, the United States had defaulted in meeting its dues to the United Nations because it found the UN rather a hindrance to the increased American influence on a global scale. Thirdly, such a supranational organization happens to be neither a state nor a nation by itself. So, the United Nations have to depend, especially, either on the consensus among great powers or on a stronger power for its existence and upkeep. Stalin had remarked in the same speech that I have quoted from Hunt a little earlier, that the world organization could be sufficiently effective if the great powers continued to act in a spirit of harmony and accord. It is on this general consensus that the survival and function of the UN depended. Now that there is only one superpower, the United Nations is faced with a difficult choice: either to follow the United States and restructure itself, or what Condoleeza Rice had foretold about the prospect of gradual liquidation.

Many politicians who would like to see the UN as an alternative to the US world leadership can least expect that to happen, at least, in a unipolar world. The United Nations can at best be a tool and a means but not a decisive institution in serving as the beacon of civilization. That responsibility lies with a superpower, the United States. The North Atlantic Treaty Organization (NATO) happens to be its 'fist'.

From the above it is clear that the futures of the UN, the EU, the Truman Doctrine, NSC-68, and NATO depend on a single assumption: the American presence. These post war institutions and doctrines may prove to be a transient phase in the history of international politics if the United States chooses to withdraw from international politics. Conversely, the American supremacy is still extremely dependent on these post 1945 doctrines and institutions.

Korean War

Korea had been under the Japanese domination since the early decades of the last century. The nationalists, though divided, continued their struggles against the Japanese occupation of the peninsula since 1910. With the Japanese defeat in WWII, the Soviet and the US forces occupied the northern and southern parts of that country, divided at the 38th Parallel. For the next three years, efforts at unification seemed illusive and both the United States and the Soviet Union installed puppet governments in their respective zones that claimed authority over the entire peninsula. It was in 1948 that the South proclaimed the Republic of Korea. North, in turn, set up the People's Republic of Korea. Bolstered by the Chinese communist success in 1949 and supported by Stalin, the communist North invaded the South in the hope that the United States, already bogged down in Europe, would not be in a position to intervene.

However, the United States had more than one reason to act. As mentioned earlier, the need for the creation of a permanent military-industrial complex to bolster its economies and to counter the growing Soviet threat was uppermost in the minds of the post war US policy-makers. Moreover, there remained the issue of the American credibility and willingness to defend Europe from any possible Soviet aggression. Like in the Berlin crisis, the United States wouldn't let go this opportunity to enhance its global image as the liberator of the oppressed people. Such a far-away flash point as the Korean peninsula had little chance of developing into a super power confrontation, at least, closer to Europe. On top of it, getting NSC-68 approved by the Houses remained at the back of Truman's mind.

The war lasted for about three years with fluctuating fortunes as the initial advantage that the North had as an aggressor to overrun Seoul was neutralized by Macarthur's forces a few month's later in 1950. For most of the war years, a condition of rough stalemate developed as the Chinese forces intervened on behalf of the North to beat back the UN forces heading dangerously close to the Chinese borders, thanks to Macarthur's misadventure. According to the Department of Defense reports, 54,246 American servicemen and women lost their lives during the Korean War alone. Korean casualties exceeded 4 million with civilian casualties comprising two thirds of that figure. Further discussion on the Korean War could be found below in the section dealing with the Eisenhower era.

European Integration

American initiative in integrating Europe happens to be another milestone development in the US post war foreign policy. Forcible attempts of a single power domination of Europe were made since the era of the Mediterranean-centered Rome. Later on, Charlemagne's Frankish empire, the Holy Roman Empire, the Christianity in the Middle Ages, the formation of the Customs Union in 1806 in Napoleon's Continental System and the Nazi German proposal in 1943 for a European Confederacy were all efforts in this direction.

Victor Hugo was the first to put proposals towards peaceful and cooperative ways of unifying Europe on the basis of equality of membership in 1847. Further attempts made in 1860s towards a sort of European integration failed, as did the period of economic interdependence prior to the First Great War. The 1923 Pan-European Union was another effort towards European integration. André Malraux and Georges Bidault in 1941 made similar efforts prior to the WWII – excluding the Soviet Union.

The United States was more interested in creating an American version of the United States of Europe that would allow free flow of trade without tariffs within the Continent. According to Paul Hoffman, "The substance of such integration would be the formation of a large single market." In the aftermath of the two devastating wars in the last century, European nations looked for united efforts at harnessing the resources within the continent. With the loss of the overseas colonies, European powers needed to compensate that loss by merging their markets.

The Council of Europe was the first post-war organization of European unity. However, the American objective of creating a unified zone permitting free and uninterrupted flow of capital required, first of all, the circumvention of the objections by the dissident British and the Scandinavians who along with Portugal, Austria, and Switzerland, in 1960, went on to form their own European Free trade Association (EFTA). To realize its objective, the United States, thus, had to rely on two major European countries: war ravaged France and Germany. Both these countries had the urgent need to resolve their long-standing problem of shortages of coal and steel that had led to frequent wars between these two nations. The European Coal & Steel Community (ECSC), consisting of six European countries, formed in April 1951, was supposed to eliminate France's chronic energy crisis and tie Germany in a web of interdependence, making it impossible for Germany to launch any aggression on France. For Germany, this proposal meant a good opportunity for its much-needed industrialization and a revival of its lost prestige . The aim of the ECSC, a brainchild of the French economist Jean Monnet and the French Foreign Minister Robert Schuman, was to reduce trade barriers in coal and steel within the six signatory states and to regulate policies in regard to coal and steel. For the first time, a higher and a supranational authority was established to deal directly with companies, labor unions and individuals. In the same year these same six states, France, Germany, Italy, Netherlands, Luxemburg, and Belgium signed another treaty for creation of the European Defense Community (EDC) to bring the European military forces under a single command, but the French Parliament failed to muster enough consensus in ratifying that treaty.

In July 1957, as per the Treaties of Rome (implemented on 1st January 1958), France, Germany, Italy and the Benelux countries formed the European Economic Community (EEC), and the European Atomic Energy Committee (the EURATOM). European Common Market (ECM), as the EEC also came to be known, incorporated the concepts of free trade and a Customs Union (a common set of tariffs on goods imported from countries other than the members) to facilitate free movement of goods, people, labor, and capital. Simultaneously, a Common Agricultural Policy (CAP) was established that ensured equal subsidy to all the farmers for all the member countries. The CAP has in subsequent years absorbed most of the EU's budgets (and now amounts to about two-thirds of the EU's budget) and has been the real bone of contention between the EU and the United States. Some critics of the Marshall Aid lament the failure of that program to create a tariff-free united Europe by pointing to the EU's protectionist Common Agricultural Policies.

France under General de Gaulle continued to deny the merging of EFTA with the European Common Market and any extension of that supranational body. Eventually, Britain along with Denmark and Ireland were included in 1973. After some uneventful years, the process of integration gained momentum with the establishment of the Single European Act of 1985, the European Community (EC) in 1986, and the European Union (the EU) in 1992. These were followed by the Maastricht and the Amsterdam Treaties aimed at creating a common European market through free movement of goods, services, labor, and capital, elimination of all non-tariff barriers, and the creation of the European Monetary Union. A single common currency 'Euro' came into full circulation in 2002. These treaties also addressed issues relating to immigration and criminal activities, contrabands and sex trafficking. One of the far-reaching goals of these treaties was to prepare the ground for eventual political integration and a common foreign and security policy (CFSP) and the European security and Defense Policy (ESDP) discussed in part III. Establishment of the European Central Bank (ECB) to replace the functions of individual central banks and to formulate monetary policies was another major development in the European Monetary Union.

This supranational body works through such institutions as the European Commission, the European Parliament, the Council of the European Union, the European Court of Justice, the European Court of Auditors and the European Council. The 25-member European Commission works on a four-year renewable term and is supposed to look to the EU interests instead of that of the member nations from which they come. It is the Council of European Union or the Council of Ministers, presently consisting of 25 designated ministers from each member state that formulates policies to be implemented by the European Commission and also acts as a check for the EU's supranational prerogatives. The European Parliament looks after judicial and legislative matters with not much power to pass laws. But its representatives are elected directly by common European voters since 1979. The European Court of Justice (ECJ) is more eager to look after the interests of the EU even to the extent of overruling national laws not conducive to the EU and deals with both the government and the individual cases.

However, the lack of a strong centralized authority has been a hindrance to the fiscal management of the Union. Even today, the EU budget is a tiny fraction of total government spending and the recent row over the EU Constitution and the recurrent problems about the EU budgetary issues have cast doubts regarding the EU's future. What is more, the coexistence of the developed and the poor members in the same organization has rendered the task of monetary management all the more difficult since the increased fund ($25 billion) to assist these poor members have to be borne by the rich members. A benchmark was thus created to restrict membership in the Union, like, maintenance of the level of budget deficit to within 3 per cent of the GDP and national debt not to exceed 60 per cent of GDP after making allowance for an inflation level of 1.5 percentage points above the average of the three lowest inflation members, and ensuring stable interest rates.

The EU has currently twenty seven members with many others in the queue. These are nations belonging to the erstwhile second world communist bloc and the rim states like, Turkey. Spain and Portugal were admitted to the EU in 1986 over the original ten members. Austria, Finland, and Sweden joined in 1995, while both Norway and Switzerland stayed away because of domestic compulsions. The EU expanded its membership to its present twenty-seven through incorporation of Poland, Czech Republic, Slovakia, Hungary, Slovenia, Estonia, Latvia, Lithuania, Malta, and Cyprus in 2004.

The EU is still evolving and there are differences as to the nature and future course of the European integration. Some countries, for example, France, want limited number of members and deeper integration through monetary union and other measures suggested by the Maastricht Treaty while others like Britain favor a broadening instead of deepening the process of integration by inducting more and more new members in Europe and its fringes. No doubt, the new entrants would be the backward nations and this would slow down the process of integration. France is concerned with cornering most of the agricultural benefits from the Common Agricultural Policy. New entries would definitely divert resources from agricultural allocations and that might pose problems for the future of the EU. On the other hand, given the greater inclusiveness on the part of the EU, Russian entry could make the dream of a common European House a reality.

Joshua Goldstein sums up the European position in the following lines: "Beyond the EU itself, Europe is a patchwork of overlapping structures with varying memberships. Despite Single European Act, there are still many Europes. Within the EU are the "inner six", and the "poor four, and the possible new joiners, each with its own concerns. Around the edges are the EFTA states participating in the European Economic Area. NATO membership overlaps partly with the EU. Russia and even the United States are European actors in some respects but not in others." Russia is more in favor of discharging of European obligations through another intergovernmental Organization, Conference for Security and Cooperation in Europe (CSCE)

German Foreign Minister Joschka Fisher favored a federal Europe with the federal institutions, elected European executive and legislature as a precondition of total political integration. Tony Blair, on the other hand, favored a confederal type without a core group: issue based and greater autonomy for the individual members. Some others prefer a "multispeed Europe" in which only the core fifteen member nations would be involved directly with the process of political and economic integration. The idea behind mutispeed Europe is that members other than the core members would have varying needs and interests in non major issues and hence there won't be any uniform speed with which the European integration could take place.

The success of total European integration depends on the EU's internal development, NATO and the EU enlargement, the Russian factor, endemic Balkan crises, intriguing issue of the Turkish membership, and above all the direction of the future American foreign policies. Deep sense of nationalism in many European countries and other international developments may either lead to a single power domination of the EU, say, Germany, or the European nations may decide that a critical point has reached in the process of integration to act as a limit.

All of these two possibilities, in turn, are dependent on the American factor. If the United States prefers to withdraw from the anarchic international field or if it thinks that a united Europe no longer serves its interests but rather acts to the detriment of the US interests, then Europe may once again be the cockpit of intense international activity, desirable or undesirable. Likewise, the EU expansion in breadth and thoroughness (in terms of laying stress on its defense preparedness) may complicate and disrupt the NATO- EU relations, viz., unwarranted duplication of structures and costly investments, and miscalculations about political and nationalistic trends in various European countries. Above all, it must be borne in mind that except Britain, no major power in Europe has got any sort of sentimental attachment to the United States.

European integration can be seen from another direction. Alliances and economic interactions have taken place since earlier times and these were carried further in the last three centuries. That way, the drive for European integration can be seen as a continuation of the past. What is striking is the nature of political integration. All such previous attempts relied on force and subjugation. The present wave of integration had started some six decades earlier in a peaceful manner. Yet these are liable to change with time. The chances are that, given Europe's history, the EU may either disintegrate or be rendered more and more inactive as divergences in interests manifest over time. If one takes into account the two primary conditions that led to European efforts at integration, then the future of the EU seems uncertain. Of those two primary conditions, one is that the Soviet Union no longer exists, while the other condition on which much depends is the American presence. It is strange and perhaps ridiculous that a trans-Atlantic partner could continue to influence the course of Europe indefinitely!

Another point of consideration is that when the EU becomes a truly global power what would a common European identity look like? Here lies the difference of Europe with the United States. Originally, comprised of several colonies in the Eastern seaboard, America had all the elements of homogeneity that made it easier to frame a single constitution and in knitting new states (as a result of Frontiers expansion) to follow a single approach to governance. The EU members include and its projected expansion will include almost all the nations under the Austro-Hungarian, the Hohenzollern, and the Ottoman empires, not to speak of the mainland of the erstwhile imperial Britain and Scandinavia and parts of the Czarist Russian Empire. For most part of the last millennium, countries of Europe fought amongst themselves. The picture since the second half of the last century and in the new millennium, in particular, is just the reverse: unity and integration. The weight of a thousand years' history is, no doubt, far more imposing than that of a mere six decades or so. A common European identity based on political values seems to be a far-fetched proposition in a continent already built on heterogeneous ideals, values, priorities, and interests.

Eisenhower Era

It remained for Eisenhower to bring an end to the Korean War. The post armistice position was hardly any different from the pre war position. Korea remained divided at the 38th parallel. With the death of Stalin, with Truman out of office, and with the hectic and intense Cold War years in the initial round sapping the energies of both the super powers, Khrushchev was more willing to do the job of thawing the strained US-Soviet relations. Eisenhower, through his New Look strategy, sought to lower defense spending within a range of $35-42 billion. After all, it was time to contract a bit once the elasticity of the initial years was stretched to its utmost limit.

The new US president was reluctant to spend much on 'unwinnable' war and favored a balanced budget and tax cuts. Eisenhower rather sought to spread the net of Soviet containment on a global scale, especially in the Middle East, indirectly though, through various regional alliances like the Baghdad Pact or the CENTO, the South East Asia Treaty Organization or the SEATO and the ANZUS to cover the Asia-Pacific at the same time that would be less costly and more importantly, less risky.

In most of these alliances, developed countries like the United States, France, Britain, Australia, and New Zealand were the common members. The geographically distant United States found it difficult to cope with another super power having overwhelming geographical advantages in that the latter's borders touched most of the continents of the world and comprised eleven time zones. The United States, in order to minimize the cost and risk of its earlier anti-Soviet policies, resorted more and more to indirect, covert and even pre-emptive actions during the whole of the 1950s, e.g., CIA backed coups in Iran, Guatemala, Indonesia, and Cuba in 1953, 1954, 1958 and 1961 respectively and the adoption of a more militant posture in the Quemoy and Matsu island disputes with China to assure Formosa of the American support. However, most of the above alliances and treaties during the Eisenhower administration proved ineffective and a burden on the United States and most of these had to be disbanded within a quarter of a century after their formations as they failed to contain the Soviet globe-trotting in the 1970s. Thus, Eisenhower's New Look has been described by Alan P. Dobson as 'containment on the cheap'.

Both Eisenhower and his Secretary of State Dulles preferred deterrence through massive nuclear retaliation to relying on the more expensive conventional weapons that required 'bases' abroad. The US nuclear stockpile doubled within two years of Eisenhower's assumption of presidency and in keeping with Dulles' famous rhetoric of brinkmanship, the United States even deployed some 'low-kiloton nuclear warheads in Europe'. Such a policy rested on the simple assumption that nuclear deterrence was adequate to make the Soviets think several times before embarking on any misadventure. Interestingly, Dulles' anti-communist rhetoric, however, got punctured in the 1956 Suez crisis and in the American ineptness during the Hungarian crisis, the same year. Alan P. Dobson and Steve Marsh aptly gives a break-up of Eisenhower's containment strategy into three components, viz., reliance on nuclear weapons, insistence on burden sharing on the part of the allies and 'covert, economic, and psychological warfare.'

There is another explanation for this game of brinkmanship fancied by Dulles. Long before, Adam Smith in another of his classic work, Theory of Moral Sentiments (1759), dwelt on the effect of 'finger' cutting. He reasoned that the news of the collapse of a far-flung empire like China wouldn't create so much worry in the minds of the Westerners because they would calmly go to bed with their fingers in tact. Likewise, nuclear deterrence afforded both the superpowers the time and luxury to indulge in all sorts of hyperboles to unnerve each other, psychologically. Both the superpowers 'insured' their heads by an extra cover of 'hair': their respective 'spheres of influence'. Since hair is no organ of human body, no pain or loss would accrue if it is shed. That is why the Soviet Union could afford to relinquish its empire 'voluntarily' in the hope of preserving its inner core.

Truman and Eisenhower administrations' ambivalence towards the Soviet Union were due to a strange 'respect' for that enigmatic country, because the rise of the Soviet Union coincided with the declining 'charisma' of its Western allies. Moreover, the Soviet Union was viewed as a potential balancer in Europe, in the coming days. To that extent, the entire logic of the US response to Soviet behavior in the Cold War era rested on the Kennan assumption that the United States ought to register maximum gain by changing the nature of the military 'heavy' Soviet society through some dogged and persistent policy of containment and balancing the Eastern colossus with the growing power of the industrialized nations of Europe. It rested on the assumption that if the Soviets did change, well and good, and if they did not, then the Western alliance must confront them to their logical end. Yet the bottom line was that the United States of the 1950s could well make 'swords' in place of 'plows, and created a 'permanent armaments industry of vast proportions'. The United States during these years enlarged its defense establishments far beyond the limit recommended by the founders and by the end of the 1950s, covered three and a half million men and women at a cost exceeding the 'net incomes of all the US corporations.' However, no serious effort was made to 'roll back' the iron curtain during that era.

President Eisenhower used the 1956 Suez crisis as an opportunity to atone for America's past 'sin' committed in 1948. Egyptian President Abdul Gamel Nasser needed resources to develop the Egyptian economy. As the United States declined to help Nasser, he sought to raise resources by nationalizing the Anglo-French dominated Suez Canal Company in 1956. The United Kingdom and France, in connivance with Israel, carried out the campaign against Egypt. The United States was reluctant to lose the psychological initiative that it gained at a time when the Soviet tanks rolled through the streets of Budapest. Another important reason might be that the United States did not want the erstwhile European powers to reassert their control over the oil-rich Middle East. Equally important for the Americans was to anoint the deep Arab wound caused by the creation of the Jewish state in the very heartland of Islam.

Eisenhower's policies seemed to work for the Middle East but another development, nearby, dented the US prestige. The United States failed to repeat in Cuba the success story of Guatemala. Let me briefly describe the Guatemala episode, first. The United Fruit Company (UFC) controlled about sixty per cent of the arable land in Guatemala. The UFC paid low wages to the agricultural laborers, deprived the government of its legitimate revenue, left vast lands in an under utilized condition (the company continually reported only a fraction of the value of its land and exports) and became the target of the vast landless agricultural population in that country. In 1951, Jacob Arbenz, a reformist leader was elected to lead one of the most backward Central American countries. Arbenz seized a quarter million acres of land from UFC for a price of $600,000. The UFC claimed $15.8 million for such a confiscation of its lands. In the subsequent months, the United States charged Arbenz government with having communist links and found an appropriate stooge in colonel Aramas. The CIA trained some Guatemalan exiles in the nearby Nicaragua, then ruled by Samozoa, and on 8 June 1954, these dissidents, with the American help, isolated the military from Arbenz. The code name of that successful operation was PBSUCCESS. On assuming the charge, Aramas obliged the UFC by returning all the land appropriated by the Arbenz government and, in the process, pacified the Secretary of State Dulles whose interest in the UFC was already well known.

Cuba, traditionally the exploited, was another troubled spot in Latin America. The Cuban rebels used to carry out intermittent insurgent actions against Spain since the 1820's. The same story was repeated when the United States established its Cuban Protectorate following the US-Spanish war. Cuba's resentment towards the United States assumed a new dimension in the late 1950s with the US backed Batista regime losing its credibility. Fidel Castro emulated what his ancestor failed in one such earlier attempt and overthrew the corrupt dictator, Fulgentio Batista in a 1958 uprising. The United States was annoyed to see an ally replaced by a nationalist and anti- US leader in its backyard. Castro appropriated all the private lands held by the US wealthy class and nationalized all the industries belonging to the US business interest groups. The United States was alarmed at the prospect of a regime about to turn pro-Soviet.

Eisenhower administration had sharply reacted to Castro's Soviet overtures by lifting the sugar quota and by imposing economic embargo. The United States severed diplomatic relations with Castro's Cuba in 1961. Eisenhower even authorized the CIA to prepare and plan for an invasion of Cuba. I'll return to this episode a little later as it remained for the Kennedy administration to follow up this abortive coup attempt.

Africa proved to be a classic example of the US inability to match its Cold War politics based on anti-communism with non Cold War issues. The Dark Continent offered the United States an opportunity to burnish its idealistic image further as the famine-stricken undeveloped continent needed economic help. African nations were a bit unfortunate to see the light of liberation after WWII, at a time when the Cold War was going on full swing, and they were left largely ignored by both the super powers. The US policies towards Africa in the initial decades of the Cold War remained inconsistent and conflicting. For example, the United States supported the UN vote in 1961 on the liberation of Angola from the Portugal and even supported another UN Security Council motion to censure Belgian imperialism in Congo following the 1959 popular revolts and demands for liberation. Strangely, in both these cases, sensing that the Soviets were eager to cash on the anti-colonial nationalist sentiments in these regions, the United States extended its support to anti-Soviet faction in Angola and to Colonel Mobutu Sese Seko in Congo. The latter, with apparent CIA backing carried out the September 5, 1960 coup to depose Lumumba whom the US considered a Soviet puppet. The US support to the dictatorial regime of Mobutu continued because of the perceived need to protect the interests of multinationals in exploiting the mineral resources, viz., cobalt, copper, diamond, gold, cadmium, and uranium.

Kennedy era, Cuban crises, Vietnam saga, Nixon and Ford's policies

Right from the beginning, the Kennedy administration meant business. It lost no time in executing the plans laid by its predecessor to oust Castro. The ultimate aim was to eject a pro-Soviet regime from its backyard, as early as possible, to save the Monroe Doctrine from being soiled any further, to avoid a domino effect in Latin and Central American countries, and most importantly, to avoid a possible Soviet encirclement of the Western Hemisphere. As mentioned earlier, Eisenhower acquiesced in a coup attempt by the CIA trained Cuban ex-patriot dissidents. Kennedy upheld that decision and sought to execute the operation, on condition of maintaining strict secrecy. The operation took place on 17 April, 1961, when a contingent of about 1500 Cuban exiles landed in the Bahia de Cochinos (Bay of Pigs) on the south coast of Cuba. The US planes helped in the off-loading of Cuban rebels under the cover of darkness on the beach. The coup failed miserably as the rebels were small in numbers and lacked the mass support needed to make it a success. Within two to three days almost all the rebels were either captured or executed and the United States had to be content with a face-saving agreement that ensured transportation of the surviving rebels to 'safety'.

The new President John F. Kennedy had thus a baptism by fire, beset as he was, with all the legacies of a whole range of problems from the Eisenhower administration, besides Cuba: increasing tension with communist China, tougher Soviet attitudes bordering on threats because of the launching of the Sputniks, intensification of the Berlin crisis, the worsening situation in Vietnam and the 'Khrushchev' rhetoric that the American grand children would grow up in a communist world and that the Soviet Union had the capability to 'bury' the United States any time it wished. The rapidly growing 'brushfire' challenges from a growingly communist-oriented Latin America in the 1960s alarmed the US policy makers. Already, the failure of the Bay of Pigs operation, Cuba's subsequent tilt towards the Soviet camp, and the spread of the communist ideals to the neighboring Latin America, Africa and parts of South East Asia, convinced Kennedy that poverty and underdevelopment were the ideal breeding grounds of communism and that the third world countries needed a sort of Marshall Aid package, failing which they would slip into the arms of communism.

In order to cut the multifarious tentacles of communism, Kennedy relied on his doctrine of 'flexible response' ranging from the Peace Corps Program to the Green Berets counter-insurgency force in its own backyard. In order to safeguard human liberty, Kennedy's America was prepared 'to pay any price, bear any burden, meet any hardship, support any friend, and oppose any foe'. Flexible response stretched containment policy further as Kennedy felt, "The free world's security can be endangered not only by a nuclear attack but also by being slowly nibbled away at the periphery, regardless of our strategic power, by forces of subversion, infiltration, intimidation, indirect or non-overt aggression, internal revolution, diplomatic blackmail, guerrilla warfare or a series of limited Wars."

The Cuban Missile Crisis

Alarmed by the abortive US attempts at the Bay of Pigs and a couple of other attempts either to kill or 'debeard' him with poisons, the Cuban leader thought it wise to make a full fledged commitment to the Soviet Union to ensure protection of 'David' Cuba from its northern 'Goliath'. Already, by 1959, Khrushchev had come to the conclusion that future wars would go the nuclear way and hence strategic advantages and bases were crucial for the launching of intermediate and medium range ballistic missiles, IRBMs and MRBMs, respectively. The offer from Castro to install such missiles in Cuba came handy for the

Soviet Union. First, such an adventurous and surprise move would so unnerve the Americans that their policy-makers would be at their wit's end to formulate appropriate policies to counter this Soviet threat and stop thinking of 'lobbing' one or two nuclear bombs past the Soviet 'bow' right into the Kremlin.

The Soviet Union could hardly let go such a golden opportunity to blackmail its bete noire and bring its principal adversary to its knees. The United States was completely taken aback by the suddenness and 'absurdity' (earlier Kennedy administration had repeatedly rejected intelligence reports since August 1962 and rather relied on the statements by the Soviet officials that the Soviets had not the slightest intention to deploy missiles so close to the American borders) of such a 'misadventure' by the Soviets that had a vertiginous effect on the American policy makers in Washington. Such an utterly callous approach on the part of the US administration can be explained either by its over-confidence or an apparent complacency to bear with the polar bear in the spirit of the game. More specifically, such a mind-set revealed how the tensions of intense bipolar rivalry of the previous years have dazed the American policy makers and how the Soviets shrewdly exploited this subtle psychological advantage.

Kennedy was informed of the Soviet shipment of quite a number of such missiles in the Cuban waters, thanks to a U2 reconnaissance plane, flying over a construction site in Havana. Kennedy let this be known to Britain a day before the world came to know via the presidential broadcast on 22 October, 1962, about this Soviet 'misdeed'. By then, Kennedy had formed an executive committee of the National Security Council comprising of a very small number of Soviet experts and those very close to the president including his brother, Attorney-General, Robert Kennedy, who played a crucial role in defusing the crisis. It had been reported that this small group suspended all outside contacts during the brief period of the crisis. The immediate concern of this group was how to respond to this new type of fait accompli handed down by its arch rival.

The suddenness of the event deprived the United States any leeway to flash its economic and financial card to either of the adversaries. Soviet presence had literally enabled Castro to twist the tail of the tiger. After all, Castro had a sound logic to justify such installation. He pointed out that it was the United States that had been the trendsetter in deploying such missiles in Europe and in Turkey. Never before, except in the Civil War, had the United States found itself a prisoner of its own doing. After remaining in a state of inaction for several days, the United States eventually drew some blood as it opted for a naval blockade and the inspection of Soviet incoming ships within 500 nautical miles of Cuban waters instead of launching a direct invasion or air strike. Kennedy acted extremely prudently in checking his impetuosity to go for an all out attack on Cuba because of the presence of forty thousand Soviet troops armed with tactical nuclear weapons. This, notwithstanding the Soviet downing of a couple of U2 planes for trespassing the Soviet and Cuban borders during the crisis days. Meanwhile, the United States took the issue to the UN Security Council as the rest of the world stood on the edge, apprehending a possible nuclear Armageddon.

On 26 February, the Soviet Union informed the US administration of its willingness to pull back and dismantle its deployments provided the latter guaranteed Cuba's sovereignty and pledged not to attack Cuba. On the next day, 27 February, Soviets made their real intentions known when they demanded dismantlement of a few Jupiter missiles on Turkey close to the Western Soviet border regions. The United States readily agreed to the first demand made by the Soviets but passed on a feeler to the Soviet leaders that the removal of Jupiter missiles would take place in camera in order not to weaken the US commitment to its allies. Thus, curtains were drawn on one of the Cold War period's closest encounters. But the Cuban missile crisis had a positive effect in ushering in an era of detente as the superpowers felt the need for closer coordination, like the installation of the hot lines in emergency situations, the need for arms control measures like the Partial Test Ban Treaty in 1963, later on, the Non Proliferation Treaty (NPT), and above all the Strategic Arms Limitation Talks (SALT).

Kennedy had no option but to adopt a flexible approach – a mixture of 'charioteering' and 'defense' to leash Soviet communism at a time when both France and Britain, bastions of capitalism, had been reeling under an unprecedented rise in the numbers of sympathizers of leftist dogmas in their intellectual circles. The strategic parity between the superpowers following the Cuban missile crisis had two consequences: the need for arms limitations talk to avert nuclear showdown and the adoption of MAD (Mutual Assured Destruction) theory. The United States felt the need to develop a 'second strike' capability to survive a first attack and to retaliate at the same time in order to deter the Soviets from committing any misadventures. Such an approach was obvious in view of the cold nature of a conflict that bordered on brinkmanship but never resulted in a war. The post Cuban missile crisis era saw an unprecedented rise in arms race even during the Kennedy era. The US defense budget shot up and the number of Polaris submarine fleet and Minute missiles doubled by 1964.

As for quarantining the spread of communism through means other than war, Kennedy took several measures: sending about 9,000 American volunteers in various fields, by 1963, to over forty countries, under the Peace Corps program; the Food for Peace project to supply the developing countries in need of food out of the American surpluses; and the Alliance for Progress to support progressive movements in Latin America for winning the 'hearts and minds' of the people of the Third World. To this end, Kennedy proposed $20 billion of aid over a period of ten years. Alan Dobson writes,

> The Alliance for Progress failed. It helped to increase Latin the American economic growth to about 5% per annum by the mid-1960s, but wealth accumulated in the elite, not the people and there was very little land or tax reform. Effectively, the Alliance for Progress strengthened and enriched the forces of oppression. By 1970, there were over a dozen more military regimes in Latin America than in 1960.
>
> —*Dobson and Marsh, 2001, p.68*

Like Europe of the 1940s, Latin America in the late 1960s offered a model of how the communists could capture state powers in various parts of the world through propaganda and guerrilla warfare.

President Johnson inherited the same problems in Vietnam and Latin America, in a bigger way. The defeat of Joaquin Balaguer, Trujilo's heir, in an election at the hands of a leftist reformer, Dr. Juan Bosch, seemed to the US like a fire to the burnt child coming as it on the heels of the repeated American failures in Cuba. In response, Johnson sent the US forces to invade and occupy the Dominican Republic to stop what it called a "Communist rebellion," with the help of the dictators from Brazil, Paraguay, Honduras, and Nicaragua. At the back of Johnson's mind was the fear that any failure in Dominican Republic to 'protect the American lives', would have spill-over effects on his Vietnam campaign.

The Vietnam Episode

Unnoticed amidst the ensuing feverish arms race of the 1960s and overshadowed by the Cuban and the Berlin Wall crises, another crisis was brewing up, yet again, in the Chinese neighborhood that proved to be the phase of a great 'eclipse' in the American history. The United States survived that self-inflicted 'crucifixion' in Indochina through a resurrection bathing in the blood of communism in the early 1990s. It was the United States that had the last laugh so far as Vietnam was concerned. The United States pulled up one of the great miracles of history, largely through its economic muscles, to convert the traditionally and fiercely independent-minded bete noire of the 1960s and 1970s into its handpicked tool in the 1990s. This also underlines the fact that despite the heroic struggles waged by the Viet Minh forces, the US army could easily have overwhelmed the North Vietnam absent Soviet and Chinese supplies to that country during the US-Vietnam war. This claim is further reinforced by the fact that once the United States succeeded in isolating the Soviets and the Chinese from Hanoi in the closing years of the 1960s, Hanoi was compelled to take part in peace talks to resolve the issue. Today, in a complete turnaround of events, it is the old enemy, the United States, that happens to be Vietnam's ally, as China grew more and more hostile to its past ally and Russia stands marginalized in Indochina.

Vietnam has got a strong nationalistic past as that nation had incessantly fought against its neighbors to defend its sovereignty. Vietnam, once upon a time, happened to be an empire. It was in the middle of the nineteenth century that Vietnam became a French colony and remained so till France ceded most of its control of Indo-China to Japan during the Second World War, retaining to itself only the nominal administrative control of the region. In 1941, Ho Chi Minh set up a nationalist organization, the Viet Minh (Vietnam Independence League) and provided the allied forces in their fight against Japan with intelligence information. Apart from supplying information to the US military Intelligence wing, Office of Strategic Services, OSS, Ho's party used to harass the Japanese rear with guerrilla maneuvers. It was hoped that Vietnam would be free once the Japanese occupying forces left. On September 2, 1945, the day Japan signed its surrender agreement that formally ended the war in the Pacific, Ho Chi Minh declared the independence of Vietnam and became the first ever president of the Democratic republic of Vietnam.

The French administration under De Gaulle was unwilling to cede France's colonial rights in Indochina. As WWII was drawing to a close, Roosevelt, and later Truman, repeatedly asked France to forsake its colonial rights in the region. The First Indochina war spanning 1946-1954 took place since France was reluctant to let Vietnam free. Vietnam remained virtually divided between Ho's forces controlling the North and those in the South under the control of 35000 French troops.

Given the memories of the North Korean offensive over the South in the early 1950s and given the Vietnamese Communist Party's agenda and Vietnam's proximity to communist China, there was enough cause for the United States to fear that a united Vietnam under communist rule might have a domino effect in the entire South East Asia. Accordingly, the United States rendered all sorts of help to the French forces. The traditional US opposition towards European colonial rule in Asia and Indo-China changed overnight and the American policymakers thought it prudent to let France have another opportunity in carrying out the war against the Viet Minh forces to arrest the spread of communism in Asia. By the time the Korean War came to a conclusion, the US aid to France stood around $500 million that was to rise to about $800 million in 1954 to cover the entire French cost of conducting the war in Vietnam. Some scholars point out that the US eagerness to secure French support for the European Defense Program had led the former to have a 'double take' at 'nationalist' Ho Chi Minh and rather to brand the latter as pro-communist. Hastedt remarked, "In a virtual quid pro quo, the United States agreed to underwrite the French war effort in Indochina the same day France announced its intention to participate in the plans for the defense of Europe." (Hastedt, p.104)

In the decisive battle at Dien Bien Phu in 1954, North Vietnamese forces, bolstered by the infiltration of large number of Chinese Red Army released from the Korean front, besieged the French army and a hapless France intimated America that it needed urgent help. Eisenhower administration was reluctant to oblige France and the French army surrendered. The Geneva Peace Accords partitioned Vietnam at the 17th parallel through the establishment of a provisional line of demarcation between communists and pro-French elements in the northern and southern halves respectively and promised a national election in August 1956 to decide who would rule the unified nation. That means the United States never said that Vietnam would be divided. Laos and Cambodia, freed from the French forces, were to stay as neutral zones. Though, the United States refused to sign the Accord, it promised not to use force to disturb the peace process even though some American troops remained in Vietnam after the French withdrawal. However, the United States flouted with the provision of the Geneva Peace Accord when it created the SEATO, soon after, and sought to cover both Laos and Cambodia through a separate protocol. This was done to separate these two countries from the communist influences of North Vietnam and further steps were taken to ensure that a separate state of South Vietnam be formed under the leadership of Diem. Later on, the Communists also violated the Neutrality of Laos and Cambodia by using them as supply routes to their southern communist brethren through what came to be known as the Ho Chi Minh Trail.

The United States was well aware that given Ho's popularity, the communists would corner 80% of the total votes should a national election take place. Such an unacceptable situation led the United States to back Ngo Din Diem who had become the leader of South Vietnam by replacing emperor Bao Dai. The United States provided him with all military assistance and set the stage for a protracted and atrocious war in Vietnam. The United States sent a military mission comprising one thousand American non-combatant military advisers. Taken as a whole, the American engagement in Vietnam was both a war between the two Vietnams as well as between the American and the North Vietnamese forces.

The Kennedy administration escalated the US involvement in Vietnam. Acting on the recommendations of the Taylor Rostow report that required at least 8,000 American combat troops, Kennedy increased the number of the US military advisers by an additional 15000 to score a win over the hostile North. It remained for President Johnson to make the US engagement in Vietnam complete when he sought the Congressional approval to use force following the Gulf of Tonkin affair that remained as mysterious as the Maine affair, some six decades ago. The war in Vietnam had begun as the Congress gave its nod to the Gulf of Tonkin resolution and authorized the President to do whatever he deemed.

The first sustained US bombing operation rolled like thunder over the Vietnamese sky in retaliation to the two Viet Cong offensive on the US base at Pleiku, in February 1965, in which the US casualties ran to dozens. As the war progressed, the United States became desperate to end it as swiftly as possible with the injection of massive ground forces that grew to about 5,40,000 at the end of the war. Meanwhile, goals kept changing as the war intensified. According to a Pentagon Paper revelation "70 per cent of the US priority was to avoid a humiliating defeat; 20 per cent to keep South Vietnam from China; and 10 per cent to permit the people of South Vietnam to enjoy a better, freer way of life." (Hastedt, p.105-06) This and subsequent expositions by the American Dailies were aimed at demonstrating how the US administration, since the first Indochina war, misled the American people.

The failed communist-led Tet offensive in 1968 revealed their (North Vietnamese fighting forces') will to stake everything to overrun Saigon along with other provincial capital, through concerted efforts. The United States reckoned that its time for withdrawal had come. In order to save face, it had started to normalize and improve relations with both the communist giants to isolate them from Hanoi and opted for Vietnamization of the war in which it would be the South Vietnamese forces, henceforth, who would have to do the fighting with American financial and military assistance. Domestic pressure kept mounting that called for withdrawal of all the American troops from Vietnam. McNamara repented that henceforth America won't go to war in other parts of the world, single-handed.

Nixon era

Vietnamization, one form of Nixon Doctrine, hardly worked for America, as the corrupt leadership in the South pocketed most of the American money, instead of using them in war efforts. Moreover, South Vietnamese forces were ill-prepared to fight the far more organized North. The United States, in sheer desperation, invaded Cambodia to flush out communist hideouts there and intensified the bombing of North Vietnam in the hope that this would give time to the South to regroup its forces. Undeterred by such indiscriminate and random US bombing, the North Vietnamese forces launched their offensives across the demilitarized zone (DMZ) compelling the United States to reenter the war with massive bombing of the North Vietnamese targets and to resort to what came to be known as infamous mining of its ports. After several rounds of massive bombing of Hanoi and Haiphong (hitherto off-limit to the US attacks) in the closing months of 1972, a peace treaty (talks for which had begun as early as 1969) came into place on January 31, 1973. South Vietnamese resistance ultimately succumbed in 30 April 1975, the day after the last remaining of the US forces and non-military personnel 'fled' that country.

Nixon had one more boil in the American neighborhood that required to be surgically removed. This time it was Chile that fell to the pro-Marxist regime of Allende and the United States once again apprehended a red star over the Andean. The United States poured in enough money to foster opposition and to sabotage Allende's economic policies. Just at a time things seemed to be getting out of Allende's hands and he was becoming unpopular, the Chilean General Augusto Pinochet, reportedly, with the support of CIA, carried out a military coup in which Allende was killed. The US Congress decided that henceforth it wouldn't endorse any individual killing of leadership.

While Nixon Doctrine did not work in Vietnam, its general message was clear. Unprecedented domestic pressure and an utter disillusionment with an 'ungrateful' Europe confirmed the American belief that Europe never wanted the United States to play a bigger role outside its hemisphere (European acceptance of Atlanticism, though a matter of dire necessity, was also an age-old European ploy to engage America in European affairs). Nixon Doctrine conveyed to Europe that the latter couldn't continue to be a free rider so far as security matters were concerned and that henceforth they would have to rely on their own forces with the US financial and technological assistance only. The United States, however, pledged to adhere to its earlier treaty commitments. To add to the US discomforts, Germany and France tried to negotiate their outstanding issues, separately, with the Soviet Union under what had come to be known as Ostopolitiks.

The United States under Nixon hoped to reduce its reliance on its European allies and, instead, opted for Détente with both the Soviet Union and China. First such opportunity came during the Strategic Arms Limitation Talk in the Moscow summit in 1972. Both the superpowers felt the need to cooperate on various international issues and the need for coexistence, and de facto power sharing arrangement on the basis of status quo. Both these countries refrained from taking advantage of the other's domestic problems through mutual restraints. The Helsinki Accord of 1975 was a pointer to the realization that the two opposing socio-economic systems could coexist and, what was more, this coexistence and cooperation must be nourished. While, détente helped the United States save its face in Vietnam, it proved costly in political terms as the decade of 1970s rolled on. The Soviet Union took this as a sign of the American weakness and a possible rupture in the trans-Atlantic unity. The Soviets leaders were further emboldened by the US recognition to treat their country as its equal. The United States, on its part, hoped to have some respite in the financial front as the crisis in international financial system and the recession in most western countries tempted the Group of 77 to float their dependency theory demanding greater concession from the developed countries.

The two traditional US economic prescriptions of generous foreign aid and proliferation of multinational corporations, in various parts of the world, to lift mankind from their poverty yielded little results in the 1970s. The demand of the era was rather to alleviate poverty, hunger and economic inequality in a post Vietnam international ambience marked by utter disregard for the American imperialism. Most of the third world nations, rather, wasted these financial aids in unproductive sectors and in debt servicing.

Meanwhile, the American Middle East policy initiated by Kissinger successfully marginalized Soviet influence in the region for the rest of the decade. Aware of the problems created by the OPEC nations in the oil sector, the Soviet Union tried to preempt both the American and Chinese designs to control the Middle East oil resources by a policy of encirclement of the region through various overtures in Angola, the Red Sea region, and the Horn of Africa. Soviet timing of the invasion of Afghanistan can also be well explained by the Soviet desire to exploit America's difficulty with the Iranian hostage crisis and to move closer to controlling the Gulf region and, not the least, to counter the growing Chinese influence in the region.

Détente on America's part can be best explained by an old Sanskrit proverb that the wise don't mind parting with half of their resources, when in distress. In that sense, détente was aimed at keeping America afloat for some time. That is why Robert Tucker thought of détente as more of a "holding operation than a settled strategy". Soviets might have got the feeler that if the Vietnam debacle could reduce 'containment' to the level of détente, then a further nudge in another key area might put the United States, acting under Congressional restrictions, to be more defensive.

The Nixon-Ford administrations' emphasis on a more multi-polar type of international order almost negated NSC-68 Resolutions' main tenet of making ideological conflicts between the two opposite systems the basis of the post war American foreign policies. While NSC-68 unwittingly put the American foreign policies in the straitjacket of anti-communism, thereby, making it dangerously rigid and lop-sided, the post 1945 United States had little interest in continuing with policies that would make it look like a stranger and more 'exceptional' in an international political system defined by mediocrity, power and national interest. To the extent that Nixon and Ford were trying to bring 'exceptional' America more in line with the majority of 'ordinary' nation-states, this implied that the hitherto moralistic-legalistic American approach must give way to stark realism. The United States in the 1970s found itself in a similar position that the Soviets happened to be under Gorbachev a decade later. Meanwhile, Congressional pressure on the Executive kept mounting in the aftermath of the

Vietnam War and with the coming into being of the War Powers Act in 1973. Congress linked the granting of most favored nation (MNF) status to the Soviets with permissions for Jews residing there to immigrate to the United States under the Jackson-Vanik Amendment in 1974.

President Carter restored the ideological content of the American foreign policies by emphasizing the centrality of human rights that had also been one of the cardinal messages of the Declaration. However, Carter's emphasis on human rights undermined the continuity in the post war US foreign policies based on realism. NSC-68 proposals meant that every other consideration including human rights must take backseat to the policy of containment on a global scale. Since the Soviet Union was going great guns in the 1970s, the introduction of a different variant of ideology, human rights, rendered the American foreign policies less focused on realistic goals. Kennan, as the Director of the Policy Planning the US State Department, way back in the late 1940s had warned in the following lines:

> To maintain this position of disparity (the US economic-military supremacy)...we will have to dispense with all sentimentality and day dreaming...We should cease to talk about vague and unrealistic objectives such as human rights, the raising of living standard and democratization...The day is not far off when we are going to have to deal in straight power concepts...The less we are then hampered by idealistic slogans, the better.

The United States was too concerned with Soviet overtures in Africa in the mid-1970s. As the Portuguese left Angola in 1974, the infighting between the three factions, the Union for Total Independence of Angola (the UNITA) the National Liberation Front of Angola (FNLA), and the Popular Movement for the Liberation of Angola (MPLA) grew more intense. The United States supported the UNITA and, later on, the Chinese backed FNLA while South Africa sent 2000 troops in response to Soviet-Cuban support of MPLA. Cuba sent about 14000 troops in addition to an earlier consignment of 250 military advisers. Just as the Cold War rivalry was getting hotter, Congress intervened and declined any further assistance to the US backed factions. The United States had to retreat.

References and readings

Edward Pessen, Losing our souls, The American experience in the Cold War; Ivan R Dee, Publisher, Chicago, 1993.

the Truman Doctrine, Truman Presidential Museum and Library, www.trumanlibrary.org/whistlestop/study_collections/doctrine/large/indx.php

Michael H. Hunt, Crises In the US Foreign Policy Yale University Press, New

Haven & London.

George F. Kennan, 'X', "The Sources of Soviet Conduct" Foreign Affairs, 25, 1947.

Alan P. Dobson And Steve Marsh, the US Foreign Policy since 1945, Making of the Contemporary World ed., Eric Evans and Ruth Henig, Routledge, 2001, London.

Cold War Chat, CNN Perspective Series, Albert J.Beveridge III in a chat moderated by the CNN interactive Associate Editor Andy Walton, www.cnn.com/

Fred Block, Economic Instability and Military Srength: The Paradoxes of the 1950 G. John Ikenberry, NY, Longman, 2002, Rearmament Decision, in the American Foreign Policy, Theoretical Essays, Fourth Edition.

Berlin Airlift 1948-1949, Sponsors of u-s-History.com, www.u-s-history.com//pages/h1758html

Bruce Kennedy, CNN Interactive, Episode 9: The Wall, CNN perspective series, CNN.com

Armed Conflicts Events Data, Berlin Wall Crisis, www.onwar.com

Truman Presidential Museum and Library, 50th anniversary of the North Atlantic Treaty, http//www.trumanlibrary.org/nato/nato.htm

Josse Joffe, "Continental Divides", The National Interest, (Spring 2003).

Excerpts from NSC-68, April 14, 1950, http//www.mtholyoke.edu/acad/intre/nsc-68/nsc68-1.htm

http://www.un.org/Overview/achievement.html

http://www.en.wikipedia.org/wki/United_Nations#success_of_the_the UN

Joshua S. Goldstein, International Relations, , 5th Edition, NY, Longman, 2004.

Henry Kissinger, Does America need a Foreign Policy, Toward a Diplomacy for the 21st Century, NY, Simon and Schuster, 2004.

Max Boot, *The Savage Wars of Peace, Small Wars and the Rise of the American Power*, NY, 2002.

H.W. Brand, What America owes to the World, Cambridge, 1998.

Robert W. Tucker and David C. Hendrickson, *The Fall of the First British Empire: Origins for the War of the American Independence*, Baltimore, 1982.

Richard D. Burns, eds., *Guide to the American Foreign Relations since 1700*, Oxford, 1983

Arthur B. Darling, *Our Rising Empire, 1763-1803*, New Haven, 1940.

North American Review, vols1-20, Ithaca, Cornell University Press, http//cdl.library.cornell.edu/moa/browse, journals/nora.html

Norman Graebner, eds., *Traditions and Values: the American Diplomacy, 1790-1865*, Washington, 1985.

Richard W. Van Alstyne, *The Rising American Empire*, NY, 1960.

Albert Bushnel Hart, *Foundations of the American Foreign policy*, NY, 1970.

Richard Olney, *The Growth of Our Foreign Policy*, Atlantic 85, 1900.

William Graham Sumner, *The Fallacy of Territorial Extension*, Forum, June, 1916.

Richard B. Morris, *The Peacemakers: The Great Powers and the American Independence*, NY, 1965.

Jerald A. Combs, the American *Diplomatic History, Two Centuries of changing Interpretations*, Berkeley, 1986.

Tyler Dennet (John Hay: From Poetry to Politics) and the Americans in Eastern Asia: A Critical Study of the Policy of the United States with reference to China, Japan, and Korea in the 19th century , NY, 1922.

Charles Tansill, *America Goes to War*, NY, 1963.

Charles A. Beard, *Devil Theory of War*, NY, 1936.

Newton Baker, *Why We Went to War*, London, 1972.

Ernest May, *The World War and the American Isolation, 1914-1917*, MA, 1959.

Thomas Bailey, *Woodrow Wilson and the Great Betrayal*, NY, 1945.

Blum Schlesinger, Jr., et al, The National Experience: A History of the United States, 6th Edition, NY, 1985.

Charles C. Tansill, *Backdoor to War: The Roosevelt Foreign policy, 1933-41*, Chicago, 1971.

Frederick Mark, *The Manifest Destiny and Mission in the American History: A Reinterpretation*, NY, 1963.

Reginald Horseman, *Race and The Manifest Destiny*, Cambridge, MA, 1981.

Foster Rhea Dulles, *Prelude to the World Power: the American Diplomatic History, 1860-1900*, NY, 1965.

James MacPherson, *Ordeal by Fire: The Civil War and Reconstruction*, NY, 1991.

David Healy, *the US Expansionism: The Imperialist Urge in the 1890s*, Wisconsin, 1970.

Alexander Deconde, *Ethnicity, Race and the American Foreign Policy*, Boston, 1993.

Arthur S. Link et al, eds., *Woodrow Wilson, The Public Papers of Woodrow Wilson,* Princeton University Press, NJ, 1967.

Samuel Bemis , *Jay's Treaty: A Study in Commerce and Diplomacy,* NY, 1923.

Alfred Thayer Mahan, *The US Looking Onward, 1890, in the collection of essays, The Interest of America in Sea Power, Present and Future,* London, 1970.

Major Problems in the American Foreign Policy, vols. 1&2, Edited by Thomas G. Peterson, MA, 1989.

Glenn P. Hastedt, the American *Foreign Policy, Past, Present, Future,* 5th Edition, Prentice Hall, NJ, 2003

CHAPTER V

CARTER, REAGAN, AND BUSH ERA AND THE END OF THE COLD WAR

American foreign policies were more meaningful under the Nixon and the Ford administrations. Policy of détente and cooperation pursued by Nixon and Ford were meant to give a more human face to the American foreign policies. But a policy based on human rights and morality already presumes the very stage it hopes to attain. This visible gap between future visions and present realities was evident as Carter projected his own 'doctrine'. Consequently, most of Carter's policies remained inconsistent, simplistic, whimsical, and even contradictory. In trying to discipline its own house, the Carter administration reduced arms sales to South Korea, Indonesia, and Zaire, thereby, removing the latter's principal incentive and motivation to protect and enhance the American 'interests' in their respective regions. Such a callous neglect of the interests of the regional allies elsewhere, drove the latter to turn more 'promiscuous' in their conduct of foreign policies.

In another diplomatic bungling, both the United States and the USSR demonstrated narrow national interests as they traded places in their support of Somalia and Ethiopia during the Ogaden crisis in 1978. The United States, since the time of Emperor Haille Selasi, had supported Ethiopia. The Soviet Union began to take care of Ethiopia's neighbor since 1963. Following the Somalian encroachment of Ogaden, the Soviet Union switched its support to Ethiopia, thereby, putting the US on the wrong foot. The United States, much to its embarrassment, now found itself supporting the aggressor, Somalia. Cuba, as usual, sent 10000 troops to assist Ethiopia. With South Yemen as a Soviet ally, there was a distinct possibility of a Soviet control of the Red Sea and monitoring of the flow of oil to the West. Carter displayed realism by curtailing aids to Somalia and the United States once again suffered a loss in the Horn of Africa.

Overemphasis on the observance of humanitarian ideals rendered the Carter administration a prisoner of its own policies. The United States was unable to lend a helping hand either to the Shah of Iran or to the Samozoa regime in Nicaragua because of rampant corruption and cronysm in the ruling circles in these two countries. Carter's inconsistent foreign policies distanced its allies as the US wrath and displeasure now turned against them even before the end of the Cold War was in sight! To maintain its 'progressive' image, the United States even supported the rebels and insurgents trying to overthrow the above two regimes. The United States provided the newly installed Sandinista government in Nicaragua with millions of dollars of the US aid. Such an extremely volatile policy, bordering on whimsicalities, rather upset America's minor allies. The American efforts at elevating its 'humane' image recoiled on its credibility. National interest and values intersected, often. It appeared that the United States, as if, had a point to prove to the Soviet Union regarding its 'humanitarian' and 'social' goals. Carter hoped to geld and even change that country through the force of liberal economic and moralistic principles. Paradoxically, Carter remained passive towards the poor human rights records in China, the Philippines, Pakistan, Iran, Indonesia and South Africa.

However, Carter was more successful in respect of the Panama Canal treaties, the Camp David Accord, and the SALT II talks with the Soviet Union. The United States secured the right to construct a Canal from Panama (thanks to President Theodore Roosevelt's support for a secessionist rebel group in Colombia to create an independent state of Panama out of Colombia) as per the Hay-Bunau-Varrila Treaty signed on 3rd November 1903. Nevertheless, Panamanians had for a long time been resenting the US rights over the Canal. In the post-war decades, Panama took the issue to multilateral forums to redefine the treaty of ownership of the Canal. Once in office, President Carter felt it imperative to resolve the dispute. Carter's signing of two new Panama Canal treaties in September 1977 in which America retained its right to manage that waterway till December 3, 1999, created large furor in both the Houses. Thereafter the control of the Canal fell into the hands of Panama. The second treaty about the Permanent Neutrality and Operation of the Panama Canal came into effect in 2000 that made both the countries responsible for maintaining the safety and free movement of vessels of other nations through the Canal.

Camp David was a major achievement for the Carter administration, as it became the trendsetter for subsequent peace processes in the Middle East. While Carter's Camp David left the Palestinian issue in the backseat, it remained for Clinton to take up the issue in the 1990s. Both Egypt and Israel, the two arch rivals since the creation of Israel in 1948, became the greatest beneficiaries of the US largesse. Egypt under Nasser wielded considerable clout in the Arab region but its economy declined in the subsequent years. Egypt desperately needed foreign capital to revive its economy, as it turned to America for help in the 1970s. This was an opportunity both for the United States and Israel to isolate Egypt from the Arab world and to weaken the Arabian unity by playing on the Syrian-Egyptian rivalry over the control of the Arab world.

Secondly, if a peace process got under way, other non-reluctant Arab nations might follow suit and the Middle East deadlock could thus be broken. The all-important issue of Arab recognition of the state of Israel was of paramount importance.

Carter made personal trips to meet various leaders in the Middle East to resolve the Arab-Israel issues. He took personal efforts to persuade both Begin and Sadat to sign the treaty before they left Camp David. On September 17 1978, both the Egyptian President Anwar Sadat and the Israeli Prime Minister Menachem Begin signed the Accord. The Israeli-Egyptian portion of the agreement required Israel to remove all its troops and settlers from Sinai while turning over the control of the peninsula to Egypt and restricting the number of Egyptian troops there. Egypt, in turn, granted Israeli vessels passages into the Suez Canal and other waterways besides recognizing the Jewish state and assuring normalization of diplomatic relations with the state of Israel.

Shah of Iran didn't have the luck it had in 1953 when the CIA-led coup reinstated Reza Shah Pahlavi to his throne. By the early 1970s, the regime that had taken up the job of modernizing a traditionally conservative Iran, degenerated into a corrupt and repressive state machinery. Frequent popular demonstrations took place in the streets of Teheran in the 1970s. In a backlash to Iran's modernization in the past two decades, the Iranian clergies rallied round the central figure of Ayatollah Khomeini who used to conduct his operations from his exile in France. The United States deliberated in intervening even though Shah's Iran, one of the 'twin pillars' for the US in the Middle East, had proved to be the largest provider of oil to the western nations. The Shah fled Iran. The United States thought about giving asylum to an ailing Shah. The Iranians threatened the US Embassy with dire consequences if the autocratic monarch was given asylum in the United States. After much deliberation the United States allowed the former ruler on humanitarian grounds. Iranians retaliated and seized the US embassy and took sixty six Americans as hostage. This hostage crisis continued for 444 days despite the US sanctions and an abortive rescue attempt by the Carter administration to free the hostages.

It remained for Reagan to secure the release of the hostages on his inauguration day. However, at about the same time, the Soviet Union was having its own problem in its neighborhood, Afghanistan. The two time Afghan premiere Daud Khan, initially pro-Soviet, later turned a pro-Iranian. He was ousted by a military coup backed by the pro-Soviet and pro-Maoist factions (then the Marxist People's Democratic Party of Afghanistan (PDPA)) in 1973. However, over time the two factions, the Parcham (pro-Soviet) led by Barbrak Karmal and Khalq (pro-Maoist and ultra leftist) failed to maintain their unity. Maoist Khalq faction engineered a successful coup in 1974, initiated many radical reforms, and signed a 20-year peace treaty with the Soviet Union. The Soviet policy makers did not like the pace of reform. When their advice to slow down the process went unheeded, the Soviets began sending in military equipment and combat personnel to meddle in the Afghan affair. Cyrus Vance, Secretary of State, though suspicious of Soviet intentions, had the impression that the ultra left rulers of Afghanistan wouldn't help further the Soviet interests in the region. Another Maoist faction seized power in 1979 and refused to listen to the Soviet recommendation to slow down the reform process. In December 1979, the Soviet Union invaded Afghanistan and installed Babrak Kamal, the leader of the pro-Soviet Parcham faction as the new Afghan president.

Soviet intervention remained limited to helping the Karmal regime to stall anarchy and civil war in Afghanistan (as evidenced during 1980-86) and to prevent an economic collapse. However, the United States felt otherwise and this led to the promulgation of the Carter Doctrine that read:

> Let our position be absolutely clear: an attempt by any outside force to gain control of the Persian Gulf region will be regarded as an assault on the vital interests of the United States of America, and such an assault will be repelled by any means necessary, including military force.

SALT II was put in abeyance. Grains embargo and a ban on the sale of high technology to the Soviet Union took place. Rapid Deployment Force was established to make up for the insignificant military capabilities in the region. The Soviet move alarmed two other countries close to the Soviet-Afghan border. China and Pakistan, together with the United States, combined all their efforts in providing the local insurgent groups, including the fundamentalist Mujahiddeen, with training, sophisticated arms like the Stinger missiles, and sanctuaries and bases. As the war dragged on, the Soviet Union found it extremely difficult to tame the rebels who took advantage of the rugged mountainous terrain and jungles. With intense pressure from various international bodies, forums, and other countries and with no prospect of ending the stalemate, the Soviets finally withdrew in February 1989, just as the Americans did in the Vietnam War nearly two decades back.

Some scholars felt that the Soviet campaign in Afghanistan was brought about by the need to save its southern Socialist Republican states from slipping into the hands of the surging Islamic fundamentalism at Iran's behest. The Soviet leader Brezhnev cited another reason for the Soviet intervention: the humanitarian needs to save a country from poverty and deprivation. The Western leaders, on their part were concerned by the presence of Soviet troops within 300 miles of the Persian Gulf and the threat it posed for Pakistan. Iran, too, had the same security concerns. Moreover, President Carter, in many of his speeches, referred to the growing Soviet military influence and the excessive dependence of the Western nations on oil from Middle East as his main foreign policy challenges, apart from the threat of religious fundamentalism in that region. All these led Carter to proclaim his doctrine and to act accordingly.

The Reagan Administration

'Cometh the hour, cometh the man'. Ronald Reagan entered the White House with a 'bang' and possibly with some 'divine blessings'. The 40th US president's day of inauguration was also the day of liberation for the 53 remaining hostages in Iran, after they underwent 444 grueling days of ordeal. All the hostages were released under the conditions agreed by the outgoing president Carter: (1) the United States won't interfere in the internal affairs of Iran; (2) Iran would remain immune from any trial and accusation regarding the hostage crisis; and (3) Iranian frozen assets were to be released. The United States released $8 billion in Iranian assets on the same day of inauguration, 20 January 1981. Some scholars suspect that Reagan might have pre-empted an 'October Surprise' of the previous administration by postponing the release of the interned Americans by a month. Whatever be the truth, the Reagan administration had been acting on a déjà vu right from the word go in countering the threat of the 'evil empire' that had cast its 'spell' on every region from Latin and Central America, Asia and the Middle East, to Europe and Africa.

It was perhaps a great paradox of history that it fell on the lot of an amateurish, rather, 'jingoist' and 'romantic' personality like Ronald Reagan, who preferred to rely mostly on the leads from his subordinates and on his warm and deceptive smile, to bring about the fall of an 'empire' in a peaceful manner! The 'Potemkin' and the 'Tefflon' president, as he came to be known, exercised little control over the affairs of his administration officials. According to Chomsky,

> For eight years, the US government virtually functioned without a chief executive. It is quite unfair to assign to Ronald Reagan, the person, much responsibilities for policies enacted in his name. Despite the efforts of the educated classes to invest the proceedings with the required dignity, it was hardly a secret that Reagan had only the vaguest conception of the policies of his administration, and if not properly programmed by his staff, regularly produced statements that would have been an embarrassment, were anyone to take him seriously.
>
> *—Chomsky, June 2004, znet foreign Policy*

Reagan's knowledge of history and geography proved to be no better than those of William Bryan Jenkins about seven decades ago when the latter pleaded ignorance about the location of Sarajavo in Europe's map. On February 18, 1982, Reagan remarked:

"If I recall correctly ... North and South Vietnam had been, previous to colonization, two separate countries [and] provisions were made that these two countries could, by the vote of their people together, decide whether they wanted to be one country or not. Ho Chi Minh refused to participate in such an election...John Kennedy authorized the sending of a division of Marines. And that was the first move towards combat troops in Vietnam.

—Hastedt, p.102

Nevertheless, Reagan was marked out by fate to pull down the formidable socialist empire, riding, as he was, on the accumulated accomplishments of the decades-long post-war American foreign policy achievements to contain the Soviet communism. By the time Reagan assumed the American presidency, the Soviet Union was on its last legs and was nearing its total political and economic bankruptcy. I have discussed the reasons for the fall of that great empire in a separate section below.

It had become an article of faith in the conduct of foreign policies of both the Soviet Union and the United States to formulate their policies in a typical manner since the beginning of the Cold War. Both these superpowers used to attach more importance to 'intelligence' reports than relying on cool and pragmatic analyses. The Soviets backed out of the Paris talks on the issue of joining the Marshall Aid 'club' even though they desperately needed foreign capital to resuscitate their war ravaged economy. Prior to that Paris meeting, Russian intelligence had gathered that the United States wouldn't accommodate the Soviet bloc countries in the aid package. Likewise, in the late 1960s and the early 1970s, as Iran was trying to wean away Daoud Khan from the Soviet fold, Leonid Brezhnev reportedly shouted at the Afghan premiere basing his allegations on intelligence reports that the Afghan army was' infested' with NATO officers and that he must steer clear of them. There are numerous such instances when sheer intelligence report guided last minute important policy decisions of the super powers during the entire Cold war period. The United States acted on its own intelligence sources during the last Iraqi campaign, defying the views of the UNSCOM (United Nations Special Commission) and the world body, the United Nations.

Reagan admitted in his autobiography that he had prior information that the Soviet economy was like a "basket case" and on the verge of a collapse. In his autobiography he had wrote:

Soviet economy was held together by baling wire. In Poland and other Eastern-bloc countries, the economies were also a mess, and there were rumblings of nationalist fervor within the captive Soviet empire. If they didn't make some changes, it is clear to me that in time that communism would collapse of its own weight, and I wondered how we as a nation could use these cracks in the Soviet system to accelerate the process of collapse.

It is this with this 'prophetic' vision that Regan formulated his 'hard-soft' foreign policies in contrast to what he held the policy failures of past administrations in containing the Soviet Union.

The United States entered the 1980s with an inflation-ridden and unemployment-stricken economy and was virtually pushed to the wall by Soviet 'advances' in all international theaters of operation including the Western Hemisphere . It is important to note that the former USSR had always chosen to enhance its territorial and geopolitical influences whenever the Western powers found themselves in trouble, e.g., in the immediate post WWI and WWII years and in the post Vietnam crisis when the anti-capitalist and anti-imperialist sentiments ran extremely high, everywhere. Incidentally, these were precisely the times when the Soviet Union faced their crises for survival also. After the two World Wars, the Soviet economy stood in dilapidated conditions and there was the fear of a rapid German revival with the US help on both the occasions. The Soviet aggressiveness in the 1970s could also be traced to its economic and domestic policy bankruptcy.

American moral hubris, and power touched its nadir in the early 1980s thanks to some inept policies pursued by the successive US presidents in the 1970s. Reagan was bolstered by his intelligence report that an extra nudge by the US may unsettle the Soviet economy. So, he initiated a three-pronged assault on his rival superpower (as evident from the NSDD-32, that is, National Security Decisions Directive) – economic, military, and ideological – to enhance the odds against the survival of the Soviet system. Reagan knew that the Soviet economy was on a steep slope carried down by the weight of its vast overstretch and its various other commitments in the previous decades. On top of it, the Soviet economy suffered from severe malfunctions in its centralized and planned economic structure because of inefficiency, corruption, and wastage.

By the beginning of the 1970s, the Soviet Union badly needed high technology and massive injection of foreign capital to revamp its economy, hitherto financed mostly by its revenues from the sale of oil to the West. Reagan sought to discourage its allies to sell such high-tech items to that country and even dampened the value of Soviet products, especially, oil, in the world market. As for the Eastern bloc countries, the United States and the Federal Republic of Germany provided loans and financial assistance to Poland, Hungary, and even to GDR to help their economies grow along market lines. As a result, by the mid 1980s, all these nations faced serious debt problems and needed more foreign assistance that forced the Soviet Union to spend more on these countries, thereby, putting an additional burden on the Soviet economy. Already the subsidization of the Cuban economy and the costs of continuing covert or overt operations in the Horn of Africa, Latin America, and in Afghanistan had ballooned off the Soviet defense budget.

On assuming Presidency, Reagan struck at the Soviet Achilles' Hill and declared a most ambitious defense plan to force the Soviets to spend more on defense. Reagan proposed that a sum of $1.6 trillion be spent over a five-year period for a defense project aimed at producing B1 bombers, deployment of MX missiles, modernization of the Navy, the nuclear submarines and the ICBMs, the upgrading the Rapid Deployment forces (RDF). (Hastedt, p.60) The most sensational of Reagan's declarations in March 1983 was the Strategic Defense Initiative (SDI), popularly known as the Star Wars program that shook the confidence of the Soviet policy-makers. For Reagan, Mutual Assured Destruction or the MAD concept was no foolproof guarantee that the United States wouldn't be subject to a surprise Soviet nuclear attack. He had already reasoned and consulted some scientific and defense experts, that if the threat of Soviet incoming missiles destined for the United States could be minimized and even eliminated by a network of 'Laser' defense system in the space or by a sort of 'Astrodome', then these missiles could be destroyed in the air before they reached the American soils.

The major European powers were worried that Reagan's Star Wars program would undermine and even nullify the 1972 ABM treaty. The perception of the European allies was that such a program would lead the United States away from European defense commitments. Secondly, they saw little rationale for Star Wars and even for the US insistence to deploy Pershing Missiles in their own borders. They felt that the numerical superiority of the Soviet SS-20 missiles with triple warheads and a range of 5000 km from its launching site inside the Soviet borders would render the emplacement of fewer Pershing II missiles of not much consequence. The Star Wars program, in its turn, would encourage another round of unprecedented arms race.

European nations believed that negotiations and arms talks were the best course under the circumstance. If history was any guide, the American strategic and tactical superiority had always been neutralized by the USSR, sooner than latter. The issue of installation of intermediate range nuclear missiles in Europe threatened the NATO alliance. Henceforth, it would be Europe rather than the United States that would be the target of the Soviet Union, the European nations reasoned. Europe always worried about a possible decoupling of the United States from Europe because America, in the first place, had always the option of arms limitations negotiations with the other super power and secondly, the Soviet Union hardly had any interest in getting distracted by its American 'engagement'. It was Europe that had always been the main concern of the Soviet Union. That is why the Soviet General Secretary Brezhnev once wondered how the emplacement of intermediate missiles would affect the Americans. On the other hand, the Soviet Union was alarmed by the prospect of deployment of Pershing II and cruise missiles close to its borders. Arms limitations talks during the early years of the 1980s remained stalemated, mainly, over the issue of intermediate range missiles. After a deadlock for about two years since the Soviet withdrawal from Reykjavik summit meeting in 1986, it remained for a new Soviet leader, Mikhail Gorbachev, to conclude an INF treaty on the basis of Reagan's zero option in Washington in 1987.

On the ideological front, Reagan upheld the traditional American values of democracy, freedom, and individual rights in his speeches and urged the freedom loving people of the East European countries to rise up against the totalitarian Soviet rule. Reagan mentioned in his farewell address about one incident of how some ordinary Soviet citizens hailed him and the first lady in a little street called Arbat Street, just off Moscow's main shopping complex. These people took him, perhaps, as the messiah of peace, freedom, and prosperity. Reagan realized the real needs of the Soviet people and their disillusionments with the communist system. Reagan, like all his predecessors, was convinced that the inherent desire of all men and women to be free would certainly blow off a social system based on oppression and tyranny. In his farewell address to the nation, President Reagan mentioned, "Countries across the globe are turning to free markets and free speech and turning away from the ideologies of the past. For them the great rediscoveries of the 1980s has been that, lo and behold, the moral way of the government is the practical way of the government: Democracy the profoundly good is also profoundly productive".

Already, Regan had denounced the Soviet perfidy in taking advantage of the American open-ended approach during the period of détente. Reagan felt that Soviet expansionism was driven more by a pervert mind-set fostered by the dogma that capitalism happened to be the root of all evils and that mankind would truly feel emancipated only when communism replaced capitalism on a global scale. Reagan, accordingly, set out his third world policies through the Reagan Doctrine to neutralize and even roll back communist influences in these regions. Reagan intensified his efforts at funding the insurgent and anti-communist rebel groups from Angola to Afghanistan, Nicaragua to Cambodia and from Iran to Poland. Reagan, in his first term, targeted the left-oriented and communist backed governments in Nicaragua, Grenada, and El Salvador. He was scared that Central and Latin America might see efforts at 'Cubanization' with Soviet backing. Once he quipped that for the communists, Nicaragua and El Salvador were only a 'down payment' with Honduras, Guatemala, Costa Rica, and Mexico to follow.

Reagan was convinced that the Soviet ploy to intensify their 'communist' drive in America's backyard was to bog down the United States in the

Western Hemisphere and isolate it from the rest of the world including Europe. This Soviet ploy was reminiscent of the days when older European colonial powers encircled the fledgling United States on all sides after its independence. In that sense, the Soviet counter containment drive against the United States was about to unleash a second wave of forced isolation on the United States, but with an important difference. While Europe hoped to nip the newborn republic in the bud, the Soviet Union had the daunting task of containing the numero uno power in the world. Where Europe had failed against a relatively weaker United States, the Soviet Union with its hundreds of miles of 'antenna' fields close to the US border for surveillance and intelligence purposes was up against a formidable opponent.

Jeane Kirkpatrick, the US Ambassador to the United Nations under Reagan administration, hypothesized that the left-oriented dictators must be demonized and the rightist dictators ought to be nurtured. Reagan found the leftist guerrillas fighting against pro-US dictatorships in El Salvador and Honduras or the ANC and other anti-apartheid forces or even the Hezbollas and the Palestinian guerrillas fighting for their territorial rights against the Israeli occupation in the West Bank and the Gaza strip, to be enemies while the various pro-American dictatorial regimes in Pakistan, South Korea, and in the Middle East happened to be America's true allies. Despite arms sale to Iran in the Iran contra affair, the United States provided all sorts of help to the Iraqi dictatorial regime under Saddam Hussein during the Iran-Iraq war. These included 'dual use' materials, military weapons, logistic and intelligence supports to cut off Iran's access to weapons (Operation Staunch) for fear that the regimes in Saudi Arabia, Jordan and Kuwait would surely fall like ripe fruits into the lap of the Islamic fundamentalists.

The Bush administration

In contrast to Reagan's volatility, hyperboles, rhetoric, contradictions and inconsistencies, George H. Bush acted without impetuosity at a crucial juncture in world history. He simply let the developments in Eastern Europe, including those within the Soviet Union, to unravel of their own. As one author rightly says, President Bush rather represented the other extreme of the containment spectrum: integration of a more socialized Soviet Union into the community of nations. For him Soviet containment became a matter to contain the fall of Soviet empire lest anarchy and secessionist movements got out of control.(Dobson and Marsh, p.42) President Bush kept his cool and reserve amidst Soviet overtures in Lithuania in response to the latter's breakaway proclamation. The American president also dampened the Ukrainian effervescence by his speech in the Ukrainian parliament discouraging its independence from the Union. Nevertheless, the new American president cared for the economic and political transformation in the newly liberated countries in East Europe through financial aids.

Bush administration's ambivalence towards the Soviet intentions continued as the president adopted a policy of 'wait and watch' in response to the developments in the Soviet Union following Gorbachev's 'New Thinking'. The United States delayed granting the most favored nation status to the USSR and deliberated in expediting the process of granting agricultural credits that Gorbachev desperately needed to salvage his prestige in his party and country. Alan P. Dobson and Steve Marsh sums up the policy perceptions of the Bush era in these lines:

> The unimaginative 'status quo plus' was replaced by a slightly more optimistic approach based upon five objectives: to encourage Gorbachev's reforms; to maintain the territorial integrity of the USSR; to conclude arms control favorable to the US lest Gorbachev be replaced by hardliners; to ensure that a reunified Germany obtain NATO and EC membership; and to achieve a stable and democratic Eastern Europe.
>
> —*Dobson and Marsh, p.41*

Nevertheless, Bush hoped to socialize Gorbachev's reformed Soviet Union and bring it into the "family of nations." He hoped to build a world 'swayed' by a new breeze and 'refreshed' by freedom. He described his era in these lines "There are times when the future seems thick as a fog; you sit and wait, hoping the mists will lift and reveal the right path. But this is a time when the future seems a door you can walk right through into a room called tomorrow."

He did not want to destabilize the Soviet Union by taking advantage of the waves of disintegration rocking that country. There were two reasons for this cautious approach on Bush's part. First, the USSR had large stockpiles of nuclear weapons spread over several republics, Kazakhstan, Ukraine, and Byelorussia. Any outbreak and spread of secessionist disturbances would jeopardize the American efforts to gradually pull all the nuclear weapons from the peripheral republics to the center, that is, to the Russian republic. Secondly, there remained the question of German unification: would a unified Germany remain within or outside NATO? After some patient persuasion on Bush's part, Gorbachev agreed to a NATO membership for a unified Germany. In May 1989, Bush proposed to withdraw troops from Europe and submitted another 21 proposals comprising military reductions and more economic aids in December 1989 meet at Malta. Superpower rivalry had come a long way from Yalta to Malta and Bush was contemplating a 'new world order' to replace the bipolar international order.

Bush had delayed the American involvement in the Yugoslavian crisis in the early 1990s when the Serb-dominated Yugoslavian army ransacked its constituent republics that had demanded independence from the federation. Bush settled the contra affair in Nicaragua by convincing the Congress to extend the US aid for non-military purposes to Nicaragua. Bush invoked the Panama treaty to justify its 1989 intervention in Panama to forcibly remove Noriega and his forces from administering that country despite condemnation from the Organization of the American states. Noriega was charged with drug trafficking in February 1988 and he disbanded the May 1989 election that the US observers believed the General had lost. On December 1989, 24,000 the US troops invaded Panama and Noreiga was captured in January 1990 and sent for trial to Miami, Florida. Bush proposed $1 billion to Panama to make good its war damage and lifted the economic sanctions imposed on the Noriega regime. Another success for the first post Cold War president was the signing of START II in July 1991 that sought to reduce the number of delivery vehicles and nuclear warheads to 1600 and 6000 respectively. The Senate, however, ratified START II, in October 1992. One offshoot of Bush's foreign policy indecision was that much of the credit due to the administration regarding the German unification was taken away by the dynamic initiatives of the German Chancellor, Kohl. Nevertheless, minus US support that unification would not have come about so rapidly and smoothly, in view of the French and British reservations.

One of the chief areas that reflected Bush's policy indecisions was China. In 4 June, 1989, the world was shocked to learn of the Tiananmen Square incident in which hundreds of pro-democracy student demonstrators were massacred. This had terribly upset the Bush administration. The United States imposed economic sanctions on China and barred high-level governmental contacts and the sale of arms to China. But he had only to eat the humble pie barely a year later because of intense lobbying by American business lobby. In the next chapter I have dealt at length with the first Gulf War that had made the president more famous than any other of his foreign policies.

Nuclear issues

In a sense, the Cold War disproved Clauswitz's famous dictum that war happened to be a continuation of politics. None other era experienced such intensified, 'hot' and hectic political activities on a global scale as the Cold War period did. Paradoxically, it was rather a far more destructive 'weapon' of war that ensured the long peace after 1945! Well into the WWII years, both Germany and the Allied Powers were frantically searching for ways to terminate the war to their respective advantages and as quickly as possible. All of these warring countries looked into the world of 'atoms'. Germany eyed Norway as its possible supplier of heavy water that would be needed to produce enriched uranium for producing the bombs. Hitler's Germany could not create that elusive bomb but the irrepressible Americans pulled up a miracle in war history as the Manhattan Project realized that American dream. The United States detonated the first ever weapon of mass destruction at the Mexican desert on 16 July, 1945. Roosevelt's America had little interest in dragging the 'apocalypse' once America acquired the 'divine' capacity to stop the six-year war forthwith, particularly, after the German surrender. The twin cities of Nagasaki and Hiroshima were unfortunate to receive the wrath of God, as they became the real testing grounds for 13 and 22-kiloton bombs named 'Little Boy' and 'Fat Man', respectively.

Of course, by that time the conventional fire powers of the Allied Forces had all but ended the war. One political implication of Nagasaki and Hiroshima bombing was to tame and terrify the Soviet Union. However, Stalin remained unruffled at Potsdam on hearing from Truman about the news of the American detonation of atom bomb. The Soviet Union ended that US monopoly four years later. Thereafter, it became obvious that the power with greater stock and better delivery system would be in a singularly advantageous position to force the post war issues according to its liking.

The production of hydrogen bomb in the early 1950s by both the super-powers was but a logical corollary to intense early post war tensions. H-bombs were capable of unleashing destructive energies in megatons compared to the kiloton capabilities of the A-bomb, a decade earlier. The US stock of nuclear weapons grew from an estimated 235 bombs in 1949 to about 6,444 in 1957 compared to the Soviet attainment of 660 by 1957. Side by side, the US had the lead in its more accurate and effective delivery systems from its bases in Western Europe, not to speak of the numerical superiority in delivery vehicles. The corresponding figures for nuclear stockpiles (warhead) on the part of the two super powers were 31,700 in 1966 for the US and 7, 089 for the USSR in the same year; over 40,000 for the USSR and just above 23,000 for the US in the mid 1980s; and just 10,640 for the US and 8,600 for Russia by the year 2002. The corresponding figures for ICBMs, towards the end of the last century, have come down to 550 missiles with 2050 warheads in the case of the United States and to 755 missiles with 3,590 warheads in the case of Russia.

The development of the Inter-Continental Ballistic Missiles (ICBM) and the launching of the space satellite by the Soviet Union in 1957 sent a shiver of cold wave through the spines of the US policy-makers as they found the 'missile gap' of 1957 resembling those of 1945 but in a reverse way when the United States had the monopoly of the bomb. Predictably another round of arms race was in the offing although the Soviets during the closing years of the 1950s rather chose to stay content with having that psychological superiority over the United States. The latter intensified its efforts towards the production ICBMs and, in fact, established a 226-75 advantage in this area and a 1350-190 advantage in respect of long-range bombers over the Soviets at the stroke of the Cuban missile crisis.(Hastedt, p.357) The USSR was humbled during the Cuban missile crisis when the bloated balloon of the Soviet nuclear capability was punctured by the US determination to risk any eventuality. After the Cuban episode, the USSR was determined to draw a nuclear parity with its twin super power. During the Cuban missile crisis, the US possessed approximately 1500 B-47s and 500 B-2s with 200 deployed first generation of ICBMs compared to a very few Soviet ICBMs. Thereafter, both the arms race and arms limitations talks proceeded simultaneously.

Soviet Union increased their tally of ICBM and Submarine Launched Ballistic Missiles (SLBM) in 77 submarines to 1398 and 979 respectively in 1985 compared to 1018 ICBMs and 616 SLBMs for the United States in 37 submarines. The corresponding tally of overheads for the US and the USSR remained 7654 and 9987 respectively, excluding the long-range bombers and cruise missiles. On top of it, both the super powers sought to make their missile systems more hydra-headed by emplacement of Multiple Independently Targeted Reentry vehicle (MIRVs) in the 1970s. (Hastedt, pp.357, 358)

The crux was to formulate appropriate strategies that would most effectively handle this newfound energy 'demon'. Super power interests, and priorities veered around several goals: (1) how to inflict the greatest damage on the adversary while itself escaping scot-free; (2) how to project one's power through sheer demonstration of the size and stockpile of nuclear weapons that would deter the other nuclear power from even thinking of dropping its bombs on the enemy soil; (3) how to avoid a nuclear showdown that could cause large-scale destruction of men and materials in both these countries; (4) how to avoid the hazards of killings human beings while at the same time ensuring that the leadership in the opponent country may feel compelled to terminate the war at the earliest; and finally, (5) how to win a protracted nuclear warfare, come whatever may. All these policy options haunted the successive US administrations right from Eisenhower's 'massive retaliation to McNamara's 'counter force' strategy to Kennedy's damage limitation to Carter's countervailing strategy to Reagan's dual approach of damage limitation through SDI and a more aggressive nuclear policy to actually defeat the Soviet Union in a nuclear showdown.

Most of these policy options were carried over into successive policies of the subsequent US administrations. The United States contemplated a whole gamut of possibilities ranging from a total destruction of its adversary within a couple of minutes through unleashing the unlimited radiating power of these bombs to saving its own population and its own homeland by recourse to missile shields and even negotiations at arms limitations.

As a parallel trend, both the super powers sought to channelize the destructiveness of nuclear energies into peaceful purposes that had begun in the earnest with the initiation of atoms for peace project during the Eisenhower administration and the supervisory activities of the International Atomic Energy Agency (IAEA). One offshoot of this verification mechanism between the superpowers, in particular, was the Open Skies proposal of Eisenhower to enable both the super powers to exchange information including blueprints of their nuclear installations and an aerial photographic surveillance arrangement to keep a watch over their mutual activities. However, the Soviets rejected the Open Sky proposal.

But the realization of the 'accidental' factor, highlighted by the Cuban missile crisis (in fact, recent revelations, point to the sober and humane approach of a crew member in a Soviet submarine to delay executing the order to charge at the US naval ships), led both the superpowers to make a start from the scratch by a step-by-step approach in matters of arms limitations talks. As a result, the Limited Test Ban Treaty between the superpowers in 1963 came in place that permitted 'conditional' underground nuclear tests only. Moreover, there was the concern regarding the proliferation of nuclear weapons to other nations. Consequently, the Non-Proliferation Treaty came into effect in 1968 even though many countries including, France, Britain and India, did not ratify the treaty in order to keep their nuclear autonomy. Some restrictions came in place in respect of supply of nuclear materials to other countries and of their proper utilizations as the Nuclear Suppliers' Group (NSG) was created in 1975. The United States took upon itself the responsibility to discourage the Latin American countries and other European countries not to go the nuclear way through such offers as regional collective security arrangements.

The Strategic Arms Limitations or the SALT I talks had already started around 1969 and a treaty signed in Moscow by the heads of states of the two super powers in 1972 sought to limit the number of offensive intercontinental ballistic missiles at their disposal. According to the State department web site, the numbers of the US missiles on land and submarine were limited to 1000 and 710 as against the Soviet Union's 1,410 and 950, Light ICBM launchers were barred from being converted for the purpose of heavy ICBMs. The 1972 Anti Ballistic Missile (ABM) Treaty allowed each side to have one deployment area near the national capital or an ICBM site while precluding any upgradation of ABM launchers. ABM Treaty combined the dual objective of limiting nuclear arsenals and keeping mutual deterrence in place. SALT II was supposed to limit the number of strategic launchers that both the super powers could possess and also the number of vehicles that could be MIRVed. Though never ratified by the Senate, the limits set for the number of delivery vehicles and those for the purpose of MIRVing stayed at 2,400 (to be reduced further to 2,250 by 1981) and 1,320 respectively.

The Reagan administration undertook a two-track NATO policy of installing new missiles in the West on the one hand and also to continue the arms limitations talks to reduce intermediate-range nuclear forces (INF) to a lowest level on the other to put pressure on the Soviets. After some fruitless years of negotiations, General Secretary Gorbachev agreed to a "double global zero" Treaty to eliminate intermediate and short-ranged ballistic missiles. INF treaty signed by both the super powers on December 8, 1987 in Washington sought to destroy both the Party's 'ground – launched ballistic and cruise missiles with ranges between 500-5,500 kilometers, their launchers and associated support structures and support equipment within three years after the treaty enters into force.' Unlike previous arms limitations treaties between the super powers, the INF treaty of 1987 required each party to reduce the number of missiles in their nuclear arsenals instead of putting a ceiling on future productions. By June 1, 1991 the United States had destroyed 846 such weapons as against 1846 by the Soviet Union, thereby eliminating the last of the ground-launched and cruise missiles for the US and the SS-20 for the USSR, covered under the INF treaty. INF treaty was the first of its kind to eliminate an entire class of weapons with on-site inspection provisions. INF treaty facilitated the latter round of arms limitations talks like START I and START II. INF treaty has been aptly described as the 'recent brick in the arms control foundation' by one writer.

The early years of the 1990s also saw a series of offers at unilateral reduction in the number of troops deployed in Europe and in the reduction of nuclear forces. START I went into effect from 1994 and it was an agreement between the USA, Russia, and the former Soviet republics (FSR) that allowed each side only 1,600 strategic nuclear delivery vehicles, taken together the ICBMs, SLBMs, and heavy bombers, with the first two categories allotted not more than 4,900 overheads out of stipulated 6000 overheads. START I incorporated a wide-ranging inspection regime to verify compliance with treaty provisions. START II proposed a reduction of 5,000 warheads over and above the 9,000 prescribed by STARTI, in the overall strategic forces. START II, a bilateral agreement between the United States and Russia sought to bring down the figure for deployed strategic warheads to 3000-3500. No more than 1750 warheads are to be deployed on SLBMs. START II also sought to eliminate larger ICBMs and rockets carrying MIRVs. Notwithstanding the ratification of START II by the US Senate in 1992, Russia postponed its ratification by linking it with the US declaration to abrogate the ABM Treaty of 1972. Nevertheless, realizing the US determination to negate the ABM treaty with the formal declaration by President Bush to pull out of the 1972 ABM Treaty, Russia ratified STARTII. The Conventional Armed Forces in Europe Treaty (CFE) signed on 19 November, 1990 was the last straw that broke the Soviet back by leveling the hitherto Soviet superiority in Conventional weapons in Europe as the treaty between the 22 NATO members and the former WARSAW pact sought to impose equal limits on the number of tanks, armored combat vehicles (ACVs), heavy artillery, combat aircraft and attack helicopters. However, with the dissolution of the WARSAW and the Soviet empire, much of rationale behind the treaty would now center on the security of Europe from any other single power domination.

Mentionable among the post Cold War arms treaties is the Chemical Weapons Convention (1993) seeking to eliminate production and storage of chemical weapons under the watchful eye of an international inspection organization. Comprehensive Test Ban Treaty (CTBT) of 1996 at the behest of the United Nations sought to ensure a global ban on nuclear testing even for peaceful purpose, with a surveillance mechanism to look after the issue of compliance by other nations. Neither, the United States, the main protagonist of the Treaty, nor another second tier power like India ratified the treaty, as yet. The 2002 Treaty on Strategic Offensive Reduction ((SORT) signed on May 26, 2004 with no provision of verification sought to limit nuclear arsenals to 2200 operationally deployed warheads by the year 2012 allowing both parties to keep the excess overheads into storage yet keeping the option of redeployment open. This treaty was supposed to replace START II after its ratification.

Thomas Graham sums up the achievements of the arms limitation negotiations during the entire the Cold War era in these lines:

> ...the agreements reached during and immediately after the Cold War significantly reduced nuclear arsenals and were crucial elements of the US security. By stabilizing the arms race and providing a framework for the US-Soviet dialogue, bilateral, Cold war-era arms control efforts contributed greatly to international peace and stability.
>
> —*Washington Quarterly, Spring, 2000*

The post Cold War nuclear issues happen to be more multilateral in nature notwithstanding the presence of the same two giant nuclear powers, who between themselves, as per a 2004 estimate, possesses nearly 31000 ICBMs compared to some 1200 nuclear ICBMs held by other nuclear powers, taken together. The new arms control architecture encompasses various actors ranging from the governmental and intergovernmental to nongovernmental entities. But there is a caveat: too many cooks may spoil the broth. In the absence of a bipolar world order in which the super powers exerted considerable clout over the second-tier and the developing states, the post Cold War situation may see a sort of alliance between the rogue and the revisionist states on the one hand and the terrorists and the modern local 'warlords' stoking on ethno-religious and other such issues, on the other.

One important post Cold War direction about the nuclear issues is the recent US perception and policies to put its emphasis back on its conventional defense forces. It was the nuclear factor that had guided the super power rivalry during the entire Cold War period in contrast to the multipolar rivalries of the pre-1945 era. Nuclear forces happened to be the bedrock of NATO because of the huge imbalance in conventional force strength between the NATO and WARSAW groups during the Cold War. It was the American nuclear umbrella that had ensured the post-war European security. The much talked of long peace of the post war era would not have prevailed if the security and defense equation in Europe were defined by conventional military strength.

Obviously, with the dissolution of the other super power, the nuclear issues lost much of their bite. The US reliance on the modernization of its conventional forces to match the lethality of nuclear weapons (assuming that nuclear weapons cease to exist or cease to be functional) is more in line with the post- Cold War demands contingent on vast nuclear imbalance between the United States on the one hand and other major powers taken together, on the other. That is why, the United States has more than one reason to redirect its defense along conventional lines. First, the United States does not want a second round of arms race based on the power of the nukes that, ironically, happens to be a great equalizer. Any nation can pose serious threat and challenge to the United States and the world community in general even if it possesses a minimum number of nuclear and weapons of mass destruction. Given the level of developments and scale of proliferation in modern missile technology in an interdependent world, this is quite likely.

The second reason for de-emphasizing the role of nuclear weapons is associated with the evolution of a humanitarian law to spare the civilian and even industrial resources of countries at war. Recent Gulf and Afghanistan campaigns go to show how war can be made more 'humanized'. This is not possible with nuclear weapons where accidental and whimsical personal factors have greater chances to dictate the course of the war. Thirdly, it is extremely difficult to rebuild and develop a region exposed to the effects of nuclear radiation than to rebuild regions devastated by the conventional war machines. Fourthly, there remains the sentimental and emotional factor that can carry enmity to its bitterest ends if nuclear weapons were to decide the outcome of any war. Fifthly, the more the United States relies on its nuclear capabilities to project its world hegemony from a distance, the more exposed will its geographical disadvantage be. A direct and conventional combat situation may see the physical presence of the US troops and personnel but an America with a strongly fortified missile defense and in possession of long-range ballistic missiles will not be in an ideal position to wield world leadership that requires something more than brute force and more importantly, greater US involvement. Sixthly, the United States wants to get rid of the Cold War syndrome by attaching less stress on nuclear weapons, as that would constantly remind it and the rest of the world of its erstwhile nemesis, the Soviet Union.

Nevertheless, the nature of the nuclear deterrence is still crucial in today's anarchic international situation as evident from the Single Integrated Operational Plan (SIOP-00) of the Pentagon. The American post Cold War priority is to transform the nature and scope of nuclear deterrence from its Cold War Soviet-centric responses to the post Cold War challenges and to take into account some 'deceptive' states like China and rogue states like Iran and North Korea, besides non-state terrorists. This means that in the new millennium, nuclear deterrence has to be more flexible and more target oriented. Proliferation of nuclear and WMDs obviously create the need for a far broader scale of deterrence system and that, in turn, means greater nuclear stockpile to combat multiple and well dispersed targets. Hans M. Kristensen writes, " This conversion required a reform of nuclear planning that could ensure still deeper reductions in the number of nuclear weapons while expanding deterrence and war-fighting requirements so that the planners could "go global" in pursuit of enemies and targets."

The Cold War era had been termed by some scholars as an 'abnormal' phase in traditional international political system. The United States can't hope to prolong an irrational approach to guide its foreign policies when the very threat of the Cold War era does not exist. Most importantly, the United States can't sustain a costly network of intelligence and surveillance at a time when other nations invest little on such things. It is true that such burdens are passed to some extent on others through transfer and even sale of such components and renting of such infrastructures but these are of no primary importance if any nation in possession of nuclear bombs feels that it has, at least, one solid chance out of many to lob one bomb slip through the American defense cordon. All the above reasoning lead us to one conclusion: was America misplaced in putting all the eggs in one basket of Soviet containment? Did the United States hope that the Cold War and hence the nuclear arms race would continue forever? What happened and how the Cold War ended? While I have already dealt the issue in the preceding sections of this chapter, let me deal it at length now.

Unraveling of the Soviet Empire: Developments in Poland, Hungary, GDR, and Czechoslovakia

It all started with Poland. It was in Poland that some kind of 'real' opposition against communism manifested in the 1970 Gdansk shipyard strikes. Gdansk was the harbinger of the Solidarity movement in the early 1980s, heralding for the first time, the establishment of an independent worker's trade union movement in the second most strategically important workers' state, Poland. The accession of the Polish Cardinal Karol Wojtyla to the throne of the Vatican in 1976 stoked Poland's traditional catholic and nationalistic sentiments. Pope

John Paul II is still remembered as one of the architects for ushering in Poland's liberation movements against the oppressive Soviet rule. Furthermore, a fresh round of severe economic crises in the 1980s proved to be the undoing of the communist party in Poland. Solidarity was banned after 16 months from its inception with the imposition of martial law in 1981 by the Jaruzelski government, ironically, to avert a possible Soviet armed intervention.

The Polish free underground press also played a crucial role in uncovering corruption and misdeeds in the ruling official circles to hasten the downfall of communism in Poland. On February 1989, Jaruzelski invited the Solidarity and the Christian Catholic delegates to the negotiating table. Bowing to public pressures, the Polish government had no other option but to legalize Solidarity in April that year and even promised to hold general elections in June. In that partially free election, Solidarity candidates handed a stunning defeat to the ruling communist party by winning all the seats for which they were allowed to contest and claiming 99 out of the 100 seats in the upper house of the Parliament. Once the Polish United Workers' party failed to form a government, Lech Walesa, the leader of the Solidarity movement, in a rare bit of opportunism, threw an offer to form an alliance with two other non-communist small parties, the United Peasants and the Democratic parties. The communists 'abdicated' their prolonged reign on 12 September, 1989 and Tadeusz Mazowiecki became the first ever non-communist prime minister after 1945.

As for Hungary and Czechoslovakia, their economies remained virtually 'mortgaged' to the West, in general, and to West Germany, in particular, during the 1980s. Already by 1980, Western loans to Hungary and Romania touched \$9 and \$10 billion respectively to meet their ambitious plans for modernization since the last decade. To make matters worse, the Soviet Union had its own economic problems in the wake of unprecedented rise in defense expenditures, coupled with ever-diminishing returns from its economy. As a result, the Soviet Union was forced to either curtail the supplies or charge market prices for goods like gas, petroleum, etc., hitherto supplied to these countries at nominal rates. Both Czechoslovakia and Hungary grew increasingly dependent on foreign capital from the West on 'conditions' of promoting democratization, pluralism, greater freedom, and human rights observances. Side by side, the Helsinki agreement of 1975 had the desired effect of creating 'holes' in the hitherto closed economic and political systems of the East European states.

Whatever political gains Czechoslovakia registered under the reform-minded Husak government in the 1960s were rolled back over the next two decades by the communist party censorship and repression. In 1977, the Czechoslovak police arrested several members of a rock band group called the "Plastic People of the Universe". This led to the establishment of an informal group by the playwright Vaclav Havel in the shape of Charter of 77 to express their solidarity with the members of the rock band group. The intellectuals and liberal-minded communists in these countries cashed in on the relentless pressures exerted by the Western governments on the Soviet Union to adhere to its commitments to human rights observances. Unlike in the past, the Soviet Union, this time, was rather in an awkward situation and a prisoner of its own policies. With Poland showing the way and with the new Soviet leader Mikhail Gorbachev formally annulling the Brezhnev doctrine in July 1989, the roads to freedom for these ancient 'capitals' were open.

Thereafter things started to unfold at an unprecedented scale in Hungary and Czechoslovakia. Hungarian economy, since the early nineteen sixties, had developed a mild dose of market economy. By mid-1980s Hungarian economy was in a flux as it neither followed a communist nor a market-oriented pattern. Inflation rose to 16 per cent and two fifths of Hungarians were living below the poverty line. Nevertheless the 'dissident' communists in Hungary had managed to earn some sort of freedom of expression and the legalization of the 'second economy' in the early 1980s.

As mentioned above, the Hungarian Socialist Workers' Party (the communist party) had a thin sense of tolerance within its ranks that fostered these reformist minded communists within the party. Emboldened by a brace of contemporary democratic mass movements, like the environmentalist opposition to Czechoslovakia's proposed dam construction on the Danube, and the Hungarian minority problems in Transylvania, these reform minded communists succeeded eventually, in edging out the conservative elements from the party. This was also possible due to Gorbachev's reform policies. Hungary, in the closing years of the 1980s, embarked on a course of economic and political pluralism. The most decisive moment came in the state burial occasion of the leader of the 1956 uprising, Imre Nagy, when the opposition leader Victor Orban demanded the withdrawal of Soviet troops and declaration of free elections. On 23 October 1989, Hungarian Parliament changed the name of Hungary from a people's republic to only a republic of Hungary, established a multi-party system and carried out some one hundred changes to the communist constitution.

Once Hungary decided to open its hitherto closed border with Austria, East Germans seeking to cross over to the West swamped the lawns of the West German embassies in Prague and Budapest. In both these countries mass movements and street demonstrations so demoralized the police and the security forces that they remained mere onlookers as countless East Germans 'traveled' to the West. In November 1989, following a secret discussion by the East German cabinet, Gunter Schabowsky, the GDR Politburo member, hinted at lifting the ban on migration to the West. The Berlin Wall collapsed on 9 November 1989 to be followed soon after by the collapse of a most repressive communist regime in GDR.

Czechoslovakia followed suit when the week long mass demonstration brought about the collapse of the communist regime. On the 71st anniversary of Czechoslovakia's birth as a new nation, the police charged on some 20,000 peaceful demonstrators who were demanding the resignation of the government. The 50,000 mass gathering at a student demonstration on 17 November, the same year, proved to be the undoing of the communist leadership as the police acted in a high-handed manner. Most of the politburo members saw the writings on the wall and resigned. On 25-26 November 1989, a record 700,000-800,000 people took to the streets to demand the abolition of communist rule in Czechoslovakia. Vaclav Havel took over as the Czech president.

Bulgaria, Romania, Albania, and Yugoslavia

Events in the other Soviet satellite states did not unfold so smoothly compared to Hungary, Czechoslovakia, and East Germany. Bulgarian communist party, like its Hungarian counterpart, used to tolerate small doses of dissent, opposition, and criticism in its ranks. Like in Hungary, it is the environmentalists and ethnic groups that took the lead in erecting some kind of opposition to the ruling communist party led by the aging Todor Zhivkov. This time, the environmental 'foil' was its neighbor, Romania, whose factories caused air pollution in the skies of Bulgaria. The opposition movement gained further momentum when Bulgaria's ethnic tensions with Turkey resurfaced as the Bulgarian government tried to forcibly convert the remaining 10 per cent Turkish minority living in Bulgaria, thereby, killing nearly hundred people in a riot. In 1989, Turkish ethnic leaders plucked up enough courage to wage some organized protests that resulted in the expulsion of 300,000 Turks from Bulgaria. As a result, the already decaying Bulgarian economy suffered severe setbacks. Large-scale expulsion of the Turk minorities also evoked strong resentments from the Bulgarian intellectuals. Thereafter, a series of exposition of Zhivkov regime's corruption by reformers within the Party led to Zhivkov's resignation on November 10, 1989 and ended the monopoly of the Party in December 1989. The new Party composed of the reform minded ex-communists, was renamed as the Bulgarian Socialist Party that won the 1990 elections.

In Romania, public dissent and outburst took a much more violent turn because of the deprivation of the masses that lacked the supplies of basic consumer goods. While its compatriot East European states were looking for greater openness and freedom since the 1970s, Romania under Ceausescu had no intention to do so. Besides the resentment generated as a result of draconian control exerted by its ruler over the political and social life of the Romanian citizens, rampant corruption and nepotism added fuel to the fire of public anger. It was the Transylvanian ethnic tension that triggered off a Romanian crisis in December 1989 with the arrest of a priest belonging to the Magyar community.

Rumors about larger number of casualties led to violent street battles between the people and the Securitate, the Romanian secret police, killing about 5,000 people. The party dissidents used the public rebellion to stage a coup by the National Salvation Front (NSF), a new political organization. Ceausescu and his wife were arrested and executed. Thereafter, Rumania continued to remain under totalitarian rule without undergoing any reform or pluralism.

Like in China, the Albanian communist party led by Ramiz Alia read the writings on the walls and initiated economic reforms while maintaining its complete grip on the country's polity. Ramiz Alia, succeeded the WWII guerrilla veteran Enver Hoxha as the party boss and undertook such measures as wage incentives, plant autonomy, and permitted some criticism. The communist party secured 56 per cent of votes in 1991 elections and returned Alia as the President.

Yugoslavia experienced the bloodiest of ethnic and nationalist unrests as one communist regime after another kept toppling in the Soviet dominated Eastern bloc. The signs of disintegration within the federation were evident after Tito's death. Milosevic wrested power from Ivan Stambolic in 1987 and stoked up the nationalist sentiments by making Serbo-Croatian the official language and boosting the nationalist sentiments through encouragement of the study of history and the Cyrillic language.

Croatia, inspired by the failed 1968 Prague Spring Movement, had already developed a separate student body independent of the party that helped revive its past culture and history. Croatia suffered economic deprivation as the southern regions in Yugoslavia claimed greater economic share at Croatia's expense. As early as 1971, Matica Hrvatska's proposed a new Croatian constitution that sought to support their rights to secede from Yugoslavia and to the replacement of the Serbo-Croatian language solely by the Croatian language. The Catholic-Orthodox rivalry further precipitated a crisis in which many Croat leaders were arrested, including, that of the future president of Croatia, Franjo Trudjman. Yugoslavia was already sitting on a volcano of ethno-religious conflicts. The first such eruption occurred with the arrest of 7,000 ethnic Albanians in Kosovo in March 1990. In August the same year, Croatia became the victim of Serbian atrocities. Croatia and Slovenia declared independence from Yugoslavia in 1991. The Yugoslavian disintegration has been dealt in some detail in the last chapter.

Disintegration of the Soviet Union

Geopolitical earthquakes in Eastern Europe in 1989 rocked the Soviet Union with greater intensity. The Baltic republics were the first to declare independence from the Union. In 1987 Estonia demanded autonomy. By November 1989, the Estonian Supreme Soviet annulled its 1940 annexation by the Soviets. Latvia declared the Soviet annexation illegal. It remained for Lithuania to declare outright independence from Moscow. Kremlin decided to blockade Lithuania. The Soviet army ransacked the communist party offices and TV station in Vilnus. In May, Estonia followed suit. Latvia joined soon after. Other three trans-Caucasus republics in the South, Georgia, Moldovia, and Azerbaijan had seen enough of bloodshed during the past few months triggered by the ethnic clashes in the Armenian dominated enclave, Ngarno-Karbach, in Azerbaijan. These six states rejected Gorbachev's last-ditch effort to keep the Union through a treaty in which each republic would have absolute sovereignty under a 'nominal' Soviet Socialist republic. Just a day before signing of the treaty, the lost empire struck back, in vain, when the hardliners within the Communist party staged a coup and kept Gorbachev in house arrest. The military was at a loss to support the coup leaders. Another elected Russian leader, Boris Yeltsin felt that his hour of reckoning had arrived and he rounded off the Soviet Parliament, the White house, with tanks. The coup leaders eventually surrendered and the three-day drama was over. A politically weakened Gorbachev bowed out as Yeltsin took over. But the ethnic and nationalist clashes hardly ceased. The once monolithic Soviet Union soon disintegrated into fifteen independent republics.

The episode of the end of the Soviet empire and the Soviet Union can be, attributed in the main, to intense popular craving for democracy and freedom from a single party rule in the entire Soviet led Eastern bloc. Yet, the revolutionary movements of 1989 lacked a clear guideline as regards a viable alternative. For the United States, the first and foremost concern was to let the communist regimes in the Soviet Union, in its peripheries and in Eastern Europe fall without any serious backlash effect. The United States never thought that Soviet communism would vamoose with such incredible rapidity. President Bush hoped to achieve as peaceful a transition as possible by keeping Gorbachev in leadership that has been aptly termed by some scholars, as containment of the fall of the Soviet empire.

From the American standpoint, during the closing years of the 1980s, the United States needed, above all, some more time to gauge the real intention of the maverick Soviet leader. As a result, the American policies towards the Soviet Union happened to be a bundle of contradictions. The United States withheld some vital financial assistance despite Gorbachev's repeated requests for help to prop up the Soviet economy and ensure supplies of basic goods to the Soviet citizens. Gorbachev desperately needed to show his fellow communists and to the opposition that he had strong support of the United States. Unfortunately for him, the Bush administration acted in a cautious and stealthy fashion to bring about a slow death of its the Cold War rival as the United States watched the strikes, mass uprisings and riots within and outside the

Soviet Union with expectant eyes. The sole American concern remained that the situation in the Soviet 'world' ought not to get out of hand and degenerate into anarchy. Prescriptions of democracy, individual rights, liberal capitalism, and market forces were the patent American remedy to ensure the political and economic revival of the post Soviet Russia and its erstwhile republics.

But such a policy backfired as Russia and other republics are now virtually ruled by key ex-communist personnel under the guise of mafia, oil barons, or ex-communist bureaucrats. Russian economy degenerated into 'cronyism' and 'robber' capitalism that further abetted rampant corruption and mass plunder of the country's resources. The picture is no different in its erstwhile East European satellite countries, except the three Central European countries, Poland, Hungary, and the Czech Republic. Such a return of the Cold War communist 'bosses' to positions of power in some East European countries and in the erstwhile Soviet republics reveal that it is beyond the capacity of the United States to create a more viable and peaceful international order, all by itself. Indeed, the United States might have won the Cold War but it had lost Russia and something more, perhaps.

The collapse of the Soviet empire and the end of the Cold War had many causes like, the rise of the EU in Europe, the deployment of medium - ranged missiles aimed by both the rival camps at each other during the 1980s, Reagan's Star War programs and massive rearming of the American defense, the rise of the South-East Asian tigers, rise of China as a major regional power, NATO and its projected future alliance with Japan and China to make the anti-Soviet coalition much more formidable, phenomenal decline in the Soviet economic productivity since the 1970s, its massive defense expenses, the replacement of the traditional core industries by high-tech electronic sector in other countries and the Soviet failure to do so, the human rights campaigns, the Afghan debacle, and the dismal state of the Soviet agriculture. Soviet fall would be attributed to a combination of all the above factors.

Yet none of these factors can fully explain why Gorbachev made such a sharp departure from the traditional conservative communist policies of Lenin, Stalin, Khrushchev, and Brezhnev. However, one thing must not be lost sight of. Whenever a leader undertakes any new set of policies he considers all the pros and cons and even the most far-reaching consequences of his policies. He sets a high ceiling for his success and a worst-case scenario as the floor. Every gamble or well thought out strategy follows this 'floor and the ceiling' calculation.

Moreover, it is highly unlikely that any state leader would make a calculated gamble that may jeopardize its super power status. The question of a reform or a change comes only when a leadership is faced with a fait accompli in any one direction: desperation or the possibility of scoring a magnificent strategic gain and victory. In the Soviet case, in the absence of adequate documents, one way to arrive at a sound reasoning is through observation of effects: the nature of mass discontents, political upheavals, the degree of repression and the craving for freedom.

From the Soviet leadership angle, maintaining the empire became an increasingly difficult task, if not an impossible one, over time. How could they justify their role in deciding the destiny of the 100 million freedom loving people in Eastern Europe? With time, familiarity was certain to breed contempt and the Soviet 'magic' and 'good will' earned in the WWII era faded in the succeeding decades. While the third world still provided much space for the continuation of the Cold War, the Soviet Union faced a growing isolation as others, including communist China, virtually joined the capitalist 'club'. Secondly, what was easy for the Soviet Union of the 1950s and the 1960s was not so in the 1980s. For example, the Soviet Union found it increasingly difficult to justify its interventions in Hungary, Czechoslovakia, and Poland in the 1980s with the same conviction that motivated it to do so in the 1950s and 1960s. That would have meant that nothing had changed in the Soviet world, which is against the law of nature. Furthermore, such an intransigent and bigoted approach on the part of any country's leadership would render them retrogressive and leave them behind other nations. What is more, such an approach would have required either another Slobodan Milosevick or the perpetrators of the Tienman Square massacre. Being a responsible nuclear power and a principal participant in various summitry and multilateral meetings, the Soviet Union could hardly toe such a line.

Still it does not explain why the Soviet leadership in the mid 1980s made a U-turn from their previous foreign policies. Why such a change of policy perceptions didn't happen earlier? This leads us to conclude that a revolution is always a matter of time over which no authority has any control and the closing years of the 1980s happened to be those historical moments. It may be that the Soviet leaders feared that they would miss a golden opportunity of 'return' if they proved to be laggards in a rapidly changing international environment. They must act before it was too late. The Soviets, indeed, retreated in good order by deciding to withdraw instead of losing it through another devastating war. It had least intention of destroying or sufficiently weakening itself by engaging a non-European country like the United States. Rather, the Soviet leadership preserved their strength to be able to negotiate with other European powers from a position of respectability. In that respect, the Soviet restraint or retreat, whichever way one may call it, might have strengthened Kennan's logic of containment. Nevertheless, the single most factor that contributed to the downfall of the Sovietica is that the Soviet Union was dangerously close to becoming an isolated nation as communism was fast losing its legitimacy because of the breakup of the monolithic component in the communist world.

A look at the capitalist camp led by the United States would help in understanding the issue. Capitalism survived because of diversity and tolerance within that system that helped to bind the capitalist states with diverse interests in a common bond: freedom and prosperity. In contrast, lack of diversity and over-reliance on dogmatism proved to be the undoing of communism. If a former ally, say, China, collaborates with forces hostile to the Soviet Union and if the Soviet forces had to intervene each time to repress freedom movements in its satellite states, this creates a situation of forlornness for the Soviet Union.

The United States completely wrested the initiative from the Soviets as the Cold War dragged on. While America's Cold War allies had total freedom in their respective political and economic spheres, it was different in the Soviet case. The more they resorted to repression, the more they got exposed in the process (the more they had to fear) and the more the initiative went into the American hands. The Soviet leaders realized their faults, perhaps, too late. Things came to such a head that Gorbachev's glasnost and perestroika failed to contain the pent up grievances in the satellite countries and in its individual republics. This alone fully explains why a strong military and nuclear power like the Soviet Union failed to keep its empire and its components within its fold. This has a great lesson for posterity: no measure of military strength is any match for the popular craving for freedom and diversity.

The Soviet Union had an economy that was about one-third of those of the United States. Of course, there are still some states that live under despotic rules and where majority of population live below poverty lines and without the benefit of basic, not to speak of, modern amenities. But that fails to explain the fall of the Sovietica fully. It would have been possible for the Soviet Union to pursue the economic reform processes, like China, but for the ethno-religious issues that worked synergically with the craving for more freedom.

This leads us to conclude that there were four principal causes that led to the implosion of the Soviet regime. These are ethno-religious issues, economic stalemate, craving for freedom among the Great Unwashed and the increasing Soviet isolation and loss of legitimacy within international community. But all these would have been in vain had there been no alternative power and system in the shape of the United States. Just remove the United States from the Cold War scene and that would have meant perpetuation of the Soviet reign. If one has to explain the Soviet debacle in one word, it is: the United States.

But America, too, had to pay a heavy price for this super power rivalry. Had the Soviet Union been able to hold a bit longer, it could well have been the end of the United States as a super power. The protracted mega contest between the two superpowers had virtually drained both of them. It was a protracted heavy weight boxing bout between two strongest contestants whose outcome could have gone either way. Most Cold War historians attribute the fall of the Soviet empire to the bad shape of the Soviet economy. But, few of us look back on the pitiable state of the American economy. Walter LaFaber has captured this brilliantly in the following words:

> By 1985 their (American) (parenthesis mine) borrowing, especially from the Japanese and Western Europeans became so heavy that, for the first time since 1914, the Americans actually owed more money overseas than they were owed from abroad. After seventy-one years, they owed more than $40 billion to foreign lenders and were the world's most indebted people." And again, "As the US domestic debt soared toward another trillion dollars in the 1990s, young Americans faced a lifetime of paying Japanese and European creditors, while cutting back not only on their spending, but on spending for their national defense.
>
> —*Lafeber, the American Age, (pp. 711, 712)*

One of the chief causes for this economic decline was the massive military spending undertaken by the Reagan Administration that amounted to $300 billion. Like the Soviet Union in the 1970s, the United States was spending far more on defense than on the civilian sector. The financial costs of maintaining puppet regimes in many parts of the globe including the loans and 'bribing' sky-rocketed the American deficit. Since the end of the Vietnam War and the beginning of the oil crisis in the early 1970s, the US economy kept faltering as repeated recessions hit both the West and the Orient. Yet it is equally commendable that the United States recovered that shock in a few decades as Clinton found time to focus on the economic front. By that time gains from its Cold War victory started to pour results in the form of securing hitherto closed markets in Europe and Asia. The wounded Eagle drew blood and waited for another take-off with the message of globalization in its beak.

References and readings

State of the Union Address on 23rd January, 1980, http//www.jimmycarter.library.org

The Reagan Era, Excerpted from Deterring Democracy, 1991, Noam Chomsky, June, 2004, Znet Foreign policy.

Glenn P. Hastedt,the American Foreign Policy, Past, Present, Future, 5th ed., Prentice Hall, 2003.

Alan P. Dobson and Steve Marsh, the US Foreign Policy since 1945, Routledge, London, 2001.

Ronald Reagan, Anthe American Life, Simon and Schuster, NY, 1990.

Inaugural Address, 20 January, 1989. President George H. Bush, http//www.

bartleby.com NRDC: Archive of Nuclear Data, From NRDC's Nuclear Program

State Department Web site, http//www.state.gov

Major Timothy C. Jones, Arms Control In the 80s, GlobalSecuirty.org

Thomas Graham, Washington Quarterly, Spring ,2000.

Hans M. Kristensen, March 2000, the US Nuclear Strategy Reform in the 1990s, The Nautilus Institute, www.nautilus.org

Beyond the Wall, Germany's Road to Unification, A Twentieth Century Fund Book, The Brookings Institution, Washington, DC.

Robert Pastor, *Condemned to Repetition*, Princeton, 1987.

Jimmy Carter, *Keeping Faith*, NY, 1982.

Gaddis Smith, *Morality, Reason, and Power: the American Diplomacy in the Carter Years*, NY, 1986.

Strobe Talbot, *The Russians and Reagan*, NY, 1982.

Jeane J. Karpatrick, *Dictatorship and Double Standards*, NY, 1982.

Fred Halliday, *The Making of the Second Cold War,* 2nd ed., London, 1986.

Strobe Talbot, *Endgame*, NY, 1979.

Lou Cannon, *Reagan*, Perigee, 1982.

Reymond L. Garthoff, *Détente and Confrontation*, NY, 1985.

The Soviet Invasion in Perspective, Stanford, 1985.

Stephen J. Cimbala, *The Reagan Defense Program*, Wilmingdon DE, 1986.

William B. Quandt, *Camp David*, NY, 1986.

George Bush and Brent Scowcroft, *A World Transformed: The Collapse of the Soviet Union. The Unification of Germany. Tiananmen Square. The Gulf War,* Washington, 1991.

Major Crisis in Contemporary the American Foreign Policy: A Documentary History, Ed. By Russell D. Buhite, Westport, 1997.

D. Mervin, *Ronald Reagan and the American Presidency,* London, Longman, 1990.

Paul Kennedy, *The Rise and Fall of Great Powers,* NY, 1987.

Richard Ned Lebow & Janice Gross Stein, *We All Lost The Cold War,* Princeton, 1994.

J.F. Spero & Jeffrey A. Hart, The Politics of International Economic Relations, 5th Edition, London, 1997.

G. Lewy, America in Vietnam: *Illusion, Myth, and Reality,* NY, 1978.

H W Brands, *Into the Labyrinth: The United States and the Middle East, 1945-1993*, NY, 1994.

Ronald Reagan, And the American Life, Simon and Schuster, NY, 1990.

Walter Lafeber, the American Age, The US Foreign Policy at Home and Abroad, 1750 to Present, 2nd Ed., W.W. Norton & Company, NY, 1994.

CHAPTER VI

THE UNITED STATES IN THE POST COLD WAR ERA

Post Cold War realities and the US priorities

One of the major American foreign policy perceptions of the post Cold War years impinged upon the American belief that it was possible to create a US-centric liberal democratic and capitalist global order through a combined application of hard and soft powers. 'The end of the history', or the 'fullness of time', seemed to herald a new global human civilization. But such hopes were all but belied as the United States, the engine behind such progressive ideas, experienced the vengeance of history on September 11, 2001 and woke up to the stark reality that the international realm is still fraught with anarchy, betrayal, and petty national interests.

The deceptive 'zero year' (following the official signing of the end of the Cold War) seemed to promise the elimination of all divisive ideologies and the flowering of universal peace and prosperity under a single system. The messages of the American Declaration reverberated once again as President George H. Bush, the only the US president privleged to preside over two historical epochs aptly summarized the international situation in his first inaugural address on January 20, 1989:

> For the first time in this century, for the first time in perhaps all history, man does not have to invent a system by which to live. We don't have to talk late into the night about which form of government is better. We don't have to wrest justice from the kings. We only have to summon it from within ourselves. We must act on what we know. I take as my guide the hope of a saint: In crucial things, unity; in important things, diversity; in all things generosity.

The nation that was born against history, at last, saw itself not only on the right side of history but also felt able to act as what Madeleine Albright termed as the 'authors of history'. The former National Security Adviser and the present Secretary of State, Condoleezza Rice affirmed that the United States had got to accept that responsibility to avoid the future charge, " why we were on the right side of history, and did not take care of this." The geopolitical shake up that followed the end of the Cold War offered a unique opportunity to the United States to realize its 'divine' mission. In reality, however, weight of history prevailed as the United States found its hands full with the job of exorcising itself of the sins and ghosts of the just bygone era. Instead of rewriting history the United States became its subject and prisoner.

During the era of bipolar rivalry, many responsibilities were shared by the two super powers under many compelling and extra ordinary circumstances. The very nature of the Cold War drove both the super powers to the limits of their sacrifices and commitments. Once the Cold War ended, the United States felt that it was high time that it should rid itself of the Cold War 'blackmailing' by its allies and partners, spread over various parts of the world, and who still cherished a sort of dependency on the United States. *The post Cold War international politics came to be defined among other things by the age-old and classical pattern: every other power, not excluding Europe, wants to increase themselves at the existing hegemon's, that is, America's expense, while the United States is equally careful not to fall in that vicious circle in which the demands of the 'parasitic' , 'self-interested', and 'rentier' states would act as dead weights over the American dynamism, and its global influence*. The obvious outcome has been a series of disagreements on various issues ranging from environment, trade and international justice issues to weapons of mass destruction (WMD), rogue states, and terrorism, between the United States and the rest of the world on the one hand and the growing embitterment of America's relations with its allies, on the other.

Fortunately or unfortunately, the United States happens to be the only superpower in a far more politically charged and complex international political milieu than was the case with any other great power any time in human history. Contemporary international politics is now rent apart by two apparently opposing trends: increasing democratization and increasing American assertion to project its 'ways' and 'ideas', on global scale on a rather reluctant and impervious international community long programmed with preconceived historical images and memories.

These opposing trends have been aggravated by two expectations. While the US allies expected some more peace dividends from the United States, the latter felt the other way. The nations of the rest of the world had little doubt that the United States in the post Cold War period would be extremely dependent on them and hence it could not go it alone in managing international affairs. These nations still aspire for a more democratic and multipolar international order. The United States feels that it is the only reliable guarantor of 'democracy'.

Another chief feature of contemporary international politics is that it continues to evolve by freeing itself progressively from the fetters of 'bureaucratic-elitist' influences of all the previous eras. As mentioned above, it moves towards greater democratization. Developments in science and technology and the accompanying knowledge and its proliferation help in dispersing the fruits of modernization – once accessible only to the 'exclusive' club of elites – by bringing them to the doorsteps of the common people, cheaply and abundantly. The post Cold War era has come a long way from the days prior to the invention of printing to one of widespread use of computers and the Internet that has virtually broken the stranglehold of the above elitist groups in 'information manipulation'. For example, media searchlight deprives them, the luxury of the earlier times to formulate their hideous designs in the secret recesses of their 'backroom' chambers to 'hoodwink' the common masses. Today, people and leaders alike, eat the same food, watch the same TV channels and browse the same websites to get a real time picture, sitting in the farthest corners of the earth. Like space, no country colonizes 'time', any longer. The disappearance of the enchanting 'distant' factor has eroded much of the charisma that surrounded the once 'tight lipped', 'all-knowing' and the fancied (because these policy-makers carried some mystery around them) industrial-military-bureaucratic elites and made them look less whimsical, more predictable and caring about the common people.

The role of the media in influencing the contemporary international political developments can hardly be underestimated. The days of the 'hegemonic' approach – so often discussed in the scholarly circles of political communications researchers – of keeping important information within the policy-making circle from being leaked to the public, seem to be over. Modern media persons are ever busy with sensational expositions and leakages of secret agreements, documents, and tapes, tapping of telephonic conversations, and flirting with both the ruling and the opposition groups to get ready access to policy secrets in lieu of generous offer for more propaganda coverage. Another feature of this information-cum-political democratization is the exposition of the elites' disagreements on many foreign policy issues. This is known as the indexing approach. Rapid democratization of information and politics has thus become the defining feature not only of the American domestic politics but also of contemporary international politics.

The United States feels that it is the American dynamism and ideas that are behind such increased democratization on a global scale. They are the champions of the freedom of speech and the press. The United States has thus no compunction in claiming itself to be the citadel of liberal democratic forces. On the other hand, most other nations feel that the once isolationist United States needs to be further 'socialized' through more interaction with the world community of nations. It is this dilemma that characterizes the post Cold War international politics in which the interests of the United States and others tend to pull in different directions on a variety of issues, referred above. What has given spices to such a drab 'tug-of-war' situation is the coexistence of the 'tiger' (the United States) and the lamb (other nations) and the uneasiness of the tiger as the lambs often dare to tread on its tail. Interestingly, both the tiger and the lamb have their own justifications. But the American concern is how long other powers would prefer to remain as lambs.

The United States feels that recent happenings in international politics vindicates the American political, economic, and even cultural supremacy over those of others and hence contemporary international order would remain more peaceful, prosperous, and free from any kind of oppression under the American leadership only. The rest of the world feels that such a development would invariably create a single power domination of the world that would put democracy and freedom in jeopardy. This difference in perceptions between the United States and others has already created tensions along ideological and cultural lines. Carried to the extreme, anti-American ' terrorists' and Islamic fundamentalists feel that they alone are the 'angels' of the Allah with the divine responsibility to 'destroy' the American ideals and values, while the United States is equally determined to eliminate these 'barbarians' that had precipitated the downfall of many a great powers in history. The battle is now between the United States and the forces of divisiveness and fundamentalism, both claiming to be the real messiah of the mankind. Other countries are either caught in this whirlpool or they are simply waiting on the fence (despite America's best efforts to enlist them into the anti-terrorist camp) for the appropriate moment to step in to maximize their interests.

Another major American priority in the conduct of its foreign policies after the end of the Cold War is to ensure that the US status quo in international affairs endures. The United States hopes to do this in two ways: first, by cornering as much overseas markets as possible and secondly, through policies aimed at preventing the rise of a challenger to the position of world leadership. Needless to mention, the game of international politics is played on two key assumptions: first, to hold on to one's own advantages and secondly, to deny any space to any other rival and revisionist power. The underlying logic is that if an incumbent hegemon leaves the field, other powers will fill up the vacuum, soon. Moreover, quitting would mean marginalization because 'out of sight' is 'out of mind'. The United States engages itself in various ways on a plethora of international issues that may or may not be its own making so as to keep track of events and to remain at the center of world politics. *The United States intends to create a US-centric world order based on the American republican values. At the center of its republican model lies the rational for the propagation and perpetuation of its liberal democratic capitalist ideals.* In the worst possible scenario, it could leave the field only for an ally having cultural and religious similarity. These are the broad perceptions that guide the foreign policy conduct of the United States in the post Cold War decades.

American policies to mediate in every conflict situation in various parts of the world during the 1990s with such 'prescriptions' as confidence building measures, mutual dialogues, treaties, joint military exercises etc., were dictated by the above negativism: to deny other powers from stealing the limelight. The United States, in the new millennium, doesn't want any situation that would permit any other power to wield its regional hegemonic sword over its weaker neighbors. In that case, the United States would have to face growing oppositions in other regions as well: a sort of 'domino' effect. Why the United States is so prone to mediate in conflicts even in areas that hardly affect its national interests and security? The answer is that the United States being a very large country is destined to have a global reach and for that it has to pierce the net of regional and national boundaries and above all to overcome its own fear of isolationism. It is all but a truism that a great power must either expand to 'survive' or contract to 'die'. That is why Robert Jarvis in American Foreign policy in a New Era, thinks that the world happened to be the hegemon's neighborhood, and Waltz felt that for the United States "the interest of the country in security came to be identified with the maintenance of a certain world order". (Robert Jarvis, p.95)

There is also a compelling logic, especially, on the part of the United States. For great powers, 'global' is more fascinating than 'regional'. The Western Hemisphere happened to be the terra incognita-a self-contained enclave-sandwiched between two oceans that for eons of time escaped the notice of other older civilizations as the latter developed far greater geographical, commercial, military, and cultural contacts amongst themselves. Belated discovery of the New World and its more recent interaction with other cultures made the United States an upstart in international affairs for Europe and a stranger for the Orient. On the other hand, these two disadvantages, geographical and cultural, (discussed in detail in the introductory chapter) have created a subconscious fear of isolationism in the minds of the Americans.

Paradoxically, this same feeling of isolationism renders the once 'pariah' United States to be more 'sociable' now. The United States thus is driven by its inner compulsion and an inner sense of insecurity (in the sense of being a loner and being often misunderstood) to constantly engage and entangle other nations in very many activities. *This pathological fear of getting marginalized in international affairs has been one of the chief causes for the spread of the American globalization.* Notwithstanding the fact that globalization has compressed time and space, has made the two encircling oceans look like 'ponds', and other distant lands its nearby 'neighbors', the 'distance' remains, nevertheless, as the United States now has to cohabit with others in a jungle full of 'poisonous snakes'.

Interestingly, it is the same United States that in a different historical setting found it convenient to court isolationism. As I have written earlier in this book such an isolationist approach was forced on America by Europe and *it is this 'imposed' confinement that generated such a resilience as to make the United States the most 'involved' and 'inclusive' nation in the world, over time*. The United States hardly forgot the ordeals of its colonial confinements. As a result, even in victory, this individualistic and the freedom-loving nation came out with a set of interlocking policies after 1945 that were supposed to banish its fear of isolationism, forever. Even the occasional tendencies towards the American assertive unilateralism in the post Cold War era can be seen in this backdrop.

The above discussion leads us to another vital aspect of the American post Cold War priorities already mentioned above. This aspect is again linked to the Declaration and unravels in a different color in an altogether new situation: war, regional or otherwise, simply cannot be allowed to take place. While the rationale for abolishing war remain unchanged, they need 'new' interpretations in the changing international scenario and serves as the principal political logic on which to base the post Cold War American foreign policies. For example, the United States denounced war, earlier, because that country happened to be an insignificant power vis-à-vis its European counterparts. Morality, the last resort of the weak and the poor, had been the American 'anti-colonial' shield in deflecting European bullying from the Western Hemisphere .

Now, the reason is as much political as economic even though the US policy makers point to economic interdependence in ensuring peace on a global scale. From a more political perspective, the United States does not want war to take place in any other region simply because that would divert the attention of the rest of the world from the US-centrism. Conflicts during the Cold War were tolerated and even encouraged, since, in most cases, these were regulated, conducted, and mediated by the superpowers. The post Cold War United States has taken upon itself the task of guiding the destiny of every other nation through policies that run into the arteries and veins of their political and economic systems through the juice (or bitter pill?) of 'Americanization' that tend to even undermine the 'sovereignty' and 'individuality' of other nations. Such 'possessiveness' arises out of the American fear of getting isolated and out of the American conviction that its own ways are superior to those of others and that it would be a sheer waste of time and energy to allow others to have their 'disorderly' ways.

The post Cold War American foreign policies, of course, are also aimed at compromising, albeit, to a certain extent, America's republican values and ideals in national interest with a view to deriving the maximum out of the current wave of globalization and to make the most of the good time that the United States enjoys at the beginning of yet another new century. However, there is a paradox. If the United States wants to change others in its mirror image then common sense demands that it's political image ought to remain fixed. On the other hand, if the United States wants itself and the rest of the non-Western world to meet half-way, then, like the former the Soviet Union (FSU), it would lose its main 'ideological' strength and would be forced to eventually opt for the 'old world' great power politics. The post Cold War situation, indeed, throws some imposing challenges for the 'American' elements or the 'American specialties' or the 'American Cavalcade' in dealing with international affairs.

Interdependence and democracy have their limits. Contemporary international politics is still defined in large measure by national interests, violence, hatred, race, ethnicity, and language and, above all, the need for self-preservation. In short, historical and nationalist considerations still guide human behaviors and continue to remain the chief 'tool' for the political leaders in various parts of the world to frame their respective policies. As a result, the post Cold War American foreign policies also respond greatly to individual ideas, from James Baker's 'denuclearization to Anthony Lake's 'enlargement of NATO', to William Perry's Cooperative Threat Reduction to Sumner and Lipton's 'macroeconomic stabilization' and to the more recent Bush Doctrine. All these ideas and policies have one common objective: to enhance America's national interests. There is a curious law of international politics: nations tend to resort more to nationalistic and traditionalistic values when they are relatively weak or insignificant while great powers have little time to engage in such trivialities. Every other empire or great power in history, revealed a peculiar threshold of tolerance. This, I term as the liability and responsibility factor of a great power that feels comfortable in seeing itself in the role of a mediator and arbitrator, like the elderly chieftain.

The United States is now faced with a situation in which history has offered a unique opportunity for it to create an international system, virtually, from a scratch, but one in which the cost burdens are staggering and, even frustrating. The absence of the 'ideological' vector of the just bygone era and the liquidation of a 'definite' pattern of international structure established under colonialism, prior to 1945, have created a sort of anomie in the post Cold War international politics. On the one hand, there lurks the distinct possibility of the revival of the older powers. On the other, an altogether new type of world order based on the American creed and the American specialties, the seeds of which were sown long ago, is sprouting in various corners of the earth. It is this tussle that constitutes the real birth pangs for an emerging world order.

The United States in the new millennium, lords over every other major power simultaneously – a unique phenomenon in international political history. It is the same painful repetition of historical patterns in which an incumbent hegemon tries to consolidate its grip over others while the latter, though eclipsed by the former, looks for every possible ways and means to first leash the hegemon and thence to assert their own supremacies. As the gravity and scale of international problems grow to enormous proportions and as the number of players keep on rising, the United States, in the capacity of a de facto world hegemon, commanding a fractured and even 'deceptive' loyalty, faces four strategic foreign policy options in the new millennium: (1) unilateralism, that is, to pursue its goals in its own independent ways; (2) multilateralism based on consensus among great powers and observance of some commonly agreed rules that would act as checks and balances on any single power; (3) a power sharing arrangement with countries under the Western Civilization; and (4) isolationism or even regionalism marked by an American retreat into its own hemisphere. All these four alternatives are, however, discussed in the next chapter.

To make matters more complicated for the United States, the post Cold War situation not only offers little space for the United States to relinquish its hegemonic role but also closes all its exit doors. Former Soviet Union was 'lucky' to have escaped through the only 'opening' offered to it by *the* United States. The latter does not enjoy that privilege. It must play out its full innings: if America wins, it would successfully carry out the unfinished job of the Graeco-Roman civilization. Like Alexander the Great, who used to burn the roads to retreat, the US leaders will have to focus constantly on making the most out of this 'great entanglement'. If it loses, it will have to rot within the confines of the two oceans. Burdened as it is now with the vexing nationalistic issues left unsolved by the European colonialism and the Soviet communism, the post Cold War international scenario has presented the most difficult choice before the United States: whether to carry the yoke of its age old idealistic-moralistic values or to consign them into the flames of America's imperialistic ambitions. Would the Eagle dare to leave its solid ground of 'values' and soar into unknown heights either to 'burn' itself out or to precipitate its great fall? These are the most intriguing questions that confront the sole super power of our era in discharging its duties as a world leader in the new millennium.

Bush and Clinton era

Quite a number of problems, not related to the Cold War, resurfaced once communism found its destined place in the library books of history or made, what Alexander Hague preferred to call, a 'peaceful journey to the grave'. The collapse of the bipolar world order rendered it virtually impossible for any single nation to address all the above outstanding international issues. Such a realization lent a 'multipolar' trajectory to the immediate post Cold War international order and to the subsequent American foreign policies. Both Mr. George H. Bush and William Jefferson Clinton recognized the need for multilateral approaches in handling various international issues. Policies of 'Engagement' and 'enlargement', prescribed by individual think tanks in the United States, became the principal vehicles of the American foreign policies in the 1990s to dissipate growing fears about the declining US influence in world affairs. To that extent, the American post Cold War foreign policies were aimed at keeping the American 'empire' floating against the strong undercurrent generated by the Soviet withdrawal.

George H. Bush affirmed the US commitment to collective international security by advocating a 'new world order' that would ensure self-determination and sovereignty of nations through cooperative deterrence and even joint aggression at the behest of the United Nations against any transgressor. President Clinton's clarion call was to spread the ideal of 'democratic peace' that would bind the world community of nations in a 'family of free-market democracies'. Both the presidents sought to project a more multilateralist face by allowing the UN freer rein in creating an international coalition force against Iraq in the first Gulf War, in conducting the humanitarian relief operations in Somalia, and in encouraging a flurry of 'assertive multilateralism' through various peacekeeping and peacemaking operations under the UN supervision during the early years of the 1990s. The launching of the Uruguay round of GATT under Bush and its successful conclusion under Clinton and the formation of the World Trade Organization reinforced the American intention to go the multilateralist way. The United States sealed its European commitment with NATO enlargement plans under Partnership for Peace to enlist countries of Central and East Europe and even some former Soviet republics. NAFTA reflected the US willingness to work jointly with its neighbors to eventually create a 'Greater America' in the Western Hemisphere .

Both the presidents showed their interests and willingness to support treaties dealing with nuclear proliferation and the ban on nuclear testing, environmental and ecological problems, and to prop up the backward and famine stricken regions, and the failed states. The reason for preferring such a multilateralist approach was obvious. United states had to remain busy on several fronts after the Soviet demise: the issue of German unification and latter's retention of NATO status; disturbing developments in the former Soviet Republics and in East Europe with a view to avert the post communist chaos and anarchy; the American concern about the fate of 30,000 Soviet nuclear warheads scattered over several republics and the need to transfer these nuclear stockpiles to Russia. Moreover, the United States had to ensure that the dissolution and dismemberment of the Soviet Union didn't recoil on the only surviving super power. All these compulsions left little time and space for the United States to attend to other global problems, all by itself. The United States needed some time and respite to regroup and even reclaim legitimacy (largely eroded by the loss of a' common' enemy) and indispensability to the rest of the world by deciding to cooperate with United Nations on major global issues.

However, soon the rest of the world got disillusioned as the backlash effects of the immediate post Cold War policies overtook the Congress. John Jerrard Ruggi clearly describes the post 1995 situation in these words, " By the mid-1990s, however, a different orientation toward the post Cold War world had gained prominence...... Among the militia movement fringe of the American politics the United Nations and the "new world order" loomed so large as to trigger fears of tyrannical world government. For presidential aspirants in the Republican primaries, attacks on the UN emerged as a visceral issue eliciting foot-stomping approval." (Ruggie, p.3) The United States rounded up by cutting its foreign aids to a lowest level amongst other industrial democracies and shut down many of the State Department's overseas posts that had become useless in the post Cold War situation. However, most of these measures were reversed in the latter days and the United States began to show signs of acting in more multilateral fashion, again. The US policy makers under Gerorge W. Bush realized that their rhetoric couldn't match the more sober and pragmatic approach of its predecessors. But undergirding the US decision to get more involved in world affairs was another epoch making event: globalization. Let me first deal with globalization from a different angle than had been done so far.

Globalization: A different perspective on globalization

Globalization is usually viewed as the brainchild of the West and thus contains some 'grudge' element. The North-South divide, the legacy of colonial exploitation and anti-imperialist communist propaganda, have all fostered anti American sentiments in the minds of the people in the developing world. But the real truth behind this process of globalization that had started (with many interruptions in between) since the days of the silk route has never been explained in a comprehensive manner. Industrialization, one of the principal components of globalization, means, in simple terms, application of improved techniques to better harness the natural resources within a given territory in a more organized way, including the agricultural sector. With globalization, such 'harnessing' of natural resources in common becomes a prerogative for human kinds and nations, in general.

More specifically, globalization can be defined as the united human endeavor to harness the earth's resources for the material prosperity of greater number of inhabitants in various parts of the globe. Globalization, like industrialization, takes place partly out of necessity and is driven by the barometric pressure generated by developments in science and technology, at a given period. Globalization also ensures a 'perpetual' improvement of the means of production through new researches. *Given the finiteness of the earth's resources and the danger of its fast depletion in the wake of population bursts and other natural and man-made 'calamities', the issue becomes one of ever increasing numbers (people) vying for a limited or an extremely inelastic pie.* Thus the problem has always been either to increase the size of that pie or to establish the law of the strongest and the most worthy to corner the largest booty. Let the devil take the hindmost.

Medieval empires resorted to extra-territorial occupations and plunders to satisfy their needs. But these despotic rulers did little to enlarge that pie that I am talking about. Population pressures were held in some check by constant wars, natural calamities, and pestilence. Colonialism was the first organized and large-scale, yet, incomplete endeavor to harness the earth's resources in a systematic manner. Since modern civilization and history starts with colonialism and since colonialism happened to be a European concept, it is Europe, spurred by the 'principles' of Renaissance, Enlightenment and the Industrial Revolution that pioneered every other form of global activity. In a word, Europe was emerging out of its 'feudalistic' culture to subdue the rural and the rustic Orient. In that sense, colonialism marks the first departure from traditionalism in terms of risk-taking and adventurism.

With decolonization and the birth of many new nations and subsequent growth of population due to various other factors, like improvements in medical science, better health care and sanitation, greater job opportunities, etc., the demand over this 'fixed global pie' became more intense. This affected both the developed and the underdeveloped nations, alike. Obviously, the need was felt after the Second World War (because of the collapse of colonialism and because territorial occupation was rendered impossible) to focus attention on more efficient exploitation of natural resources within a given region, that is, a shift was from external to internal form of 'colonization' of the factors of production.

It must be remembered that the twentieth century fin de siècle international trade and trade related theories do not have much resemblance with those of the classical economists like Adam Smith and the Physiocrats because of several reasons. First, many earlier economists were biased towards their respective countries' world status that limited their long-term visions about the most viable alternative. Secondly, technological factors were not given due weight because they were supposed to be controlled by the government, in large measure. Thirdly, the limited vision and paucity of knowledge about the fullest interplay of economic forces (because it was not until recent past that the vast undeveloped regions have entered into the calculation of the developed economists) hindered the development of more open and comprehensive economic theories based on free market mechanism. The late arrival of the American republic with all its enlightened values rendered previous trade and economic theories inadequate in explaining the prevalent economic practices.

However, the message remained clear: human beings need more resources for propagation, preservation, peace, and prosperity commensurate with developments in political, economic, and social systems resulting from scientific and technological advancements. An additional urge on the part of the developed countries to do so is to maintain and enhance the standards of living of their citizens even at the expense of their developing counterparts. On the other hand, the share of the people of the underdeveloped and the developing nations in enjoying the fruits of modernism couldn't be ignored any longer in so far as the industrialized West had *got to depend* on the resource-rich developing world in a far more democratic international political system.

For the post war Europe, efforts at efficient harnessing of natural resources meant that European nations, bereft of their colonial possessions, have to look for ways of cooperation within their own continent only, albeit, for the time being. At the same time, it dawned on these former colonial powers that if they hoped to share in the resources of the developing world, they would have to adopt a far more soft procedure of commercial arrangement with these regions on a win-win basis – a sort of neocolonial approach more suited to American economic models. Richard Rosecrance felt, "In the past, it was cheaper to seize another state's territory by force than to develop the sophisticated economic and trading apparatus needed to derive benefit from commercial exchange with it." As a result, the leading European nations gave little thought about developing their colonies except those areas settled by the Europeans and they got concerned with territorial expansion only. Naturally their sins visited upon themselves as they lost their overseas colonies after WWII. With no immediate outlet in sight, they had no alternative but to seek cooperation within their own continent.

In keeping with the law of the strongest, the Western nations were long accustomed to the logic that a territory might be inhabited for long time by a particular group of people but that doesn't guarantee them any claim over their territory. This was the real meaning of colonial 'settlements'. Moreover, they reasoned that those non-Western countries did not even belong to the category of nation-states, until recently. So the European powers had a right to occupy overseas lands, more so, in the name of Christianity. The real issue, they thought, was not to inhabit a territory but the competence and strength to defend that territory. If the natives failed to defend their territories then the colonial powers had the 'right' to occupy (by overt or covert means) that land, harness it to their hearts content till it is worn out and, thereafter, run away with the gains from native lands and other natural resources which, being gifts of nature, ought not to be any respecter of 'native' inhabitants. Unlike the previous empires, outright plunder was not so much the aim of the colonial powers as to create some permanent source of raw materials and overseas markets. Europeans came to stay and settle in these lands. Where settlement was not possible, due to either over crowdedness or hostile man-made or natural environment, the Westerners trained a group of indigenous people. This group or the class of native people was supposed to assist in the transfer of their (the natives) country's vital resources to their masters.

In any case, colonialism meant a prolonged coexistence and interaction (both economic and cultural) – sometimes, trying, irritating, and painful – with native populations than was the case with any other classical empire in history. Colonial powers reasoned that the colonies would have, any way, remained in poverty and exploitation even if the Europeans had not arrived in these lands. After all, these people always remained in a state of perpetual destitution under exploitative and ruthless 'indigenous' despots. By assuming the charge to administer these colonies, Western nations felt that they had done them some good by familiarizing them with forces of modernism, a view echoed by Teddy Roosevelt in the early twentieth century. On that logic, the natives must either submit to Western political, economic, and cultural domination or fall into retrogression. The message was loud and clear: if the native people hopped into the bandwagon of the colonial powers then well and good. In that case they would get some pittance. *But if they prove recalcitrant then they had to either to be forcibly thrown out of their territories or left alone in their own world of ignorance and darkness. Western countries desperately needed overseas land and raw materials. It was a matter of survival for the latter, too. No less important was the Anglo-Saxon ethic to work harder and court pain in order to enjoy pleasure. Colonial powers henceforth won't allow the indolent natives to indulge in reveries and remain satisfied with little and small things.*

Such a European perception had a purpose, mentioned a few lines earlier: upliftment of at least a segment of 'intelligent' native population and to incorporate them into the mainstream of economic and political activity. This was supposed to facilitate colonial administration, as well. Even the non-colonial United States justified its expansions on the same ground in Cuba, Hawaii, and the Philippines, a century ago. McKinley remarked that his decision in respect of the Philippines emanated out of the concern for the well being of the native population and to prepare them to develop and administer their lands. *Thus the main thrust and message of modern globalization remains the same – more efficient harnessing of natural resources.* Apart from deeper European integration, the EU's proposed eastern enlargement and the

Northern Defense Initiative (NDI) are glaring examples of the grand design to exploit the natural resources in the hitherto 'inaccessible' northern-most parts of Europe. The creation of numerous free trade blocks all around the globe bears out the truth of the above analysis.

Two things follow from the above discussion: western nations are the engines behind globalization and that interdependence, integration, and contemporary globalization, all mean more efficient exploitation of resources, both natural and man-made (because some of natural bounties don't exist anymore) in any part of the world. While colonialism lent a deliberate purpose to globalization, it proved inadequate to sustain the same. It was a partial defeat for the European political thoughts and values. 'Partial', because monarchy, on which the edifice of colonial system stood, was not the only political system prevalent then. The other half manifested in the writings of Locke, Rousseau, Grotius, and Kant and was already put in actual practices on the other side of the Atlantic.

The United States stepped in where the European powers failed, thereby, underlining the tremendous resilience of the Western Civilization. Trade has always been the linchpin of that civilization. Since trade hardly remains within the confines of a definite geographical area, security risks mount for a nation to the extent its trade expands because nothing is more lucrative to the 'pirates' than to plunder a merchant vessel carrying precious goods and metals in the high seas. So the urgent need had always been to protect sea routes and the coaling stations. Efficient trade also meant greater integration with coastal and peripheral areas abroad. All these, in turn, mean the need to protect these areas with superior military power. Thus the issue of direct or indirect possession of foreign territories remains in place whether in the case of colonial European powers or a non-colonial United States. No wonder that the latter earned its reputation as an empire of 'bases'.

The post 1945 American economic policies share this logic and continuity with colonialism. While colonialism was a zero sum game in which colonial powers gained at the expense of their colonies, the American perception is different: creation of a US-centric financial order that would guarantee the fruits of development to everyone yet tying them to the American type of liberal capitalism, more specifically, the American capitalism. It is this breadth of the American perception over those of its European counterparts that accounts for the huge American success in the modern era of globalization. America's vast territory and economic diversity, its demographic composition and social mobility, and its lack of aristocratic and hierarchic class are some of the key advantages that the United States have over the European nations. Europe had its own limits and 'point of no return' because of inherent limitations of its natural and man-made factors. The United States knows no such limitation or any 'point of no return'. For the United States even the sky is not the limit.

No wonder, the United States may well be on its course to 'space colonization', someday. All these 'plus' points for the United States help create a sort of additional room of maneuver for America in international economic management. This is what I term as America's 'economic space'. To cap it up, the United States after 1945 made dollar the medium of exchange in international trade, via the Bretton Woods arrangement.

There are still some 'undeveloped' regions in America. This regional disparity in economic development is understandable if one takes into account America's vast size and constant technological growths and their uneven application because of resource and 'other' constraints. This phenomenon offers the United States a vital 'space' to carry out constant 'experimentation', wherefrom emerges new kinds of activities and dynamism that, in turn, proliferate into the other parts of the world. Britain had its Lancashire or Oxford that elongated the British imperialist domination of the world. The Soviet Union had virtually none (mainly because of its dictatorial political set-up and the poverty of its philosophy and geography) that made its reign extremely short. The United States has many such potential centers of 'economic and cultural activity' and a very liberal political system..

Now let me return to the post Cold War situation. One most important motivation for the United States in the post Cold War era not to revert back to the days of isolationism was the stark realization that an isolationist approach at such an important crossroad in human civilization would make even the American colossus fall by the way side within decades! Globalization forms the treasure trove of the post Cold War era from which every nation stands to gain. It is true that many trends and developments contingent upon globalization still remain outside of the US control. What is more, globalization happens to be an ongoing process whose future effects are still uncertain: either 'rolling into a fog' till the end of the tunnel leads to a 'gold pot at the end of the rainbow' or a maelstrom precipitating another cataclysmic war.

Globalization means increased and uninterrupted flow of goods, services, capital, technology, ideas, communications and real time information across national borders, and greater people-to-people contact. Nye defines globalization as the growth of worldwide networks of interdependence. According to some scholars, globalization happens to be the pulse of modern international activity. I look upon globalization as the course of a stream that can't be reversed and those drifting downstream stand to gain most. Not only that. Gorbachev in his memoirs referred to the example of a 'common boat' to describe interdependence of the world community of nations. No country would be spared from getting drowned should that boat capsize, midstream.

Globalization is a complex process and is not without risk. If one plays ones cards well, one can be a huge gainer. If any nation stays out of this current, it falls into retrogression and misery. Globalization happens to be the international version of the Westward expansion that has yet again provided a great opportunity for the propagation of its secret, invisible, and trade empire on a global scale. Jack Turner and Brook Adams would have liked to live for another hundred years to watch how the United States made use of this stroke of good luck in the new century. Globalization acts on a dynamism that ideally fits into the American spirit of adventurism. One sees the same zeal and spirit (that marked the era of the frontier expansion) in various American cities and its people as they ceaselessly look for newer opportunities to increase their commercial activities on a global scale. President Clinton in his first inaugural address on January 20, 1993 mentioned how the Americans can earn their livelihood in peaceful competition with the people all across the earth. "This new world has enriched the life of millions of the Americans who are able to compete and win in it." Individual states in America now vie with each other in trading with the rest of the world on a 'country-to country' basis that had lent a rare depth and integrity to the American political system. Whether it is Kentucky chicken or the Washington-based Microsoft, the prosperity of each individual state in the US is owed, in some measure, to globalization.

More importantly, globalization is the American Declaration reincarnated in so far as free trade happens to be the economic 'soul' of the United States. Dean Acheson revealed before a 1944 Congressional testimony to justify international commitments,

> If you wish to control the entire trade and income of the United States, which means the life of the people, you could probably fix it so that everything produced here would be consumed here but that would completely change our constitution, our relations of property, human liberty, our very conceptions of law. And nobody contemplates that. Therefore, you find you must look to other markets and those markets are abroad.
>
> —*Fred Block, p.170*

But there is a caveat. Globalization may aggravate the Hobbesian state of nature and render the international situation more anarchic or it may make the world more civilized, prosperous and rational. The British diplomat Robert cooper felt that globalization rather produced more new and foreign enemies 'whose motives are barely understood'.

Increased interdependence between nations may either lead to more 'Seattle' kind of demonstration or towards the realization of Kantian perpetual peace. Just as big fishes swim well in deep waters, so it is 'advantage' America in the game of globalization. Anthony Giddens writes, "The United States is easily the dominant power in the world militarily, economically, and culturally.

Most of the world's biggest companies are the American , and all the top fifty corporations have their home base in one or other of the industrial countries." (Giddens, p.xxii) According to Hubert Vedrine, the French foreign Minister, a very big fish like the United States "rules supreme in the waters of globalization."

Economic globalization is part of the story. Globalization is also about unprecedented and constant technological inventions and their applications to various other fields of human activities ranging from culture to cuisine, virtual to real world, scientific-technological to nuclear proliferation, and from the Hollywood films to the new world of fantasies. Thomas Friedman describes in his book that everywhere from Singapore to Bangladesh, from China to Latin America, the face of the common people in the streets is lit with new hopes as most of them don Western dresses, use Western calendars, observe Western customs, eat Western foods, drive foreign cars on roads made with Western help, enjoy a common vacation and tour that has become so cosmopolitan like a 'multicultural fair'. Such a homogenization of political, military, economic, and cultural activities on a global scale is something new compared to the previous eras.

In order to understand and sustain the tempo of scientific and technological developments, a nation must have a minimum level of intellectual development, openness, and breadth of vision. The Soviet Union did not lag behind the United States in intellectual field but that they had become tunnel visioned: gains from technology and science were confined to their applications in the defense sector and hardly served the diverse consumption needs of common people. Only the United States had and still possesses that capability to invent new 'high technologies' to overwhelm not only the weaker nations but also to draw the limits for other major powers. The Eagle, the great 'space' explorer, is well placed both to keep surveillance on other nations from atop as well as to maintain its superiority over other 'smaller' birds of prey. The United States constantly breathes new life and dynamism into the international system through its latest and unceasing technological contributions to globalization. This is another way of saying that the United States in keeping with its Anglo-Saxon dynamism constantly keeps the rest of the world engaged and on the move. Niall Ferguson of the Harvard University refers to globalization as "anglobalization".

But there are caveats, too. Globalization has already precipitated unrests and tensions in the developing world (hitherto unfamiliar with the concepts like 'civic' bodies, 'non-state' actors, global firms and production networks) accompanied by unprecedented rise in energy demands, environmental hazards, and demand for more clean water and food. Regular flow of labor across the border (for example, thousands of Singaporeans go to Malaysia and adjacent states by road and return the same day after performing their temporary or contracted or unspecified jobs, mostly, in a clandestine manner) in many South and South East Asian countries may give rise to organized crime or terrorism. Such a concern was voiced in the Report of the National Intelligence Council's (NIC) 2020 project regarding internal and regional migrations: "to the degree that these vast internal migrations spill over national borders-currently only a miniscule fraction of China's 100 million internal migrants end up abroad-they could have major repercussions for other regions, including Europe and North America.". The policies pursued by the IMF, World Bank, and WTO have rather widened the North-South divide.

Paradoxically, the Western world is now experiencing what Thomas Friedman calls a 'globalization fatigue' and it is Asia that has taken up the baton of globalization from the West. According to the same NIC report, "[By 2020] globalization is likely to take on much more of a 'non-Western' face." The report points to another caveat about the resurgence of an Asia-centric culture.

"Asians have already begun to reduce the percentage of students who travel to Europe and North America. A new Asian cultural identity is likely to be rapidly packaged and distributed as incomes rise and communications network spread. Korean pop singers have already mesmerized Japan. Japanese *animes* have many fans in China, and Chinese Kung fu movies and Bollywood song-and-dance epics are viewed through Asia. Even Hollywood has begun to reflect these Asian influences-an effect that is likely to accelerate through 2020."

Gains from globalization can be more fully shared only on the basis of certain conditions, foremost among them being prevalence of democracy, free trade, and rule of law. The forty-second American President Clinton summed up globalization as 'empowerment of people with information everywhere'. Clinton believed " The more people know, the more opinions they're going to have; the more democracy spreads." However, democracy, by itself, is not sufficient to sustain globalization or pax Americana, for that matter. Since globalization increases public goods, it benefits all and sundry, from peace loving common citizens to the violent terrorists. The need is to apply some discipline and curb on the 'dominating' spirit of some and to enhance the cooperative spirit of others. For example, gains from biotechnology may be used to either alleviate poverty and malnutrition or to produce anthrax, sarin gas and other lethal biological weapons.

Thomas Friedman might have this 'domination' factor in mind when he opined in his The Lexus and the Olive Tree that mutual cooperation contingent on globalization would replace Hobbesian state of war of all against all in an anarchic international arena. One important American task is to minimize the disruptive trends in globalization by helping the 'affected', 'awkward, and even 'failed' regions to develop and to make globalization more acceptable and 'friendly' for the weaker nations in order to enable them to remain in the mainstream of international political and economic activities.

One of the main planks of the post Cold War American policies is to deal with the challenges of globalization. One important suggestion comes from The Global Century, Globalization, National Security, edited by Ellen L. Frost and Richard Kuglar. "They will need adequate tools and budgets. They need to avoid preaching and practice humility. They will have to develop a thorough understanding of globalization, shared criteria of success, a more considered ranking of priorities at stake, and a more balanced application of resources, including but not limited to military forces-in short, a globalization agenda informed by strategic purpose." (Kuglar and Frost, p.70) Much depends on the United States whether globalization would turn out to be a cornucopia or a Pandora's box for itself and for the global community, as a whole. Ellen L. Frost, a visiting fellow in the Institute of International Economics is of the view, that the primary task for the US foreign policy makers ought to be to channelize globalization in benign directions.

The boat of globalization needs a strong and skillful navigator to guide through the turbulent waters of international political economy that for the most part of its history was dominated by nationalist protectionism. Like the EU or NATO, process of globalization may be disrupted if the United States is reluctant to provide the requisite leadership. The United States needs the fullest cooperation of every other nation to discharge that responsibility and it is nowhere more important than in the area where globalization faces its toughest challenge: international terrorism that can derail the march of globalization.

Terrorism and the rogue states

Since the demise of its twin super power, American responsibilities and challenges have mounted exponentially in managing world affairs. Other major powers do not always share the American priorities, interests, and responsibilities in an international political scenario fraught with several intriguing realities. In the first place, proliferation of nuclear and other weapons of mass destruction into the hands of a greater number of nations and, perhaps, in the hands of some non-state actors like the terrorists and some Islamic fundamentalist groups, have largely altered the traditional concepts of security and defense. Today, these modern 'Bedouines' roam the vast stretches of the globe through various transnational networks. Their playfields and preys are no longer the local deserts and the caravans but foreign embassies, casinos, tourist resorts, underground rail stations, places of religious worship, and centers of commercial excellence. They have no dearth of money and they give primacy to religion and communalism above the state. These amorphous and stateless terrorist groups and their followers are driven by a fanatic religious ideology for which they can sacrifice their lives in battalions. They want to redefine the concept of security in terms of human and car bombs, suicide squads and light weapons collected from clandestine arms bazaars and other sources, and hope to engage the only world hegmon into medieval war games. In that respect, the post Cold War situation reflects the tussle between the forces of the old traditional conservatism and the forces of modernization: the white man on a Pegasus and the man on the horseback: the Eagle and the Camel.

Ironically, most of the above phenomena happen to be the legacies of the Cold War policies pursued by both the super powers. When the United States made a tryst with the Mujahiddeens to wage a proxy war in Afghanistan against the Soviet occupation forces, it had little time to realize the consequences of its policies. America's most immediate and short-term goal was to halt any possible Soviet advances in the Persian Gulf region. According to Benjamin and Simson, the United States and Saudi Arabia poured some $3 billion to train and arm the Mujahedin (Benjamin & Simon, p.22). But what went unnoticed was that by lending support to Islamic fundamentalist groups to fight against the Soviet forces, the United States had created a 'Frankenstein'. What the United States did not know at that time was that its Cold War nemesis would vanish into the blue so soon and that the former rival was more preferable to its newly created 'cyclop' whose distant ancestors fought some longest and bitterest religious battles at the intersection point of the last two millenniums: the Great Crusades. The United States, perhaps, unwittingly resurrected a dead 'ideology' in trying to destroy another. The Cold War sin revisited the United States and led the US State Department decide not to disclose the data in its annual report on terrorism to Congress in April 2005. The Washington Post writer Susan B. Glasser pointed out that the number of what the State Department considered as 'significant' terrorist attacks shot up to 655 in the year 2004 in contrast to about 175 in 2003. In Iraq alone such a figure had registered a nine-fold increase from 22 to 198 over the same period.In a recent report on global terrorism , It is estimated that there had been 25 per cent rise In the number of terrorist attacks from the previous year. According to the report, Iraq accounts for about half of the 14,000 attacks that occurred in various parts of the world (Global terrorism up more than 25 per cent, CNN.com). In a recent press conference Richard Myers admitted that the current level of terrorist strikes remained as at the level of the previous year with the 'insurgency retaining the ability to surge'. The corresponding figure for Afghanistan, and in Israel, Gaza, and the West bank belt stood at 27 and 45 respectively. It is only recently that the Afghan Premiere Hamid Karzai has requested the United States to rethink its policies in respect of Afghanistan in tackling terrorism.

Like their past ancestors, these modern 'war' lords and terrorists are the natural offshoots of a combined set of international political developments marked by a strong sense of nationalism, irredentism, and virulent ethno-religious sentiments. Easier access to modern technology in some key sectors of Information and Communications, proliferation of the nuclear and other weapons of mass destructions, the spread of computers and the Internet, and the existence of an extremely 'well-oiled' international financial system provide the requisite shots in the arms of these terrorist organizations. Instead of forming the mercenary armed forces for nations that characterized its 'precursors', these terrorist 'infantry' is far more dispersed and possessed with a fanatical zeal and religious bigotry to assist brethren groups in Bosnia, Kosovo, Chechnya, Sinkiang or even in Iraq and Kashmir. They have a common objective: establishment of the solidarity of the commune, the Ummah and the Caliphate, and the destruction of the 'infidels' whether they are Hindus, Christians, or the Jews.

It is no use dwelling on morality where force and power have the last say. Whether these terrorists happen to be the 'fools' who have rushed in to tread on the American 'angelic' heartland, thereby, setting of the possibility of a very protracted and bloody 'religious' war or if they have got a definite purpose can only be tested in the imminent 'mother of battles' for which both the camps may be preparing vigorously. That purpose is to undermine the American world supremacy through a mix of intimidation and surprise, unnerve and frustrate the United States, alienate the latter from its allies, and then enlist the support of other powers to form an anti-Western or an anti-American coalition. Robert Cooper branded terrorism as 'violently anti-Western' and the 'encroachment of chaos on the civilized world'. "The new twist is that their nihilistic passion is a reaction to the progressive spread of the West's secular materialistic culture via the multiple circuits of globalization."

However, it must be kept in mind that the terrorists are not fighting out of whims, pride or fanaticism. They have their own reasoning and ideals. That reasoning had sprung from a deep sense of disrespect for the United States. In their heart of hearts they believe that the United States happens to be that great 'Satan' (no less because of their support for the heathens, that is, Israel) and that the anti-American Jihad must continue till that county is either destroyed or completely subjugated. This urge is all the more great since the United States happens to be a great stumbling block in the way of assertion of the supremacy of Islam on a global scale. Here, a simple arithmetic is at work. Prior to the rise of the European colonialism, it was the Ottoman Turks, the Arabs, the Mughols or the Mongols who held sway over most part of the globe while Europe remained busy within its continental border and the adjacent Mediterranean region. With the fall of colonialism, it was obvious that these old Islamic or Arabic rules might return, once again. But that was not to be because of the United States that took the baton of the Western Christian civilization from Europe. The frustrated Islamic fundamentalists obviously turned their wrath on the 'infidel' Yankees. Their concern now is not only to undermine the American supremacy but also to keep Europe and the United States at constant loggerheads.

Time, for the United States is short. From the US standpoint, the lone super power must either finish off this 'evil' from the earth's surface or else its 'illusive' terrorist hunt would drain away its vital resources. It seems that the contemporary American foreign policy makers are well aware of this zero sum situation and it is in this backdrop that the American policies in the Gulf have to be judged. In simple terms, the US policy makers would like to either 'colonize' the Middle East for several decades as it had done in the case of Cuba, the Philippines and Japan or revert to a League-based (now the UN-based) Mandate of the strategically important Middle East or initiate a proxy rule in this region through establishment of puppet governments as they have done so many times in Latin America and in Shah's Iran. Going by that reasoning, a US led alliance campaign against Iran and Syria are very much on the cards. But one thing is certain: unlike its Cold War strategy, mere waiting or containment would not serve the purpose. Since the able-bodied and youthful groups in the Muslim world continue to far outstrip their Western counterparts and since the widespread proliferation of technology and weapons for destructive purposes can't be effectively curbed without a strong international consensus, each passing day plants an additional 'mine' in America's way. More importantly, moral support may shift from America to its adversaries if its terrorist engagement becomes a long-drawn affair.

The United States has got one of the two options in this regard: either forge a strong international anti-terrorist alliance in carrying out the job of destroying terrorist hide-outs and bases or delegate much of its responsibility in fighting terrorism to individual nations and helping the latter with all sorts of help. Such a decentralized approach on America's part has two advantages. First, it would remove the United States from the 'frontline' so that it ceases to be the cynosure of the neighboring eyes, that is, a common target. Secondly, such a 'problem' transfer from the American point of view would give it more respite.

Terrorism has already become a global phenomenon and there is hardly any nation that is not touched by it. The United States enjoys the advantage of its geographic 'protection' compared to any other state. If, as a result of above policies, individual nations can do away with terrorism, which has got far greater chance on a regional level, it is well and good. Conversely, if the anti-terrorist campaigns on a regional basis become protracted it is once again an advantage for the United States. That would simply make these nations mentally and morally far more committed to the United States than now. This would also alienate the terrorist groups further from the common people everywhere because in most cases of regional engagement, it would remain confined within the people belonging either to the same culture or the collateral non-Western cultures. Most terrorist activities and organizations met with this fate, over time.

One thing must be remembered: while anti-Americanism happens to be the watchword of the terrorists, much of it is due to the 'super power' overstretch. International terrorism these days rather feeds and thrives on anti-American sentiments and tirades. It is simply because the United States happens to be a global power that it attracts public attention, good or bad, everywhere. Joseph Stiglitz, Nobel laureate in economics correctly says, " Because we are the strongest country in the world, others look to us to falter. Our hubris fed their hostility." That means the United States has always got some extra space of maneuver if it decides to act from behind the scene.

The theory of domination addresses the contemporary problem of international terrorism, more thoroughly. The above-mentioned strategy of decentralization would benefit the United States in an important way. As the United States shifts its policies from direct confrontation to indirect ways of getting things done by other 'affected' nations with greater regional and territorial stakes than the United States, the latter reduces its own domination instinct.

The only point of consideration is whether such a 'minimum' withdrawal on America's part would embolden the terrorists and other nations to further marginalize the United States and whether this would disrupt international trade, reverse the trend of growing interdependence amongst nations, and derail the process of globalization. The first concern is imaginary because, no other country would like to enjoy the kiss of the terrorists. There is simply no love lost between these two entities. As for trade and globalization, this has become a global concern only. Today, most nations crave to have their parts in this process of commercial integration. Today, civilizations are far more interactive and interconnected; common masses are far more conscious of the gains of peace and prosperity contingent on globalization; and there are world bodies in the shape of the United Nations and the WTO that can address political and trade injustices. Most importantly, contemporary world is so interconnected that other nations would rush in to help any nation in trouble to keep its trade doors open.

Conversely, if any set of policies prove to be a persistent burden on a country, it is wise to change or modify it. If the United States finds itself in some trouble through its active intervention in many conflict prone regions, it may need to reduce those engagements, at least to some extent, in order to avert a far more catastrophic situation in which it loses its total credibility in the eyes of other nations through arrogance. This temporary and selective retreat is a tactical one and does not mean the American disengagement from the world affairs.

But the all-important question is one of the second line of defense. The United States must first ensure its full national security as it is now doing through its missile defense program despite the absence of threat from any foreign power. Secondly, it must ensure free and uninterrupted flow of its trade, the live wire of the American system. This may require occasional sending of the American fleet even to other regions to guarantee 'freedom of trade' notwithstanding the existence of international agreements and rules. In that case, the United States would be acting on a purpose and that will be its main moral forte. The next step is to build and protect institutions and regimes that perpetuate trade, like the spread of democracy, rule of law, transparency, and ways of punishing those who disrupt these processes. The United States has been doing all these jobs in the post Cold War period. Where the United States goes wrong is in overstepping certain limits: that 'zone of uncertainty' separating forces of disruptions from those of the civilized societies. The United States ought to make every effort to isolate terrorists from these errant states.

The theory of domination helps to solve this problem. Although commonly agreed rules go some way towards solving some problems, they can't replace the importance of the force component. For an international order to prevail it needs a leader, say, the United States, and a leader, in turn, requires force to ensure that order. This is best done when that leader has firm support of an important section, in this case Europe and some other allies. That too, would prove inadequate if the United States, in the meantime, fails to weaken the terrorists through, of course, its hard power. That is what I meant when I stated above that the United States must hurry up things in its 'terrorist' angle.

Like any other phenomenon, terrorism has got its own duration and it can't be eradicated overnight. For that, it must ensure that it does not fall into the trap of the terrorists by getting alienated from its allies. Rather it should place a trap for them by a temporary and selective reduction of some of its 'unimportant' global engagements. This would also allow new contradictions to develop within the terrorist ranks (because the terrorists would lose an important motivation to justify their activities) that it can exploit later. Moreover, purposeful waiting has got its rewards. One must not lose sight of the fact that many a terrorist network vanished overnight once their leaders disappeared from the scene.

Regular and organized internationalization of terrorism took place, mainly, after the end of the Cold War. There are several reasons for this development. First, the collapse of a bipolar world order created uncertainties about the future of a viable international order. Secondly, globalization already in vogue for almost a decade or so before the end of the Cold War, gained momentum only after the collapse of the Soviet empire. Space or the sphere of influence increased exponentially for the sole 'liberal capitalist' super power as it did for the terrorist organizations and the rogue states, as well. These two conditions, that is, the breakup of the Soviet empire and the Soviet Union and globalization helped these rogue states and terrorist groups to acquire nuclear technology, materials, and expertise from the erstwhile Soviet republics and its East European satellites.

Since the Al Queda and other Muslim fundamentalist organizations have taken upon themselves their sacred job to restore the Caliphate lost some eight decades ago and the sole responsibility to destroy the global infidel, the United States, more and more followers of Islam, who had been initially apathetic to the call for "Jihad",are swelling the ranks of these organizations. The American determination to fight the terrorists and destroy their networks have further steeled the determination of the ever growing young recruits. In the same report on global terrorism referred above, it is said that the nature of terrorism is shifting towards "global insurgency". In the backdrop of this rapid globalization of fundamentalist and terrorist activities, it would be a folly on the part on the United States not to decentralize the job of combating terrorism, as I have written a few lines earlier. Only then would the peace loving people all over the world be convinced thoroughly of the perils of international terrorism.

"Things won't be the same again" was how the US President reacted after 9/11. This statement was sufficient to convey not only a qualitative change in the US perception towards terrorism after the incident, but also the American resolve to fight terrorism to the finish to ensure safe and peaceful living conditions for everybody on earth. Mr. Bush quipped in his speech following the September 11 incident, "How will we fight and win this war? We will direct every resource at our command—every means of diplomacy, every tool of intelligence, every instrument of law enforcement, every financial influence, and every necessary weapon of war—to the disruption and to the defeat of the global terror network." Colin Powell in the preface to the same report remarked:

"In this global campaign against terrorism, no country has the luxury of remaining on the sidelines. There are no sidelines. Terrorists respect no limits, geographic or moral. The frontlines are everywhere and the stakes are high. Terrorism not only kills people. It also threatens democratic institutions, undermines economies, and destabilizes regions"

The US anti-terrorist policies have yielded some success so far. However, eradicating terrorism and chastising the rogue states can hardly be a one-nation affair. Proliferation of weapons of mass destruction happens to be a direct offshoot of huge arms sales by various countries of the capitalist West, not to speak of other countries like Russia and China and the breakaway republics of the former the Soviet Union (FSU). As of today, there is little congruity amongst nuclear powers in formulating an effective policy for limiting and banning of such sales. Ironically, the United States, on its part, happens to be the largest supplier of arms and training facilities even in the post Cold War era. The pressure of arms business lobby has always been great in the history of twentieth century America. Since 1992, well over $142 billion dollars worth of arms have been exported by the United States to various parts of the world, most often to conflict areas and to non-democratic regimes. As per the Fast Facts estimates, "in the period from 1998-2001, over 68% of world arms deliveries were sold to or given to developing nations, where lingering conflicts or societal violence can scare away potential investors." The US share in the global arms exports rose from 35% in 1990 to 50.4% in 2002.

Another overriding concern for the United States and the European countries is to ensure the supply of oil and natural gas so that they don't fall either into the hands of the rogue states or the terrorist groups. Now-a-days, even a handful of terrorist fellows can disrupt or even cut off this vital source of energy – the bedrock of modern civilization – by simply bombing or laying mines all along the pipe lines or blackmailing with WMDS. After all, terrorists need the money whether from the oil barons or from other sources. According to the same source, out of 346 terrorist attacks in 2001, 178 of the attacks were bombings against a multinational oil pipeline in Colombia—constituting 51 percent of the year's total number of attacks. In the year 2000, there were 152 pipeline bombings in Colombia, which accounted for 40 percent of the total number of attacks the same year. By the by, In July, 2007 the US intelligence uncovered a plot to blow off the oil supply line leading to the JFK air port.

While conventional attacks can be identified and crushed through direct wars, it is very difficult to fight a stateless enemy having no accountability to common masses except creating confusions in their minds. Now-a-days, terrorists don't need fleet or organized armies to attack the heartland even of a super power, thanks to globalization. Nor a retaliatory attack can act as deterrence against these handful and extremely 'mobile' die-hards. The US efforts to cut off their 'oxygen', that is, money supplies by freezing assets and bank accounts in various countries with a view to marginalizing and corralling them within their 'pockets' have yielded good results so far. But would the ever-changing international political situation allow America that much time before another rival power center makes its appearance felt?

Secondly, if such proliferation of lethal weapons, referred above, can't be contained, 'because private arms dealers have tremendous clout in the Pentagon, Congress, and the White House', the United States must make sure that the rogue, errant, and autocratic states don't acquire them without the American knowledge, as this may prove dangerous for the security of the US and its allies. It was recently that under pressure from the giant US arms dealer,

Lockheed Martin, the Bush administration had agreed to resume supplies of quite a large number of F-16s to both Pakistan and India. The same lure for money by the US companies like the Westinghouse led Washington to sign a multi-billion-dollar deal with Iran under the pretext of building its future energy reserves. It had come to light only recently from a declassified document (thanks to a Washington Post revelation) that the Ford administration in the 1970s, under intense lobbying from the interested groups, strove to make a $6-7 billion deal with Iran to facilitate plutonium reprocessing in that country. However, President Ford reversed this decision after eighteen months as he did not allow 'economic interests' to get the better of the 'non proliferation' issue.

The essence of the American response to terrorism can be summed up as a combination of homeopathy and allopathy: surgical and medicinal applications: using force, like administering the bitter pill, to kill the germs or to operate away the gangrenes on the one hand, while using its 'ideology' and 'carrots' to cure that evil from its root through the use of soft power. The crux is to determine which one is more effective, force or ideal, stick or the carrot? Since force is always a short-term phenomenon, it would be necessary to anoint the wounds through carrots for winning the hearts and minds of the aggrieved fellows. The problem is that the United States is not sure of the proper mix of force and values in the new millennium. Whenever the American casualties, whether in men or materials, rise abroad, the US attitude toughens and it is driven to act unilaterally. Whenever, the United States acts unilaterally, a strong anti-American sentiment develops within the ranks of its friends and foes alike. Conversely, whenever, the United States relents, the terrorist groups tend to strike at the American targets or those of its allies. Terrorism is thus at the heart of another principal debate whether the United States would act unilaterally or multilaterally.

Importantly, one way of explaining the recent spurt in terrorist activities against the Western powers is the lack of a non-Western 'secular' power to effectively counter the West. During the Cold War it was one Eurasian superpower, the Soviet Union that had held the international order together along with the other super power, the United States. Another important explanation for the spurt in recent terrorist activities on a global scale is the absence of the balance of power politics. Let me explain this briefly below.

Terrorism on an international scale did not happen even during the era of interdependence prior to the First World War. While it is true that revolutions in Information and Technology spearheaded by the computers and the Internet might have helped tremendously in lending a transnational dimension to terrorism, that does not fully explain the spread of global terrorism after the end of the Cold War. One may also point to the unbridled and even rampant illegal spread of the arms market and easy availability of finance as possible causes for the spread of terrorism on a global scale. That too, may not be the primary cause to explain the terrorist phenomena. It has always been found that great power or the balance of power politics, mostly, absorbs ethno-religious and even fundamentalist grievances. Two examples come to mind among numerous ones. The 1956 Suez crisis, when the United States took the side of the Arab countries vis-à-vis Israel. If one takes the oil factor as motivating America to do so, it revealed a balance of power politics in that the US wanted to deny great powers like the USSR, Britain, and France, any significant strategic and economic leeway in the Middle East, then. Many a times the super powers went to the brink over the Arab-Israeli issues. Even during the first Great War, the battle lines were drawn on ethno-religious lines. History repeated, when a more or less similar situation again led the great European powers to resort to the same ethno-religious lines in their support of the contending parties during the Balkan crisis in the 1990s. That way, the rise of terrorism can be largely, attributed to the end of the balance of power politics.

The Onion Riddle

The US foreign policies from its early days can be well explained by the well-known 'onion' riddle. Since its independence, every American gain in international politics occurred at the expense of the European powers. With the liquidation of the European monarchic system, one major bulwark against the forces of anarchy vanished exposing the next or the second layer of the 'onion'. Since independence, the United States, consciously or not, had been engaged in peeling off the 'pungent' layers of the earlier international political systems in the hope that only republican America can best arrive at that 'elusive' center or discover the hidden and 'golden' seed of international politics or even the 'secret of history and civilization? This 'peeling off' process goes on as the United States pursues its new Manifest Destiny on a global scale in the new millennium.

Domestic and foreign policies of nations, these days have developed a tendency towards responding more and more to the next or the second layer (beneath that of the political layer), that is, cultural factors. The United States, on the other hand, sought to address the issue of culture in terms of superiority of American political values and through spreading of the ideals of free trade and liberal capitalism on a global scale. The American effort had so far been to go on filling up those traditional 'nationalist' layers with its liberal democratic cover.

The United States wants to wrap that 'second inner layer' in a neo-liberal and neo-colonial fold by creating and sustaining a 'trade' empire based on the American capitalism. The neo-liberal perception is that reliance on internationally agreed regimes, viz. the rule of law, democracy, liberal trade, and transparency would create congenial conditions in various countries so that people in these countries would be used to greater interdependence and, eventually, abandon their schizophrenic traditional ideals and values. It is this effort to virtually transpose the American ideals and cultures on others that poses serious problems for the execution of an appropriate foreign policy suited to the new millennium.

Whenever, the United States decided to go it alone in managing world affairs even to the extent of defying its allies, the latter perceived some secret designs in the American foreign policies. That means, as the United States gets busy with scratching the next layer of the onion, (because political 'expansionism' invariably precedes cultural domination) it exuded more pungency, thereby, blurring the American vision to arrive at that illusive center. The American foreign policy think tanks believe that it would be better if the United States remains satisfied with the opening layer only and desist from influencing the cultures of other regions by not scratching the next layer. Thus one important lesson from the onion riddle is that constant peeling off would only fill up the international political ambience with the smell and misty vapor of extreme pungency while the gains will be zero in that culture forms the soul of every other nation. It may be possible to do so but at the expense of the nation-states, themselves. The United States, rather, should focus on the outermost 'political' layer of the onion, that is, explore every other possibilities of holding its lead over other major powers in view of the fact that it is these latter powers that make or break an international order. Let the second layer or the deeper layers remain largely undisturbed. One can't just separate the nuclei from the encircling electrons without splitting the atom.

More specifically, America hopes to attain something for which there is no realistic or historical precedence. It Is one thing to focus attention on great power politics that prevailed prior to the end of the Cold War. It is another thing to proceed further in order to intrude into the cultural domain of other countries in order to impose American values. The bottom line is that habits, cultures or the age-old customs of other countries have crystallized sufficiently to form a sort of 'super ego' for every country. To do away or deny that ego is to deny the existence of human beings since ego can be refined but not replaced. Since such ego is formed over centuries of habitual and repetitive practices, the people in any historical epoch have no power to change it altogether because it was already formed much before they themselves came into being. How can a person transcend era and his life span? The most that can be done is to refine such ego and hence the domination spirit only to a small extent.

Likewise, another extremely important area that lies outside the American control is the American expectation that peace would reign everywhere through adoption of the American ways. As discussed in the above paragraph, war, violence, and anarchy far antedated international politics. That means, the United States have only to accept this objective situation because it was not responsible for the prevalence of such a state of Hobbesian anarchy. To deny one's social milieu is as impossible as denying one's consanguinity

The Onion riddle has got one important lesson for powerful nations: do not go in for absolute answers to problems but take a rather relative, detached, superficial and even 'patch-repairing' approach to any problem or crisis. Leave it to heal for itself once that temporary repair has been done. Probing further deep would get a nation nowhere. In other words, reduce the 'domination' instinct as and when necessary, whenever a certain threshold is crossed but not the domination instinct per se. Instead, it is wise to regulate domination instincts. This may require complex diplomatic maneuvering but that is what adds spice to the prevailing international order. For example, the post Cold War situation reveals a peculiar 'chameleon' syndrome in contrast to the just bygone era. The United States is left wondering about the true nature and interests of its potential rivals, Europe, Russia, China, and Japan as they enter the new millennium in a very cautious manner.

Europe

The United States is doubtful and unsure of the role of Europe in the post Cold War era. This Europe is different from what the Americans had known it prior to 1945. Intense bipolar rivalry of the Cold War decades and its spread elsewhere left little scope and time for the United States to understand the real import of the political transformations that the post war Europe underwent, during the post war decades. The United States wanted a united Europe to counter the growing Soviet menace in the post war period and perhaps to find a way to revert back to its 'proxy' role, mentioned earlier. While the first objective was fulfilled with the victory over its Cold War rival, the second proposition, that is reverting to its 'proxy' role and of being the country of the last resort to restore order and freedom on a global scale receded into the background, in part due to the post Cold War realities described above and in part due to 'smell of the empire'. Yet the United States can't take Europe for granted.

Europe has got nationality, history, and what not! Europe is situated in an ideally geographic position that gave it easy access to both the New World and the ancient lands of the Orient. Its history is written in letters of blood. It formed a part of the cradle of civilizations that emerged in the Mediterranean, long ago. Hostile and powerful neighbors surround each European country and its continental borders. It has stood on the edge of the Persian, the Arabic, and the Turkish invasions. The barbaric invasions of the Gauls, the Vandals and the Visigoths and the nightmarish memories of the Vikings are still vivid in the European minds. The Romans, The bourbons, the Teutonic Knights or the Habsburgs, the Spanish and the Austrian, marauded the length and breadth of

Europe and established the fact that brute force happened to be the only reality in Europe.

In contrast to America, Europe developed a second nature to respond to and respect heroism, conquest, and endurance as described in their various myths and folk tales. European politics was defined by dynasty and monarchy over the centuries. In the United States, the family politics of the Habsburgs are unthinkable. Compared to the millennia old monarchic history of Europe, the US republicanism is just centuries old. Compared to about half a millennium of imperialist-colonial international relations, the bipolar world order or even the multipolarity of the early twentieth century was barely half-a-centuries old. It is in this backdrop that one has to view Europe's perceptions about contemporary international politics.

Modern European culture is a mixture of Greaco-Roman and Arabic cultures. While Renaissance, Reformation, and Enlightenment, all had tremendously influenced the European culture, monarchy remained the kingpin of the European polity. Aristocracy and hierarchy happened to be the chief features of the various European countries, till 1945. Historically, the US-Europe relationships have never been based on equal terms. Relationship between the United States and Europe is still evolving, as both these continents are left guessing about each other's goals, interests, and priorities.

It is only after the end of the Cold War that we see two powerful blocks of nations, the EU and North America, seem to be working on an almost equal footing, for the first time in history. The new millennium promises a far more competitive US-European relationship. This change has been brought about by several developments. First, a fundamental change has occurred in the European outlook as its monarchic and colonial structure fell off. This means that one of the principal charges leveled by the American forefathers in the past that the European nations were decadent, worthless and 'constantly brandishing their weapons' at each other is no longer valid. Secondly, since 1945, these erstwhile European powers have come to live together under the American arbitration and protection and engaged in harnessing Europe's resources jointly instead of wasting colossal amounts in wars. The beggar-thy-neighbor approach of individual European powers prior to WWII has given way to cooperation and mutual helpfulness.

Thirdly, as referred above, America rose to position of world leadership because of Europe. Europe would like to recover its past glories because of its history and geography: history, because, apart from its rich heritage and pedigree, Europe had built the American civilization as another wing of the Western Civilization; and geography, because the former is situated in a central position between the Orient and the New World. It is Europe and not the North American continent that is ideally placed to carry out its historical missions.

Even the Sun happens to be at the center of the universe. If this happens to be the case in nature, how much it would be true about human and international affairs? On top of it, Europe has moral justification in wresting that initiative of world leadership from America.

It was to Europe's credit that it has succeeded at last in drawing the 'reluctant sheriff' into managing European and world affairs after 1945. The old balance of power politics in the first half of the last century proved incapable of providing a viable international order. The addition of a new player in the shape of the United States injected vitality and vibrancy to international politics. This has the additional advantage of further strengthening and insulating the Western Civilization from 'barbaric' Oriental attacks. Its geographic importance is significant, too. Add Europe and North America (and perhaps, the entire Western Hemisphere) in a single Western Civilizational block and one will find a reasonable territorial and demographic parity with other civilizations taken together.

The crux is to forge and ensure a sort of permanent unity within this civilizational block. If past is any guide, this can happen only when there is a 'common' non-Western target that may threaten the Western Civilization. The Soviet Union served as that common glue during the Cold War when unity of the trans-Atlantic partners was assured. In the post Cold War decade; now, terrorism is being projected as a real menace not only for the Western Civilization but also for mankind as a whole. Prior to 1945, international order was dictated by colonialism. The post Cold War global order is dominated by the liberal capitalist democratic system of the same Western Civilization.

Europe, after over four decades of Atlanticism is out to reassert its identity, gradually though, by marginalizing the United States in world politics and by proceeding along the lines of least resistance instead of confronting it directly. It does so by entering into various agreements, economic and political, with other European nations through enlargement of the EU on the one hand and by interacting with its erstwhile colonies, on the other. The EU had sent a 'conciliation' team to find possible outlets for ensuring peace in a most volatile region in the world, the Korean peninsula, at a time when the United States was seriously contemplating a military action against that country. French and German disagreements with the United States over Iraq's possession of weapons of mass destruction and over the likely action to be taken against it also proved that the perceptions of the two continents differ on many issues of global importance. In the recent Iranian crisis over the latter's nuclear programs, it is Europe that has taken upon itself the job of arbitration. The recent Iranian episode typifies the traditional European efforts at replacing the United States in playing the lead role in global affairs and an equally determined US effort to thwart the same.

But that is seeing one side of the coin. The other side promises cooperation and a grand design. European Commission President Romano Prodi highlighted this trans-Atlantic commonality in March 3, 2004 in the following lines:

"On both sides of the Atlantic, we share two aims: to build a peaceful and ordered society for our citizens, and to lay the foundations for stability and development in other regions of the world. We are driven by the same ideals and a shared awareness that a world which is more stable and more just is a condition for our societies' well being and security....

"What we want is to see liberty flourishing and peace and quality thriving. Both Europeans and the Americans must put all their efforts and all their energies into that."

A peculiar situation has arisen in the post Cold War international politics. While the United States happen to be the unquestioned world leader yet it feels bound to Europe as ever. While, it can't go it alone in international affairs bypassing Europe with which it still has the largest trade volume, it can hardly rely on Europe's judgments and policies that have brought about the latter's downfall on several occasions in the last century. The United States wants that Europe must fall in line with what America does. Cold war legacy still pervades the American perception as it struggles to formulate its foreign policies in the new millennium. Europe, too, is not free from its Cold War spell.

One offshoot of this 'dependence' is that European countries have become more peace oriented (at least for the time being) and less willing to go to war as Robert Kagan rightly stressed on his Power and Paradise. Europe has grown more cautious and less adventurous. Conversely, America's vicarious attitude has imbued that country (that is, the United States) with original European traits and vices. Prior to 1945, it was the United States that held Europe to be the main culprit for creating international instability. Now the situation is reversed. It is the United States that has become more jingoistic and is more eager to carry out aggressive foreign policies. Incidentally, the American history had never been free from interventionism, if we consider Latin America.

An undercurrent of traditional rivalry between these two continents is visible after the end of the Cold War: the race for global supremacy and 'leashing' of one by the other. In fact, such differences began to manifest within two decades after 1945 once Europe recovered from its wartime wreckages. That is why one of Gorbachev's close aides Georgiy Arbatov hinted at the Soviet withdrawal in 1987 when he remarked that the Soviet Union was doing a terrible thing by depriving the United States of an 'enemy'.

Europe is well poised to wrest back its global supremacy from the United States since its chief advantage lies in its centuries-old familiarity with the rest of the world. Two adages are extremely relevant in this connection: (1) public memory tends to be short. As a result, countries under European colonial domination and its new generations may not be so averse as to accept European leadership if they find the incumbent world leader too possessive; and (2) familiarity breeds contempt. Most countries, by now, may have seen the better part of America and they may be craving for something new. Europe has another additional advantage over the United States in this respect. Europe has proved vulnerable on many occasions and this has given the impression that the European hegemony won't either be prolonged or that it can be terminated, anyway. On the other hand, nobody is sure about the duration of the American hegemony. The very fact of its size, unity, and near absolute supremacy in economic and military matters might have added to that 'uncertainty'.

One of major trans-Atlantic differences center round European Union's defense initiative and move towards a Common Security and Foreign Policy, CSFP. The need for creation of a 'substantial', 'autonomous', and 'collaborative', military capability was felt by both Britain and France once the European inability was exposed in managing the Balkan imbroglio in the 1990s, especially, the Kosovo crisis in 1998. The result was the Saint Milo agreement between France and Britain towards erecting an 'European Pillar' in the transatlantic alliance. During the formative years of NATO, its European members foresaw the need for the integration of the defense sector as a long-term objective. An independent European security structure commensurate with a united Europe was supposed to 'lighten' much of the American responsibilities in carrying out the cold war. As the Cold War ended, Europe drew blood and increased the momentum of the process of European integration and moved towards a common European Security and Defense Policy (ESDP) via the 1992 Maastricht treaty, the 1997 Amsterdam treaty and subsequent agreements reached at Saint Milo and Helsinki.

Many in the United States remained skeptical about the EU decision to go ahead with the ESDP. Stanley R. Sloane observed that the American policy towards European defense had always been set within a broader American concept of its role in the world and in the way in which the allies related to the world. The American concern is that such autonomy might jeopardize NATO, result in duplication of NATO efforts and in discriminating between the EU-NATO and the non EU-NATO members. The US senators, and members of the Congress feel that given Europe's past efforts in this direction, the chance of success is remote since European integration is still incomplete and there is no guarantee that full integration would at all take place in future. They feel that the new EU initiative in matters of defense and security would rather inflict irreparable damage to NATO and to trans-Atlantic relations.

Notwithstanding the American concerns, Europe has taken its own course. No less responsible for this decision is the US assertive unilateralism, its occasional flagrant violations of international regimes and institutions, and its missile defense program. Europe feels that now is the time to revive and project its 'identity'. Europe seemed to be touching a raw nerve regarding the US perception that multilateral institutions are rather hindrances for a US based international order. The main difference between the EU and the US lies in their respective approaches towards envisioning a viable international order in the new millennium: unilateralism or multilateralism. In plain words, Europe wants to compel the United States to accept the reality of a multipolar world order. There is another logic for Europe's more activist role in global affairs in recent years.

As mentioned in the very beginning of the book, Europe had hoped to tie the Eagle within the European orbit. Europe gets concerned when the Eagle tries to soar higher. Obviously, Europe felt that there ought to be a quid pro quo arrangement: the United States would remain Europe-centric while Europe would leave its defense and security matters to the United States. Once that unwritten 'contract' is broken, Europe feels that if it has to overcome its 'dependence' on the United States, then it must go all out instead of in a half-hearted manner. Japan would also feel the same way, as it grows stronger, economically and militarily. This means, the US efforts at leashing its major allies within its security net may be a temporary affair. A time would soon arrive when it is not unlikely that its allies would go their own ways and the bonhomie of the Cold War days may vanish. A multipolar world order, sooner or later, appears to be a foregone conclusion.

Just as the United States after 1945 has shaped Europe's attitudes and interests, the latter have also shaped the American priorities. Four decades of Atlanticism might have eroded European identity, to some extent, but the post war Europe has also made its profound impact on the United States. For example, sensing Europe's rise and recovery, the United States sought to increase its trade volumes with the Pacific countries since the 1960s. The United States took a leaf out of European page by forming free trade zones in North and South America to prepare for the unforeseen possibility of getting marginalized in Europe. The reader may well recollect one of my important assumptions: *great powers always prepare in advance for the distant future. The United States is no exception. The drive towards creating regional blocks alongside globalization highlights the American concern about the rise of Europe.*

Two important considerations remain: how the US- EU relationship is going to evolve in the coming days and what will be future of the EU? Will the EU remain integrated or will it disintegrate or will it remain like a confederate type that would exert less influence on the national policies of its respective members? As I have discussed in the previous chapter, the chance of a federal Europe is remote. Joseph Nye observed that with the incorporation of 'Britain and some other Nordic countries' in 1970s in the European Community, such a move towards a federated Europe has receded. That chance has further receded with the increase in the EU membership in recent years to 27. Europe in the coming days has its hands full with domestic engagements.

Russia

Post Soviet Russia continues to occupy an important place in the American foreign policy considerations because of its vast size that stretches over eleven time zones and that, roughly, touches the regions bordering the Atlantic, the Pacific, the Mediterranean and the Persian Gulf. There is a saying that when a big tree falls its effects are felt widely. In an Israeli television interview a year ago, president Putin underlined the fact that Russia already happened to be a great state with 'major presence' in both the "Northern" and "Southern" tier countries, in Europe and in Asia**. According to the BBC News in 5 April, 2005, Putin had alluded to the fall of the Soviet empire as 'the greatest geopolitical catastrophe of the 20th century.'** Alexander Dugin in his leading work, Osnovi Geopolitiki: Geopolitichiskoye Budushiye Rossiyi (The Foundations of Geopolitics: The Geopolitical Future of Russia), reiterates these dormant and historical Russian aspirations in the following lines: "The creation of a Russia-dominated Eurasian space, stretching from the Levant to the Asia-Pacific." Dugin believes "Russian people are ethnically, culturally, psychologically, religiously and, above all, historically destined to recreate Russian greatness, which is not fulfilled today by ephemeral constructs like the CIS and the Russian Federation." For him, Russia "cannot exist outside of its essence as an empire, by its geographical situation, historical path and fate of the state."

'Mystical' Russia still holds the magic key to future international order. For example, if Russia gains a NATO membership, this would tilt the balance hugely in favor of the West in which other great or would-be powers like China, Japan, and India would be on the defensive. On the other hand, if the 'polar bear' gets its way in the EU, this might send the United States packing to the other side of the Atlantic. The United States and Europe would like to deal with a 'humiliated' superpower with caution and understanding to relive the 'concert of Europe' arrangements and to avoid the 'Versailles' blunders.

The accession of the Baltic states in the EU and NATO coupled with the strict European standards of code, democracy, and human rights observances may go some way towards assuaging minority Russian discontent in these countries, besides facilitating Russia's integration with the both these organs. However, all such advantages depend on some 'ifs' and 'buts': that the EU and NATO would continue to develop new institutions and goals and able to work towards common goal of security, democracy, rule of law, and other humanitarian tasks. But there are disadvantages, too. Russia may feel isolated and marginalized by the 'ice curtain' separating it from the Baltic States. For example, the issue of Russian access to its Kaliningrad remains an intriguing one since Russian access to Kaliningrad runs through the borders of Poland and Lithuania, the two countries that have joined the EU. For the time being, a transit agreement has been reached in a EU-Russia summit.

Likewise, the growing American influence in Central Asia as a sequel to the NATO enlargement in these areas may create security problems for Russia. The United States needed the help of Russia in tackling such issues as terrorism, drug-trafficking, poverty and hunger, the Afghan and the Persian Gulf imbroglio and still would need the Russian support on the Iranian and the non proliferation issues. Like in the 1970s, but in a reverse way, the United States would like to play its' Russia' card to contain China.

Yet too much 'coaxing' or conciliatory approach to Russia may foster a 'Munich' syndrome in the minds of the Russian leaders and may encourage them to stoke Russia's centuries-old nationalistic feelings that may lead it to dominate and 'annex' its neighborhood, yet again. One compelling need for the post Soviet Russia is to retrieve the Czarist gains in its neighborhood, in the Near East. That is why the United States has finally shaken up its the Cold War syndrome by declaring that it no longer considers Russia a major threat to the United States. The special status enjoyed by that country for about a decade after the formation of the new republic has since been withdrawn. This seemed a very pragmatic move by the United States because it would make no sense to attach undue importance to a country that had voluntarily accepted defeat in the Cold War. Indeed, the United States needed to shake off its Cold War syndrome as early as possible.

European concern about Russian expansionism may not be unfounded in the backdrop of recent moves on the part of Russia to coerce its various erstwhile republics like Georgia, Moldova, Azerbaijan, Uzbekistan, Ukraine, and Belarus. Russia has virtually served these republics a sort of a fait accompli that it is far better to have Russia as an ally and their 'guardian' than to face a hostile Russia. Russia has historically exerted tremendous economic clout in its neighborhood because of its ability to cater to the traditional production and consumption patterns in its neighborhood. Moreover, the presence of hundreds of thousands of ethnic Russians spread over its various other republics provides a great leverage for Russia to control the 'Near Abroad'. From the US point of view, Russian influence in Central Asia and the Caucasus may not make any difference in so far as its the Cold War tirade was principally against the unlawful Soviet annexation of the Baltic States and Eastern Europe. The United States would be glad to leave that matter to Europe, as this happens to be Europe's 'domestic' affair.

Russia can hardly afford to lose its Central Asian and Caucasian republics at a time of its reduced influence in the Baltic and the Balkans. There was significant change in Putin's attitude as Russia made some recovery in economic and political field during his presidency. On assuming power in 2000, Putin declared that Communism was a utopia and that there won't be any repetition of that past mistake. Within a space of five years, the same Russian president appealed to the nationalist sentiments of Russians by saying that defeat in the Cold War and the abdication of 'super power status had been a national disaster for the Russian people.

Western efforts at democratizing and modernizing post Soviet Russia floundered on the rock of corruption, crony capitalism, oil oligarchies, black markets, rampant speculative and criminal activities, and 'state capitalism' in which it is the erstwhile influential communist 'personnel' that are now running huge industrial combines in the 'guise' of privatization. Enlargement of NATO close to Russian borders and the American physical presence in Central Asia and the Caucasus, the 'loss of the Baltic' and the 'Balkans' are few of the mortifications that a vanquished Russia had to bear in the post Cold War years as the post Soviet Russia continued to 'cede' large amount of territories in the West. The United States tried to anoint the Russian 'wound' by awarding it a special role in NATO, a membership in the G8 group of countries, and a special role for its peacekeeping forces (Implementation Force) in the NATO led campaign in the Kosovan crisis.

One of the great achievements of the post Cold War US foreign policies was the successful conclusion of the transfer of strategic nuclear arsenals from Georgia, Belarus, Ukraine, and Kazakhstan to Russia. This process was initiated by the first Bush administration in 1991-92 and completed by the Clinton administration in 1996. While Senior Bush was concerned with a smooth transition to a new kind of world order out of the wreckages of the Cold War era, his administration was stingy in giving financial assistance to Russia. The logic was obvious. Since Russia was not humbled by war, the United States had not much room of maneuver in that country's internal affairs. The United States was thus loath to spend money over a country that caused so much drain on its resources during the past forty-five years and where the future 'returns' were extremely uncertain. Instead, Russia was asked to assume its past 'debt' and to democratize. On a post facto analysis of successive Russian policies this logic might not appear unfounded. No measure of the American assistance could deflect Russia from supplying nuclear technology and materials and other military hardware to Iran and Syria or to oppose the US in its 2003 Iraqi campaign. Russia takes a lead role to erect a sort of strategic alliance to counter the US global hegemony. Post Soviet Russia is untiring in its efforts to wean away Germany from the American fold.

Russia's time-to-time warm attitude to Germany hardly escapes the attention of the American foreign policy makers. The final days of the First World

War, the happenings in the early 1920s, and the 1939 Molotov-Ribbentrop treaty forged 'warm relations' between Germany and Russia as if they were built on 'blood'. Since the early 1950s through the 1960s and again in the 1970s, the Soviet Union had enticed Germany to settle the issue of German unification, bypassing the United States. Even during the crucial years of Glasnost and Perestroika, Soviet President Mikhail Gorbachev virtually gambled with the Soviet Union's future by playing the German card. Helmut Kohl staunchly held on to NATO alliance group much to the Soviet dismay. But Russia never lost heart. Even Vladimir Putin is now very keen to have close ties with Germany, which has always been crucial to Russia.

President Clinton thought otherwise. He found it worthwhile to keep Yeltsin floating by providing generous financial assistance to post Soviet Russia in the hope that a market-oriented democratic Russia integrated to the West would lose its traditional appetite to expand in its outskirts and in Europe. Within a decade of the collapse of that empire, the US victory over its Cold War rival rather seemed to be a 'loss'. The 2000 presidential election debate on 'who lost Russia' underlined the American failures in the Russian front. There was a growing realization in the White House that it would be a wild goose chase on the part of America to focus on Russia's internal developments with a view to shaping the latter's foreign policy priorities.

Yet the recent anti-American overtures by the Russian president Putin may very well require the US to have a double take. Of late, Russia, in contrast to Western norms of secularism and democracy, has become friendlier towards the monarchies of the Middle East and to Islamist authoritarianism in Iran. Putin did not mince matters in revealing his policies in various press conferences in Jordan and Qatar and in his interview to the Al Jazeera. Putin's Russia has shocked the West when Putin promised to sell 'peaceful' nuclear reactors to Saudi Arabia in addition to 150 T-90 Tanks. Russia is out to create a new geopolitical space by bringing the 'disgruntled' Middle East into the net of Russian arms market through such offers as sale of helicopters, building of Rocket propelled Grenade (RPG) factories and providing sophisticated anti-aircraft system. Russia has underwritten a substantial portion of huge debts that Syria owed to Russia through the former's purchase of arms in order to revive its good relations with that country. Russia has even offered to sell Syria its Strelet air defense system, much to the Israeli annoyance. Russia wants to flex its economic muscle through its energy resources like the natural gas by endorsing the idea of forming a gas cartel, the Gas Exporting Countries' Forum (GCEF) similar to the OPEC. Putin's Middle East overtures has earned him the King Faisal award from the Saudi chief,

In the post cold war ambience Russia thinks that the old balance of power politics alone can guarantee stability in the international system. No less insignificant is Russia's current efforts at revamping its military might through a projected investment to the tune of $159 billion. Russia has extended its arms market through big deals with China, India, and Venezuela, not to speak of the Middle East. Conversely, it is only in June, 2007 that Putin has asked for a change of the post Cold War economic structure at the behest of WTO. Already, many countries, including Russia and China have opted to keep their reserves in Euro instead of dollars. On a military level, Russia has threatened to pull out of the CFE and the INF treatises, the bulwark of the post cold war military balance. On a diplomatic angle, Putin grabbed the initiative by undermining the American efforts at democratization of the Middle East by pointing to the huge political gains made by the Hamas and Hezbollah in Palestine and Lebanon. The list of Russian grievances against the lone super power is endless. Importantly, the projected Russian foreign policy approaches in the new millennium not only vindicates my theory of domination but another important assumption in this book: to gain at America's expense by undermining its policies in most areas. For this, Russia won't mind being soft on various militant and dictatorial regimes.

If one has to sum up the Russian foreign policy approaches in the new century it is the continuation of its cold war policies: exploiting America's problems and helplessness arising out of its 'overstretch' that clearly exposes the limits of the American power potential and the latter's lack of legitimacy in justifying its global hegemonic role.

China

The US perception of China remained always incomplete because of distance and mystic nature of the Middle kingdom. This vision was further obscured as China gleefully hurled its red curtain before the Western eyes in 1949. Later on, despite the honeymoon of the days of the ping pong diplomacy, 'capitalist-turned' communist China ticked up the US suspicions by the Tien-En-Man's square mayhem at a time when communism as a political system was fast becoming effete in the whole of Eastern Europe. For a time, the United States was bemused and upset. How come it that the more enigmatic and the less 'friendly' Soviet Union could shake off its ideological 'complexes' but not the more close and 'knowable' China?

Chinese 'mysticism' lies in its Confucian and the Taoist culture. The Chinese people believe what their seers have taught them that one could travel thousand miles by single steps only. Kissinger most aptly surmised that while the United States seeks 'concrete solutions to 'specific problems', these are, for the Chinese but 'stages in a process' in a grand endeavor to arrive at the ultimate truth. The United States finds it extremely difficult to arrive at that illusive center of the Chinese 'onion' referred above, because of the working of the 'back to the future' syndrome in the Chinese case.

The Chinese mind has always interpreted reality from observations of the natural and the animal world. Both the martial arts and the Chinese 'astrology' testify to the above fact. For the common Chinese, it is the 'peeling' off of the successive layers that are more important even at the cost of arriving at that 'illusive' center or simply, the Tao. The Chinese mind acts on an inbuilt dynamics of caution and prudence formed over the millennia old 'grilling' under the 'superior' Confucian culture. China might have been the old grandfather of the ancient civilizations but it is a kid in the new century, marked by greater interdependence. Confucian teachings have struck deep root in the Chinese national psyche. While the American 'absolute' mind-set and its penchant to uncover the secret of an event or even a process may lead it to tear off successive layers of the onion, the Americans are flexible enough to call it a halt if they find that exercise a futile one. The Chinese, on the other hand, see the continuous uncovering or the understanding of the secret of nature a way and philosophy of life. Like the Greeks, the Chinaman is a great thinker unlike the Americans, who are, rather, men of action.

John Elster, who visited China in 1988 at the invitation of the Chinese Academy of Social Sciences, wondered if China could be transformed into a modern society:

> Chinese do not know what they are doing. First, the leaders do not know where they want to go. Even if the leaders knew where they wanted to go, they would not know how to get there. Economic theory has nothing to say about the transition from communism to capitalism, nor is there any precedent from which they can learn. The official metaphor for the reforms is 'feeling the stones with one's feet in crossing the river'.
>
> —*William Pfaff: 1989, p.218177*

The Chinese mind may not be so goal oriented but it likes to relish a kind of pride not so much in 'performance' as in the act of comprehending the secrets and truth about nature. A long period of centralized bureaucratic-administrative practice has led the average Chinese to defer to scholars and intellectuals and a 'disregard' for the business classes. Nearly four decades of 'aggressive' communist indoctrination has further increased the Chinese paranoia. It is only recently that some change could be discerned in the Chinese attitude towards leadership and outsiders as pointed out by a panel of three experts consisting of Bates Gill, Lu Ning, and Margaret Pearson in 'The Making of Chinese Foreign and Security Policy: Implications for the United States'

It is in this background that American efforts towards transforming the once 'sleeping' agrarian and nationalist 'dragon' into a vibrant capitalist 'giant' have to be viewed. Chinese leaders are more keen to see through the American 'design' to capture the vast Chinese markets knowing full well that this, too, happens to be a 'transitory' phase in the great cycle of eternity. While foreign capital and technology are needed to feed its teeming millions this may be just a means and a temporary means at that. China would rather opt again for its ancient role in the 'Middle Kingdom' to symbolize the Chinese cultural superiority even if it grows into an industrial giant.

Thus Mearsheimer's claim in his Tragedy of Great Power Politics may be, at best, partially true of China aspiring to be a regional hegemon but the 'tortoise' knows how to get back in its own shell when faced with uncertainties abroad. Even a militarily and economically strong China may prefer to remain isolated in a second Great Wall of 'protectionism' and 'defense' instead of engagement, competition, and prolonged military campaigns unless under foreign aggression or driven by 'lebensraum' or internal ecological catastrophe. Secondly, one has got to remember Chinese preference for patience in regaining Hong Kong from the British and in reclaiming Taiwan. Mao Tse Tung once told Kissinger that China could wait for another hundred years for Taiwan to merge into the mainland. It may be the Chinese goal to free the Western Pacific from the American influence but the promulgation of another Asian version of Monroe Doctrine would be anathema to the Chinese mind for both cultural and political reasons. China won't borrow philosophy from any US president because of its inherent belief in the superiority of its age-old Confucian culture. On the other hand, China would rather wait for, may be, another 'millennium' for its neighbors to accept Chinese ways rather than forcing it on them. Yet Meirsheimer's analysis highlights one important feature of the emerging international order: regional politics is going to be an important component of international politics in the coming decades.

This is not to describe Chinese simplicity. China did intervene in the Korean War, initially, but only when its borders were threatened. China never entered the Vietnam War despite apparent threats to its regional interests. This means that the Chinese leadership always acts on a matured and diplomatic principle. But how does one explain such Chinese 'simplicity' and 'Himalayan' patience when China fervently waited for a possible super power clash during the Cuban missile crisis or when Mao Tse Tung urged America to take a more direct action against the 'socialist-imperialist' USSR? The simple fact is that China wants no super power domination and bullying as it had enough of it in the nineteenth and the first half of the last century.

China is extremely sensitive to regional interests. China may have enough patience but it is equally determined to clinch the issue as Margaret Thatcher felt the hard way when Britain tried to make a last ditch and 'indirect' effort at keeping Hong Kong into its fold beyond 1997. China's time-to-time aggressive missile testing aimed at intimidating Taiwan is based on the logic that

Taiwan should not harbor its own independence from the mainland. On the other hand, China wants to reassure the Taiwanese people (to facilitate Taiwan's merging into the mainland China) by offering its markets to the Taiwanese business tycoons. The bottom line is that China may aspire to be a regional hegemon out of its security needs, but it would wait like an 'old fox' for conditions to be so conducive in crossing the water rather than taking extra steps in the 'unknown'. China's vigorous drive for the modernization of its defense sector and its increased defense expenditures coupled with its manpower potential lead others to view China with suspicion. Yet China is never cut out to play a global role. Perhaps Edward Said might be right in stressing that it is the underlying culture that guides the expansionist tendency of a great power and by that yardstick Chinese culture is inward looking.

Yet there is more to what meets the eye. China considers India as its potential regional rival and that is why it has tried to encircle India with some friendly overtures to India's neighbors, Pakistan, Bangladesh, and Iran. Not content with that and being suspicious of any secret Indo-US defense pact, like that of the 1971 Indo-Soviet treaty, China hopes to gain some territorial and hence geopolitical advantages through pre-emptive measures, viz., by its unlawful claim over chunks of the Indian territory in the North -East, in Arunachal Pradesh. The five principles of Buddha or the Panch Shila has no place before its national interest. China says it favors a multipolar international order in which there will be mutual cooperation and competition that would act as checks and balances towards maintaining international stability. China has opted for modernization of various sectors of its society, yet it is extremely conservative and suspicious of international regimes. For example, June Teufel Dreyer, in a February 2007, FPRI (Foreign Policy Research Institute) Newsletter (Vol. 12, No.5) China is extremely sensitive to any overtures made by Its neighbors towards either Dalai Lama of Tibet or Lee Teng hui of Taiwan. China is very critical of Japan developing or acquiring a Theatre Missile Defense system.

Nevertheless, one must not lose sight of the fact that the United States won't mind even to risk its survival if its vital interests are affected. The Cuban missile crisis or the massive US military buildup in the 1980s bear testimony to these facts. China knows this well. That is why it is so restrained against Taiwan. Conversely, any reduction of the US support for its allies in this region would put pay to the US vision of global domination that would rather embolden China. That is why the United States has to pacify both China and Taiwan just as it does in the case of India and Pakistan.

China wants to build its own economy through foreign capital, loans and investments and is biding time till its own day comes when it can dictate terms to the rest of the world. China is ready to dance with the wolf and when its day comes it hopes to tame these wolves. Some 300 out of top 500 transnational companies now invest in China. China has been an economic force in recent time and it Is likely to replace Japan In a few years. China's economic might became evident during the 1997 financial collapse in South-East Asia when it bailed out Asian tigers with requisite finance to tide over that crisis. More importantly, Chinese stocks in the financial markets of Japan and the United States are seen as assets to avert any financial calamity in these two countries. China has, of late been acting as a money lender to many countries of Africa and Latin America at a time when the World Bank has written off outstanding debts of these countries. Chinese exploitation of labor within and abroad have, of late, created widespread discontent within the ranks of the working classes in these countries. Corruption and crony capitalism has plagued the Chinese economy beyond measure.

From the above, it is clear that China lacks the capacity to maintain its magic 'economic' run in the long run and lacks the necessary traits to carry its 'good time' to such a height that would catapult it to the status of a super power. Given the deep distrust and the burgeoning economic growth of its neighbors, China has to perform another miracle in its diplomatic and economic maneuvering to become a regional hegemon, in the least. And remember, China is prudent enough to beat a retreat should the occasion demand. While China has not, so far, shown the kind of aggression and expansionism needed to transform itself into a global power, another Asian power has the past record of doing so.

Japan

Japan, prior to its forced opening to the West in 1853 by commodore Perry, largely remained closed within its islands. Its only contact had been with China that had influenced the Japanese culture from very early times. In the absence of external compulsions or wars that determine the military organization of a given state, Japan built its martial forces around frequent internecine and inter-island feudal wars. Japan developed a strong sense of nationalism and a unique culture by fending off foreign contacts as much as possible. Japanese culture thus became a matter of pride for its people. This explains why the humiliating defeat of the Second World War and the more humiliating American 'domination' of the Nippons drew out the 'paragon' of patience in the Japanese people to rather undergo the suffering of the consequence of 'voluntary' misdeeds that Japan committed during WWII, instead of trying so much to reform its polity and culture.

Decades of the American presence and influence in Japan hardly furthered the cause of the United States in creating a 'different' Japan. International situation after the end of the Cold War remained at the same stage where it stood prior to 1939, so far as East Asia is concerned. Japan has rather sought to pursue a more activist role in international politics by rearming its military and by its efforts towards staking claims in a chain of islands Dokdo/Takeshima held by South Korea and by holding the disputed islands of Senkaku/Diaoyu that has become the bone of contention between Japan, on the one hand and China and Taiwan, on the other. Its current defense expenditure is second or third next to that of the USA.

In foreign policy matters, Japan has become more assertive because of the presence of a powerful China in the region. Japan had declared that it wouldn't mind joining hands with the USA in the event of China invading Taiwan. Japanese overture to lend money to South East Asian nations in the 1997 financial crisis or Japan's policy of investing in the Chinese periphery 'ranging from Taiwan to Vietnam to Uzbekistan' is motivated by the Japanese concern to counter China's growing regional supremacy. In order to successfully contain China, Japan needs allies on either side of the Pacific. While Japan has a common interest with the United States in thwarting a Chinese hegemonic design in Asia and the Pacific, Japan has its problems, too.

First, its strong sense of nationalism won't permit it to play into the American hands. Secondly, much of America's claim of building a post war Japan through a 'benevolent and exemplary administration' in the immediate post war years seem to have gone awry as Japan has started to reveal its nationalistic sentiments in recent years. Moreover, the legacy of the WWII days is fast fading as the new generations in Japan take charge of their country's affairs. Japan, in the post Cold War era is smelling its chance of revival not only as regional hegemon with its 126 million population and an economy generating well over 500 trillion yen a year, but also as a global power in today's interdependent world. Already Japan's contribution to the UN peacekeeping mission in Cambodia, Rwanda, and Mozambique or its sharing of financial burdens in the 1992 Gulf War demonstrates the Japanese perception of an independent foreign policy. The removal of the Soviet threat and the weakening of Russia in economic and military terms might embolden Japan to distance itself from the protective security umbrella offered by the US-Japan treaties. Japan's armed forces are one of the best in the world and it would be naïve to think that 'martial' Japan would forego the option of developing nuclear bombs, in future.

The stark fact is that Japan felt humiliated and subjugated under the hoof of the American occupation and having to remain satisfied with a foreign policy package 'made in Washington' in the immediate post war decades. On top of everything, remains the deep scar of the Hiroshima and Nagasaki that has forever destroyed any sort of 'sentimental' attachment between the two nations. Burst of suppressed nationalism could be discerned in the more restrained but determined Japanese efforts at excelling the United States in the only field it was allowed to develop, its economy. As Japan overtook the United States in this sector in the 1980s, Japan voiced the view that America happened to be its dependency. Japan's traditional clash of interest with the United States over the Far East and the Pacific is too well known. Obviously, Japan counts on two possibilities: to match the United States militarily or getting the United States to agree to a power sharing arrangement in the region by virtue of its being America's ally.

Nationalist Japan would hardly like to remain permanently dependent on the United States and allow its fate to fluctuate with the American fortune. Japan would rather like to deal with China on its own in the Pacific because it shares many commonality with the Sinic culture. Besides, Japan's overriding regional concern may lead it to stay away from a US-centric design. On the other hand, Japan may have to care more for support from South Korea in containing China as both the latter countries share the same sentiments about Japanese atrocities committed during the first half of the twentieth century. None of them are prepared to see Japan in its pre-WWII role. Japan has moreover to take the North Korean factor into account where the role of the United States may prove to be crucial. Australia still remembers Japanese occupation of islands bordering the continent when the former's security was threatened during WWII. This means Japan would have to be more dependent on Australia and the United States. Already Australia and the United States have supported the Japanese membership in the UN Security Council that had been opposed both by South Korea and China.

What does all these mean for the American foreign policies? Who happens to be its ally in the Pacific, barring Oceania? None, in the true sense of the term. Yet there is a huge possibility of playing the role of a balancer in the region in view of the prevalence of deep distrust and animosity between the various neighboring countries. The entire geopolitical landscape of the Pacific and the Far East has changed not so much by the Cold War but by the post Cold War imperatives. Two factors are responsible for this change in the Pacific situation: the American presence and growing Chinese influence. Modern Japan has never faced a strong China since the Meiji period. Like in the case of trans-Atlantic powers in which a strong and unified Europe faces an equally formidable United States, it is also for the first time in the Pacific that two great regional powers, Japan and China, are so keen to project their regional hegemonies, simultaneously.

Conclusion

The post Cold War American foreign policies have two major objectives: first, to complete the unfinished job of the Cold War – wiping out the weeds of communism (here, too, there is difference in the US perceptions with those of its other major allies, barring Britain) from the face of earth in any of their manifestations, and secondly, in a complete reversal of its pre WWI isolationist policies, to take steps that would eliminate any possibility of the US marginalization and a possible 'rollback' into its own hemisphere. As for the first, the United States won't henceforth show any sympathy towards rogue states or terrorist groups and individuals or their sponsors. The United States would do everything at its command to prevent the proliferation of nuclear and other Weapons of Mass Destruction (WMD) on the part of these 'barbarians' who seek to add new dimension to the poor man's war – the guerrilla warfare – a stark reminder of the legacies of communism – and more importantly to deter them from becoming a source of perennial threat to free trade and liberal capitalism.

Thus the primary task before the policy-makers in Washington have been to ensure that the ghost of communism doesn't arise out of that ash heaps of the Cold War days in any of its chaotic or distant forms. Consequently, the United States and its European allies are on their jobs to further precipitate the dismemberment of Russia, a traditional despoiler of the European democratic ideals, through some systematic, cool, and deliberate policies in the Caucasus, in Central Asia and in the Baltic. These policies range from efforts at the creation of free trade zones in the Russian peripheries, enlargement of NATO close to the Russian border, Eastward 'expansion' of the EU and the promotion of the Northern Defense Initiative (NDI). The inclusion of Hungary, Poland, and the Czech Republic's both in the NATO and the EU in the 1990s had an important geopolitical bearing: to fill in the void created in Central Europe since the last century by the elimination of the Austro-Hungarian, the Hohenzollern and the Romanov empires, the Third Reich and lastly, the Soviet Empire, on the one hand, and to cage the 'polar bear' besides containing Germany, on the other. All these jobs are being carried out at the American behest, sometimes unilaterally and sometimes in league with Europe.

The unfinished job of the Cold War has another dimension: to consolidate the victory of the Anglo-Saxon liberal capitalist democratic ideals on a global scale by seizing the hitherto closed second and third world markets and creating an economic model based on 'American' capitalism. Major post Cold War American foreign policies are supposed to work on several planes at the same time towards a common objective. That objective is derived historically from the Declaration and the American Constitution. In that sense, the post Cold War American foreign policies can be viewed as further steps towards completing the unfinished job of the Declaration, at the same time. No Doubt, a grand design is at work: the consolidation and establishment of the superiority of the Western Civilization, in general, and of the Anglo-Saxons, in particular. The blue-print for a future international order was laid down in the Atlantic Charter in 1943.

Even after a decade and a half into the new millennium, the post Cold War world lacks an order that characterized its precursor. The sole super power in charge of contemporary world affairs either lacks a grand vision or a coherent strategy. For many American scholars, the US foreign policies in the post Cold War period remained, inconsistent, 'incremental' 'ad hoc', 'patchwork' and more focused on crisis management on a global scale. The American foreign policies in the post Cold War era (after 9/11) is yet to take a definite strategic shape based on an appropriate rational. But these academicians and intellectuals fail to appreciate the true import of the post Cold War situation. The fact is that there is a grand design but that design is less discernible to the common eye since it is in the process of making. That design is the gradual consolidation of the Cold War gains but with 'restraint' because the American Cold War victory was largely of the Soviet making. The 'Versailles' syndrome still haunts the United States to a greater degree now that the post Cold War situation is extremely complex and is filled with the intoxicating vapor of anti-Americanism – a legacy of the Cold War era.

The post Cold War American foreign policies are no less ingenious than the previous eras but they require more patience, tact, diplomacy, restraint, co-operation, and a judicious use of force to take shape. The American task has been twofold: to consolidate the gains of liberal democratic political objectives and to extract the maximum out of recent wave of globalization on which depends the future of its supremacy. The grand strategy behind these two policies would be clearer in the coming decades with the consummation of every incremental gain in the way. Like many other crucial periods in the American history, its post Cold War policies are no less important for the American 'survival' and security. The fact is that the post Cold War United States has a viable foreign policy whose effects would dependent on a successful conduct of a series of 'sub' or 'branch' policies.

The Eagle is in the middle of its journey, away from its root and hoping to reach its destination. In the middle of a journey one must remain patient and confident like the development of a 'film' or the growth of a seed. But the process goes on silently and inexorably towards finality. Andrew J. Bacevich found a definite 'purpose' in the American post Cold War policies. " That purpose is to preserve and, where both feasible and conducive to the US interests, to expand an American imperium. Central to this strategy is a commitment to global openness-removing barriers that inhibit movement of goods, capital, ideas, and people. Its ultimate objective is the creation of an open and integrated international order based on principles of democratic capitalism, with the United States as the ultimate guarantor of order and enforcer of norms." (Bacevich, p.3)

Joseph Nye thinks that the United States has diverse power capabilities to play the role of a balancer in regional politics on a global scale. This fits well into my suggestions that the United States in the new millennium would have to adopt an extremely flexible and open-ended strategy in which the United States remains the primus inter pares. The United States must develop into a skillful trapeze player doing all the tight rope walking yet with an eye to its goals. If others prefer to be friendly to the United States everything is fine but if they prefer the US enmity then they would have to bear the 'high-voltage' shock of the American power. This syndrome of the American 'omnipresence' may work to the US advantage but it has its pitfalls. The United States has to consolidate its world leadership more thoroughly and in a short period because of two reasons: any extra time would help its nearest rivals to regroup themselves and more importantly, the surprise and charm associated with 'globalization-Americanization' might fade over time.

References and readings

George H. Bush, Inaugural Address, Friday, January 20, 1989, http://www.bartleby.com

Robert M. Entman, Projections of Power, Framing News, Public Opinion, and the US Foreign Policy, The University of Chicago Press, Chicago, London, 2004.

John Gerrard Ruggie, Winning the Peace, America and World Order in the New Era A Twentieth Century Fund Book, NY, 1998, Columbia University Press.

Richard N. Rosecrance, The Rise of the Trading State, NY: Basic Books, 1986.

Economic Instability and Military Strength: The Paradoxes of the 1950 Rearmament Decision, Fred Block in the American Foreign Policy, theoretical Essays, 4th Ed., G. John Ikenbery, Longman.

Anthony Giddens, Runaway World, Routledge, NY, 2003.

NICD-Mapping the Global Future:Contradictions of Globalizatin,www.cia.gov/nic/NIC

Andrew J. Bacevichthe American Empire, The Realities and Consequences of the US Diplomacy, Harvard University Press, 2003.

The Global century, Globalization and National security, ed. By Richard L. Kuglar and Ellen L. Frost, vol.1, Institute for National Strategic Studies, National Defense University.

Susan B. Glasser, the US Figures Show Sharp Global Rise In Terrorism, State Dept. Will Not Put Data in Repot, Washington Post Staff Writer, Wednesday, April 27, 2005.

Pentagon Plays Down New Rise in Iraq Violence, Bradley Graham, Washington Post Staff Writer, Wednesday, April 27, 2005, Page A16.

The European Union, the United States and Liberal Imperialism, Michael Brenner, paper delivered to the biennial conference of the European Union

Studies Association.

Patterns of Global Terrorism -2001 Released by the Office of the Coordinator for Counter-terrorism May 21, 2002.

Fast Facts, fas.org/asmp/fast_facts.htm

Past Arguments Don't Square With Current Era Policy, Dafna Linzer, Washington Post Staff Writer, Sunday, March 27, 2005, Page A15.

George Kennan, 1984: 17.

Who Are We, The Challenges to America's National Identity, Samuel P. Huntington, Simon & Schuster, NY, 2004.

Ilan Berman, Institute for the Study of Conflict, Ideology and policy, Perspective, vol. XII, No.1, September-October 2001.

Henry Kissinger, Does the American Need A Foreign Policy?, Henry kissinger, NY, Simon & Schuster, 2004.

Barbarian Sentiments, William Pfaff, Hill and Wang , NY, 1989.

Ambrose S.E. and Brinkley, *D.G.,Rise to Globalism*, NY, 1997.

Seyome Brown, *The Faces of Power,* NY, 1994.

Oye, K.A., Lieber, E.O., and Rothchild, D. eds., *Eagle in a New World, the American Grand Strategy in the Post Cold War Era*, NY, 1992.

Abelson, *D.E. the American Think-Tanks and Their Role in the American Foreign Policy*, NY, 1996.

Fraser Cameron, *the US Foreign Policy after the Cold War, Global Hegemon or Reluctant Sheriff?* London, 2002.

Art R. J. J. and Jarvis, R. International Politics,: Enduring Concepts and Contemporary Issues, NY, 1999.

Brewer, T. Globalizing America: the USA in World Integration, Cheltenham, UK: Edward Elgar, 2000.

Moynihan, M, Coming the American Renaissance, How to benefit from America's economic resurgence, NY, 1996.

Chomsky, N. Rogue, States: The Rule of Force in World Affairs, Cambridge, MA, 2000.

Christopher, W., In the Stream of History, Shaping Foreign Policy for a New Era, Stanford, 1998.

Clinton B., *Between Hope and History*, NY, 1996.

Robert Kagan, *Of Paradise and Power, America and Europe in the New World Order*, NY, 2004.

Pillar P, *Terrorism and the US Foreign Policy, Washington*, DC, 2001.

Tucker, R.W. and Hendrickson, DC, *The Imperial Temptation: The New World Order and America's Purpose*, N.Y, 1992.

Zakaria, Fareed, From Wealth to Power: The Unusual Origins of America's World Role, Princeton, 1998.

Jeffrey Salamon, James P. O'Leary, and Richard Shultz (eds), *Power, Principles, and Interests* Lexington, MA, 1985.

J. Huntley, Pax Democratia: A Strategy for the Twenty-First Century, Basingstoke, 1998.

P.J. Schraeder, *the United States Foreign Policy towards Africa: Incrementalism, Crisis, and Change, Cambridge*, 1994.

M. Cox, *the US Foreign Policy After the Cold War: Superpower Without a mission?*, London, 1995.

J. Rosner, *After The End: Making the US Foreign Policy in the Post Cold War World, Durham*, 1998.

James M. Goldgeier and Michael McFaul, *Power and Purpose: the US Policy Toward Russia After the Cold War*, Washington, DC, 2003.

Thomas Friedman, The Lexus and the Olive Tree, NY, 2000.

Joseph Nye, The Paradox of the American Power: Why the world's only superpower can't go it alone, NY, 2002.

William Pfaff, Barbarian Sentiments, Hill and Young, NY, 1989.

Bates Gill, Lu Ning, & Margaret Pearson, The Making of Chinese Foreign and Security Policy: Implication for the United States, A Panel Discussion by three experts, The Nixon Center, Washington, Washington D.C. www.Nixoncenter.org

June Teufel Dreyer, The Making of Chinese Foreign and Security Policy In the Era of Reform, FPRI Newsletter, 2/2007,www.fpri.org

Daniel Benjamin and Steven Simon, The Next Attack, The Failure of the War on Terror and a Strategy for Getting it Right, Times Books, Henry Holt & Company, NY, 2005.

Robert L. Jervis, American Foreign Policy In a New Era, Routledge, NY, 2005

CHAPTER VII

THE POST COLD WAR SITUATION FURTHER REVIEWED

The second 'strategic pause' that followed the collapse of the bipolar world order (first such strategic pause occurred in the immediate post war years) continues in the new century despite the articulation of the New Bush Doctrine. As of today no viable alternative international political order has emerged. The all-important question still remains unanswered: what shape would the emerging international order assume in the coming years? Is the time ripe for the emergence of a multipolar world order consisting of several major powers? Or would matters be left to the care of the United States, for some more time? So far, the best solution has been the safest one: the maintenance of the status quo, that is, the continuance of the United States leadership in international affairs, even if that meant acceptance of the bitter pill of the Americanization and tolerating the American unilateralism.

The Eagle has yet to regain a solid ground that it lost once its rival superpower vanished from the international scene. The former Soviet leaders, perhaps, thought that they had had enough and it's no use feeding a 'teleological' (the United States works best, given a specific target) and a 'cybernetic' state machinery. It was better to stop America's anti-communist paroxysm that carried the arms race to unimaginable heights and was fast converting Europe, its closest neighbor, into a nuclear arsenal. The Soviet Union thought it wise to return to the pre-WWI days of multipolarity, even by forsaking its super power status, and thereby catching the United States off guard. The old war horses – the Cold War allies – were about to cross over to the other side of the dividing line (so long defended by the former Soviet Union), either as possible contenders to the world crown or as co-sharers of world leadership. America felt that the post Cold War power equation can't any longer be reframed on ideological issues and that the United States can face up to a resurgent Europe, China, and Japan, if it can do away with the Westphalian nation-state system, the bedrock of modern international political system. The United States had genuine cause for concern: the rise and resurrection of

Europe might undo the American efforts at creating a US-centric international order and, who knows, if Europe relives its past glories, it would throw the existing world order into the abysmal depth of chaos, yet again.

The end of the Cold War signaled the return of pre-1945 regional politics, discussed in the previous chapter. Today, Japan, after nearly six decades of its WWII defeat deems it imperative to apologize to Korea and China for its past 'misdeeds' – a clear sign that henceforth, regional issues – one of the weakest spots in the American conduct of foreign policies – would come to dominate international politics. If the EU takes care of the whole of Europe and the Mediterranean, where does the United States find itself other than in the Western Hemisphere ? If China or Japan converts the Pacific zones into their spheres of influence, will the Far Eastern door be closed to the United States? If India gets the better of South Asia and if Israel lords over the Middle East, where does the United States put its other leg (the first leg being in its own hemisphere, of course), except in the space? Is unilateralism the answer? What are the promises and prospects for multilaterlism? Then again, which type of international order best serves the above two courses: unipolarity or multiploarity?

Does America need some sort of 'plastic surgery'?

There is no getting away from the fact that the United States would be required to overhaul its previous foreign policies to suit the realities of the post Cold War international situation. The United States had and still has more reasons to create a new international order based on the American values and interests. For the American policy-makers, 'Now' is the 'Time' and if not now, then when else? The United States went from being the country of the last resort and staying on what Rostow called a "critical margin" in maintaining balance in Europe, Middle East, the Pacific, Africa and Latin America, to one too keen to establish the US supremacy on global affairs in the new millennium. This means a change of *attitude* from its age-old moralistic-legalistic principles to one based on stark national and geo-strategic interests. The United States needs not a mere face-lift or a cosmetic change but some kind of 'plastic surgery' to replace some of its earlier political concepts, more specifically, the American specialties, with borrowed logic from erstwhile imperial powers to make it look less 'exceptional' and more 'common'.

America's traditional emphasis on its messianic role and its proneness to wield its sword of justice over the 'barbarians' led others into believing that the United States should forever remain the last resort and guarantor of peace, prosperity, and stability in world affairs. So definite and familiar had been that pattern that the rest of the world is still reluctant to see America in any other role. They see little American justification to stay engaged in world affairs beyond 'requirement', which in plain terms means serving *their* 'interests'. This is a crucial area where the United States ought to focus its immediate attention – that of erasing its image of a 'thankless' performer.

On the other hand, such an approach of acting as the guardian and mediator in conflicts in every region had made the United States somewhat vulnerable. Other countries take it for granted that it is in *America's interest* to do so. Another effective way to dispel the notion of carrying the yoke of others in a vicarious manner is to band with countries under the Western Civilization so that responsibilities are broadly shared. After all, unity is strength and a collective purpose has far more credibility than an individual one. Since America has little control over such occurrences as the rise of rival power centers like the EU, Japan, Russia, or China, discussed in the last chapter, it must prepare in advance for every probable and viable future alternatives, instead of relying on lop-sided, preemptive, and unilateralist logic.

Seen from the above angle it is extremely necessary to bring the American interests and priorities more in line with the interests and objectives of other major powers as early as possible. As discussed in the earlier chapter, the United States ought to remind others of its hegemonic status by occasionally acting unilaterally to achieve its objectives while declining to intervene in every conflict situation or issue to avoid the role of a world cop, including matters related to the countering of terrorism. This means, the United States may have to reenact the role played out by every other precursor imperial great power, albeit, in a restrained, skillful, and, perhaps, benign manner. The United States ought to lead the world by becoming like them. When in Rome one must behave like a Roman. Did not Truman's America prepare itself to go to the hell to combat the 'communist' devil?

Conversely, the United States, in keeping with its belief in its lofty ideals may decide to change others in its own image. The US efforts at transposing the American ideals and values on a global scale have rendered that country susceptible to doubts by other countries. Take for example, what Wilson proclaimed in 1917, "These are the American principles, the American policies. We could stand for no other. And they are also the principles and policies of forward-looking men and women everywhere, of every modern nation, of every enlightened community. They are the principles of mankind and must prevail." This moralistic-legalistic thread ran through the New Bush Doctrine when the incumbent US president declared "moral truth is the same in every culture, in every time, and in every place." However, the entire history of the American policy as discussed in part II and Part III of this book, rather, tells a different story: expansionism. That is why George Kennan made an honest admission about the need to focus exclusively on the American national interests instead of on traditional moralistic-legalistic principles in these words:

> To maintain this position of disparity (the US economic-military supremacy).. we will have to dispense with all sentimentality and daydreaming...we should cease to talk about vague and unreal objectives such as human rights, the raising of living standards, and democratization. The day is not far off when we are going to deal in straight power concepts....The less we are then hampered by idealistic slogans, the better.

The US efforts in getting the rest of the world to embrace the American ideals or to make them believe that it is the United States that only knows the 'secrets' of history, definitely dilute the 'natural' element contained in the Declaration. Such an approach ignores and undermines the cultures, the rich historical heritages, and the values of other nations. Moreover, such an approach rests on a 'self prophecy' – the superiority of the American culture over those of others. There is, of course, no objective and scientific criteria to prove the superiority of values of one civilization over those of others except through force. Lastly, such a perception rests on an assumption that the United States is always on the side of the good and that good must always win over evil. Again, there is no way to prove that 'good' would win over 'evil' as most of the nations of the world were ruled, for the large part of history, by 'evil' despots than by 'good' democratic governments. Ironically, God may not be always on the side of good and what is evil for the United States may appear good to the other nations.

All those 'value-based' assumptions are being challenged in the post-war and post cold war period as the United States entangled itself in world affairs and increased its frequency of 'intervention' beyond its own hemisphere – into the far-away regions – in the name of regime change, democracy, and countering of communism. Another fallacy in the American foreign policy perception is to assume in a self-styled manner that the United States has got a divine mission to 'civilize' and 'uplift' the downtrodden from their miseries and that to realize this objective, the United States ought to be the pioneer and the leader amongst nations.

The Declaration's claim about the 'inalienable' rights derived from God loses its 'religious' content under the impact of American multiethnicism. Forsaking its core Anglo-Protestant cultural identity for the sake of multiethnicism blurs the 'idealistic-religious' part of the Declaration. I have already dealt with this topic in greater detail in the introductory chapter and my conclusion was that America's shift from assimilationism to muticulturalism is rather a step in the direction to dilute its republican political system in favor of a more 'imperial' type of political system: a sort of 'political' plastic surgery.

The need to reformulate an appropriate foreign policy strategy

Despite Kennan's hard 'realism' and despite the need for some plastic surgery discussed above, the United States may still strike a balance between its realistic-nationalistic interests and its values. President Clinton reiterated in his first inaugural address: "Not change for change's sake, but change to preserve the American ideals—life, liberty, the pursuit of happiness. Though we march to the music of our time, our mission is timeless. Each generation of the Americans must define what it means to be an American ." The United States in the new millennium, in keeping with its vast capabilities and widespread networks, must adopt an extremely fluid, elastic, and open strategy in which it would always be a gainer whether in the capacity of a world leader or not.

Given the tremendous American clout in various fields, such an approach is more real than utopian. All that the United States has got to do is to play its cards as if it already has answer to each and every move by other powers. The United States should create a 'world' order in which it alone would set the agenda and execute them. In other words, it has to be the supreme ruler in the true sense of the term so that in its character, principle and consistency it is always in touch and in tune with what it creates and knows the gains and failures of its policies, yet, ever ready to bear with any attendant misfortune as just another 'step' in overcoming it. That means even if it needs to modify its values, such modifications would rather serve to enrich the American values. To make this possible the United States should persevere like a 'dark man' as described in the Great Book of Changes. There the line is light (in this case, the American values) and the place is dark (an anarchic and uncertain international ambience). Through following a middle course and refusing to be drawn into wrong relationships, the United States can maintain its individuality and still impress others with its exemplary values.

By constantly reducing its errors, the United States may attain a position in which it can always do the right thing at the right moment. The United States must perform its ambidextrous role by sometimes preferring to go it alone to remind others that it is not too dependent on them to the extent they think, while adopting an open strategy that offers it maximum scope to prove indispensable to the rest of the world. It is, therefore, necessary to make a correct assessment of the American capabilities, its advantages and disadvantages that enable the United States to project a more predictable yet benign, and value based 'self image', and one more conducive to handling the complexities of the post Cold War situation. *In short, the United States may have to simultaneously play the role of a 'villain' and 'God', 'rogue' and 'friendly' super power before it attains a stage in which it can guarantee perpetual peace and prosperity to all and sundry.*

The United States has got to ensure that it pursues a foreign policy worth the name. That is what made Henry Kissinger to inquire if the United States needed a foreign policy at all. Already a large number of foreign policy literatures in their hysteric bids to uphold the declining nation-state concept have seized upon the third wave of 'globalization' as a most convenient tool. The Clinton era epitomized how globalization can be ingenuously applied to vindicate the traditional American 'missionary' approach. This has several implications for the subsequent American foreign policies. For example, it is more or less commonly accepted that the American political system and Constitution were not cut out for imperialism. Rather, it happened to be a territorial democracy whose ideals and systems were geography-specific. Little wonder that these scholars would try for the next best alternative: if not imperialism, then hegemony. After all, hegemony relates to foreign policies and foreign affairs only. The argument is that since America's *internal* political and psychological constitution precludes 'foreign' rule and territorial occupation, it is necessary to separate the 'domestic' from the 'foreign' component.

Parallels are drawn with the democratic 'imperialist' Athens and the oligarchic-'hegemonic' Sparta, the Delian and the Peloponnesian League, to prop up the declining appeal of a value based republican system that had never much meaning for other nations. Reference is made of Thucydides' observation that even a commercial giant like Athens had to turn imperialist in order to protect and consolidate the gains from an ever-expanding trade. A middle course, hegemony (Headley Bull's *dominance* and *primacy)* – was supposed to provide that illusive answer as a preparation for America's transition to 'imperialism' in case the republican ideals fall in the way side. There is nothing wrong in such an approach. I have referred earlier that nations prepare much in advance for the 'impending' and the 'inevitable'. Moreover, through this 'fire-walk', the American values would be further tested and steeled. The post Cold War international political situation happens to provide a background for such an open-ended approach on the part of the American foreign policy makers. Yet the all-important question is not one of imposing hegemony, anyway, but one of its duration. Here, the importance of 'values' becomes paramount.

The American republicanism was supposed to serve as a model of equality, democracy, liberty, and justice. That means, anti colonial America desires sovereignty on the part of other nations to the same degree as it does in its own case. Yet the crux is one of maintaining a correct balance between freedom and order since unbridled freedom may lead to disorder – a situation of 'free for all' or a 'state of nature' – at home and abroad. People must be convinced of the need to accept some kind of observance of commonly devised rules and mores under the watchful eye of an enforcing agent, or a 'State'. Such a State ought to be built around values like truth, justice, and peace, in a word, 'principle'.

Truth, justice, and peace must relate to something in order to have some 'meaning'. These values must be contrasted with their opposites, e.g., light with darkness. John pope Paul II aptly surmised, "If there is no ultimate truth to guide and direct political activity, then ideas and convictions can easily be manipulated for reasons of power." Drawing on his knowledge of history, Pope rightly apprehended that democracy without values gets transformed into dictatorship. Let me now discuss the US advantages and disadvantages in formulating an appropriate foreign policy strategy in the light of the above analysis.

The US advantages

First, the United States still stays as a superpower despite the historical precedent to the contrary that the collapse of an empire follows another. Riding on the crest of globalization, the United States has developed into a hyperpower since the last decade of the last century. The United States is well on its course to expand and consolidate its 'secret', 'non territorial', 'federal' and 'cyber' empire, to every part of the world. Already a battalion of nations in South, South East and East Asia have decided to march with the US band by accepting the American prescription of democracy, free trade, and market-oriented economy. Many of them have registered higher level of economic growth and rising living standards.

The Confucian and Buddhist culture of the East and South East Asia had little difficulty to adjust to the ideals and work ethics of Christianity. All these three religions shared a disciplined mind-set fostered by their respective 'monasteries'. The West wind continues to sweep across the Chinese mainland and Asia. India was under British domination for about two hundred years and hence had little problem in importing and incorporating the western 'ideas' into its Hindu culture. The only distinctive socio-cultural system other than communism happens to be the Islamic world guided by the Koranic verses. Earlier, the Middle East happened to be outside the perimeter of liberal democratic influences, mainly because the United States thought it wise not to take two ideological enemies, communism and Islamic fundamentalism, simultaneously, and also because of the absence of oil crisis prior to the 1970s. After Saddam's misadventure in Kuwait and the 9/11 terrorist attacks into the heartland of America, President Bush declared that this would no longer be the case. Thus it is up to this region either to remake itself in liberal democratic model or face a fait accompli.

Secondly, the United States, unlike other former great powers, is not overtly exploitative. It is averse to the zero sum game practiced by the colonial powers. It wants other regions to raise their standards of living. The non-colonial America with a democratic republican system and guided by a universal and philanthropic 'mission', appears less threatening and more reassuring to others. America's geographic location is viewed by many as a hindrance to its 'annexationist' ambitions beyond its oceanic borders. They hope that the United States would make every effort to negate that isolation and hence must depend more and more on the cooperation of other countries. The very fact that the United States has virtually no border with any other continent except the South American continent removes an inherent suspicion and fear of territorial subjugation from the minds of others. The United States, rather, acts as a 'buffer' and a mediator to restrain bullying by the stronger regional powers.

Thirdly, thanks to its anti-hierarchic and liberal democratic set-up, the United States presents the benign face of a 'common' man. It too, remained under the European domination and shares anti-colonial sentiments with erstwhile colonies in many parts of the world. This puts America on a more 'intimate' plane with the former colonies. The North American continent, by itself, offers a viable alternative to the earlier Euro-centric international political orders. People from other countries find it easier to pick the American card simply because of that country's lesser legal complications and greater individual freedom. Every immigrant knows that pedigree matters little in attaining a place of prominence in the United States. Imagination, merit, sincerity, and hard work are all that is needed to amass wealth and power in the United States. The American immigration policies are more lenient than those in Europe and Japan where nationalist feelings still remain stronger.

Fourthly, the United States happens to be the provider of public goods and services on a global scale. It creates and satisfies new consumer demands at the same time. Thus, it remains indispensable for others, and forever. *Most importantly, the United States happens to be only power to force the policy-makers in other countries to adopt ways that benefit the common masses, more and more. The United States acts on a dual dynamics: on the one hand, it appears to be the common denominator in any regional dispute settlement process since all the contending parties feel reassured when the United States acts as an arbiter; on the other, it strives to win the confidence of the people in these countries by influencing their rulers to be more transparent, law-abiding, and more caring of their masses.*

People and even leaders in other parts of the world can't ask for more. Remember, people tend to act rationally and they won't sacrifice the 'golden American goose' until they find a more beneficial 'cow' for milching. The rogues and errants find it hard to pierce this American net that they resent as an American design to bind other people in a permanent 'bondage'. Yet the United States does not occupy foreign territories and is quick to leave its 'bases' when it receives 'marching' orders from its client states.

The US disadvantages

The American disadvantages are no less either. Its geographic and cultural disadvantages lead America to constantly interact with other regions out of its compelling economic, social, and security needs. The United States is handicapped by these two factors and its foreign policy has got little relevance if it fails to add a 'security' dimension to its policies.

As referred above, others find it difficult to comprehend why the United States has got to remain as a world leader once it had done its part in demolishing its Cold War nemesis. This is the second disadvantage that I am discussing. For the erstwhile European powers, the American withdrawal would give them the much-needed freedom, so long suppressed under the hoofs of the bipolar rivalry, to develop their economies and politics, as they would like to have. As for Europe, its purpose is served. It has grown economically robust and united. Its main security threat is gone. It, too, needs more freedom of action to recover its lost glories. Europe, feels that it is high time to shake off the four decades of Atlanticism. All these desires would remain unsatisfied as long as the United States remains the focal point of world activities.

The Third disadvantage is that the American led structural reforms in various parts of the world, including Europe, since the early years of the 1980s, has spawned suspicion about the real American designs: whether the United States really means what it says all about free trade or whether it wants to further expand its trade empire based on the American capitalism. Indiscriminate use of tariff and sanction on certain food items and steel imports from Europe, the beef-hormone dispute and the "dumping" of excess steel through under pricing aggravates this suspicion as the United States strives to goad the EU and Japan to follow the VER and voluntary import quotas. Trade rivalries between the EU and the United States have intensified in the past two decades while the developing nations face increasing tariff restrictions on agriculture-related goods, cotton textiles and apparels. What is more, these structural reforms are seen to be in the interests of the American multinationals and to the detriment of the regional and indigenous economies. The tremendous dislocations created in these economies as a result of privatization, disinvestments, and deregulation have resulted in huge unemployment and yawning wealth gap in these countries, besides, adversely affecting the environment, ecology, health, and labor standards in these countries.

Fourthly, the American 'absolutist' approach to see everything in terms of black and white- unmixed good or evil- reflect a sense of intolerance that might appear to be repelling to other countries. The policy makers in the United States believe that they are doing a long-term benefit to international community and hence the United States has got to act assertively on certain intractable issues that threaten the security of the community of nations. The United States feels that terrorism must be weeded out while others feel that this happens to be an age-old problem. I have already explained that a spirit of domination acts as a spur to such activities. This can be reduced but not obliterated altogether.

The peace-loving citizens the world over is at pains to realize why innocent people would be bombed (despite the American claim to target military and industrial installations only and to limit human casualties to the minimum) in the name of regime change in 'rogue' states when the American intention is to ensure freedom. They feel that it entails enormous time, money, and sacrifices to build industries and infrastructures that could be razed to grounds in a momentary fit of frenzy and indiscretion. True, it is the United States that mostly supplies the sinews and expertise for reconstruction program but it can't return those time and sacrifices. As the American interventions in the non-Western countries keep on increasing, such grievances solidify and lead other people to make a choice: enough is enough and that the United States must go. They see a more 'jingoist' United States in place. They are even horrified at the atrocities let loose by the various ethno-religious conflicts in many parts of the world. They feel that the United States has failed in all these areas and they start to look for an alternative, as the 'benign' face of America turns 'rude'.

Possible options for the United States

Modern international order has so far followed a pyramid pattern: from mutipolarity to bipolarity and thence to unipolarity. The next stage may portend to be what Niall Ferguson calls 'apolarity' of the New Dark Age whose consequence would be far more destructive than the one that prevailed for about a couple of centuries in the post Charlemagne period in world history. Such a comparison, of course, makes little sense because the increasing odds of survival in the modern era render interdependence between nations a sine-qua-non. A world defined by a condition of 'apolarity' might be the ideal breeding ground of the modern Huns, the Tartars and the Vikings. It is thus necessary to portray such a picture from time to time to remind people about the horrors of lawlessness and disorder.

At least, four possible alternatives deserve some serious consideration regarding the shape of the emerging world order in the coming years and the course that the United States might prefer to follow. These are (1) single power American domination of world politics, that is, unipolarity; (2) total American withdrawal from world affairs; (3) multipolarism or a world order dictated by more than two power centers; and (4) domination of the Western Civilization and a power sharing arrangement between countries under that civilization. I am discounting the possibility of any Asian state or a coalition of the developing and other countries to call the shots in international politics, at least, in some foreseeable future.

Unipolarism

Unipolarity is a kind of international system or order in which a single power, largely or wholly, regulates international affairs. Unipolarity and unilateralism are not synonymous concepts. The former denotes a system while the latter is concerned with activities and courses that a country may adopt to conduct its foreign policies. A unipolar power may resort to multilateralism as the United States did in the early years of the 1990s. I have discussed some of these cases below under a separate section. Conversely, a quasi-multipolar power like France in the 1960s conducted some of its foreign policies in a unilateral manner. The previous era of bipolarity came to an end with the fall of the Soviet Union. The United States lost what one eminent statesman called its 'magnetic north pole'. On the other hand, other major powers were still unprepared and needed some more time to play the role of a balancer that created a sort of 'strategic pause' in international affairs.

Paradoxically, despite being a military and economic colossus, the United States still finds itself in a situation in which it is not able to translate its overwhelming supremacy into reality and act according to its wishes. The paradox is that if the United States prefers to go it alone on any issue that it deems vital, but against the wishes of others, it is liable to be labeled as a 'rogue' super power. On the other hand, if the United States maintains a low-key approach not commensurate with its super power status, then others would take this as a sign of weakness and would not mind 'pecking at the Eagle's breast'.

If the United States opts for unipolarity, one important question remains: does America have the stomach and the requisite mind-set to carry out such an 'aggressive' role, all by itself? The answer is no. The American values and ideals, in short, the American creed, happen to be the greatest obstacles in this direction as discussed earlier. Moreover, in military terms, this would mean a state of perpetual military burden and commitment in so far as unilateralist approach of a unipolar power means both winning the war and peace at the same time. The United States is matured enough to know that a greater burden and engagement may put too much strain on its internal political set up.

Exercising the option of 'force' is based on the key consideration of who decides what the best course for a nation is at a particular time. First, an illusion fostered by the centuries of democratic movements or 'democratic centuries' (as Tocqueville used to call) that foreign policy domain no longer remains the forte of a minority elite, must be given a double take. Despite the widespread notion that domestic 'issues' shape the American foreign policies, it may be safely said that the American people, like any other people, won't mind foreign campaigns on the part of their country if it brings about an improvement in their living standards that entails least risk and sacrifice. The problem starts when a great power fails to deliver goods to its citizens and suffers setbacks abroad as happened in the Vietnam War in America's case. The number of odds keep ticking up as the great power in question seeks to ensure a swift victory with least casualty, and as each successive campaign enhances the resistance within and abroad and further erodes that great power's legitimacy to carry out such a campaign.

Secondly, it is still the vested interest groups and not the common masses that decide whether to go to war or not. The US administration's possible plans to take on North Korea, Syria, and Iran (after Iraq) is the brainchild of the American policy makers and not of the American people who care little about politics. The American foreign policy activism was at a low key in the decade of 1990s because of the changes in the international situation following the collapse of communism. The United States was busy digesting what it could gulp and was wise enough not to pursue a penny-wise and pound-foolish policy by searching for further minor gains instead of consolidating its larger Cold War gains.

Still then, the first decade of the post Cold War era was not without blood and tears if one looks at the ethnic mayhems in the Balkans, in Africa, or in East Timor. 'Rogue' states like Iraq, Iran, and North Korea seemed to act out the historical roles played by smaller nations and the 'barbarians' of the earlier eras whenever empires did collapse. Other major powers like China, Japan or the nations of Europe kept their heads cool by not irking the United States for fear of losing their share of the 'Cold War' pie. After all, these countries did not want to throw away the gains of globalization. Modern barbarians or the terrorists chose the other end of the spectrum by focusing on the American failures and misdeeds, out of grudge and vengeance. These 'precocious' terrorists, preferred to see the forest for the wood and they challenged the United States not in its soft belly but in its forte. The US Defense Secretary, Donald Rumsfeld gleefully accepted the terrorist challenge in the hope that it would mean a return to those rewarding days of the Second World War, in a bigger way. The United States now has little compunction in placing its talons at the 'forbidden lands of the Middle East and it has now a 'theater' to experiment with its simulation based high tech and remote controlled war programs. In that sense, the post-Cold War international scenario provided the ideal setting for the American unilateralism.

Look at the American selection of targets for its armed campaigns, especially, the Middle East. In the first place, the Middle East and the Gulf happen to be strategically important for any great power. Secondly, most of these countries are small in size that would make it easy for the United States to overrun them quickly. The presence of vast deserts offers a set piece situation for demonstration of America's awesome airpower fully over a 'guerrilla-free' terrain. Middle East and the Gulf countries were never under European colonial domination except for the few decades of League mandated rule by Britain. Moreover, all these countries happen to be non-nuclear states and the American commercial stake in these regions are not much. American assertive unilateralism in this region is driven by two other considerations. In the first place, the United States happens to enjoy an absolute military superiority over all other great powers that lack the power to resist its domination of that 'key' region with the same intensity that they would have done if the difference in power potential were not much.

Secondly, the United States hopes to register its greatest gain in history by dominating the Middle East. Besides crucial oil reserves, a strong foothold in this region would give the US an important leverage to control vital access routes at the crossroads of three continents and in the very cradle of human civilization. In simple terms this means that by the time any other great power of Europe or Asia feels able to challenge the United States, the latter has 'already' got hold of an extremely crucial region to roll back such challenges easily. With assured 'energy' supplies, the United States would be in a position to carry on a prolonged war while no other great power could afford to carry on a protracted warfare in the absence of adequate energy supplies. With the entire Western Hemisphere in its bag (excepting Castro's Cuba and Chavez's Venezuela), and with the control of the key Pacific (assuming that Japan, Australia, and New Zealand would continue to support the US actions in some foreseeable future) regions, with strong allies in the Central Asian republics and in Turkey, Ukraine, Georgia, and the Baltic republics, the United States would then feel pretty safe in containing both an aspiring China and the old 'war horse' Russia. That is why the United States is in a hurry to control the key Middle East even through assertive unilateralism, as its good time may not long last. The United States hopes to attain where some former great powers like Britain, the Soviet Union, and Germany floundered.

If the United States prefers to go it alone on a particular issue, it has above all to ensure that not only it never fails in its mission but also to see to it that such a mission must be completed as swiftly as possible. The United States simply can't afford to get bogged down in any potentially protracted conflict that would render it more vulnerable to the manipulations of other major and minor powers. Such a victory can be ensured through use of the much talked of high-tech American war machine relying on a combination of accurate intelligence, excellent logistics, sophisticated weapons, a near infallible command and control system, and a military strategy based on far greater mobility and flexibility with least material damages. Nevertheless, the American stake in acting on a unilateral basis is greater because any set-back or even a stalemate situation, like in the Vietnam War, may go a long way towards crippling its freedom of action.

But the crux is how to establish peace and stability by installing a friendly government in place that may not require a longer military presence for 'peacekeeping' purpose. It is only recently that the US joint Chiefs of Staff, Myers, had admitted that the United States was beginning to feel the military overstretch while its armed forces remained thinly spread over large parts of Iraq and Afghanistan and that any contemplation of a third campaign either in Iran or North Korea would further strain its military capabilities. The unilateralist America can hardly count on the support of other countries or even its allies if the original campaign had been undertaken against their wishes. The American reluctance to involve itself in nation-building (there was much criticism on the American efforts in this direction during the Clinton era from the republicans and his successor George W. Bush), not to speak of administering the conquered territories, makes the question of unilateral foreign intervention even more tenuous. Nevertheless, unipolarity requires that a single power maintain its military supremacy far above every other power and it has to demonstrate that superiority from time to time.

As for the intermittent use of force, there is some ground for acting unilaterally. First, the United States not only happens to be a superpower but it is the pioneer and leader in most key areas in an emerging global civilization. It has the entire defense infrastructure and weaponry, built during the Cold War era, at its command and its military-technological superiority is likely to create further gap with any of its nearest rival power. Its well-advanced computerized command structure with unmatched logistics, its robust intelligence networks in land, sea, and space, its most sophisticated and ever developing precision guidance missiles and bombs, its unparalleled nuclear capability, and, more importantly, its rare kind of flexibility in mobilizing its forces in any part of the world or to a multiple destination, at roughly the same time, strikes a fear of God in others. It is a commonplace that nations and people understand the language of force in the first place. Otherwise, there would have been no need for administration. It is the fear of retaliation and retribution that happens to be final word in matters of 'rule', administration, and order.

Just imagine an economically robust yet militarily weak America. Other states would still care for it but much less than in the reverse case. An economically weak and militarily strong Soviet Union held the powerful capitalist states in ransom during the Cold War decades. Rome was not fully independent, economically, yet it could wield so much authority because of its tremendous military clout. Military-oriented Sparta was no less formidable than the commercial Athens. If that were so, how much it would be truer of an economically and militarily strong United States. While too much show of force invites retaliation in kind, lack of willingness to demonstrate raw power, sometimes, is equally dangerous. A holier than thou attitude creates a 'wimpish' impression in the minds of others.

What is more, any incumbent super power is disadvantaged by the fact that any of its 'weak' or 'soft' spot might render it liable to be ruthlessly exploited by its rivals. For example, the US decision to withdraw its troops from Somalia emboldened America's enemies and the terrorists to strike at the super power's weak spot: America's reluctance to undergo human casualties, particularly in areas not of major security concern for that country. This prompted one Chinese spokesman to say that the United States won't risk the lives of millions of its citizens in the major American cities just for the sake of defending Taiwan. Conversely, it is the same China that had been held in check by the presence of the American seventh fleet in the Pacific and the Taiwan Strait for so long. The theory of domination fully explains such behaviors on the part of the nation-states.

Another important consideration is that nations, like common people, believe in the inevitability of historical laws. For example, they know that with time Pax Americana might decline. Each time the United States runs into a trouble, economically, diplomatically, or even militarily, they feel encouraged to point out symptoms of decline in the American hegemony. It is thus difficult for the United States to stay as a benign hegemon amidst all such odds, suspicions, and ill-wills. It is a historical truth that world leadership precludes 'level-ended' politics over a longer period. Naturally, the United States has more reason to go it alone in forcing any important issue to its liking, because if it resorts to multilateralism, this would mean the rise of another power center, like the UN or the EU, for example.

Nevertheless there are caveats. From the standpoint of international politics, such an assertive and unilateralist approach is bound to evoke serious reactions from foes and allies, alike. The possibility of the formation of anti-American coalition would be greatly enhanced. What is more, it might hasten the rise of a rival power center and worse of all, it might lead to a number of countries flocking towards that new power center, by deserting the United States, as happened in a fourteen-power coalition against France during the Napoleonic wars. Both the geographical and cultural 'remoteness' of the United States would further contribute greatly to its woes. International situation, in that case, would, first, pass rapidly into chaos and then to a sort of makeshift order around another hegemon whose power and room of maneuver, in turn, would be crippled because of the burden of enormous demands made upon it by various countries that had helped it to attain that status. Or it may be that a multipolar international order led by the United Nations might replace the present incumbent, out of sheer necessity and survival. The second possibility is more probable now because, the major powers of Europe, Japan, Russia, and China already prefer some kind of multipolar international order at the behest of a world body. This means that the United States would be the odd man out in the management of international affairs.

The new Bush Doctrine takes into account the conditions and changes in the post Cold War milieu. The new Bush Doctrine strongly advocates unilateralism. It marks a sharp departure from all earlier American security policies in so far as the challenges are supposed to come more from the non-state, amorphous, fleeting, and unidentifiable enemies. These disruptive forces take every advantage of the limits of the lone super power's 'overstretch' problems in an era marked by proliferation of nuclear weapons and technology. Because of tremendous asymmetry in military power balance, the US military machinery is likely to encounter elements of surprise and harassment from its enemies.

The Bush Doctrine, therefore, rests on several assumptions: the new and non-traditional threats to security described above requires vigorous efforts on the part of America to counter them; a preemptive strike that may be undertaken on the mere perception of the threat and the need to act unilaterally. The basic premise of this doctrine is the over emphasis on domestic policies in guiding foreign policies. This doctrine was put into operation in the Iraqi campaign of 2003. This Doctrine is not about purely military measures but is couched in value terms, like, establishing liberty, democracy, and free market enterprises. That way, it is a mix of realism and liberalism. The need for preventive war arose out of the post cold war strategic realities defined by the following developments.

It is assumed that anti-American resistance may resemble the 'scorched earth' syndrome where the psychology, will, and patience of the contending parties would be tested to their utmost limits. According to Ralph Peter "The future of modern warfare lies in the streets, sewers, high-rise buildings, industrial parks and the sprawl of houses, shacks, and shelters that form the broken cities of our world." (Hastedt, p.381-82) The rationale on the part of the terrorists and the 'problem' states is to extract greater concession through intimidation and surprise. Once they are successful in this mission, their next step would invariably be to press for total American withdrawal from their lands.

The 'surprise and shock' tactics of the terrorists and the cyber and information hackers, and the proliferation of WMDs require that the United States goes for hunting down the terrorists and forestall their designs through preventive wars. The Bush Doctrine seeks to retain more freedom of action for the only remaining super power to effectively manage international affairs. It is a new version of the Roosevelt corollary but with a minor difference. Roosevelt preferred 'soft speaking' while carrying the 'stick'. Bush relies more on 'humble' ultimatums and fait accompli. But the message is common: if other nations fail to conform to certain norms of cooperation, democracy, rule of law, and free trade, then the United States has a mission to make them behave properly. The rational for such an approach can be traced to history again. The United States hopes to plug the main loopholes in the international system by denying the 'barbarians' any advantage to hold the world at ransom. History is replete with such examples when these 'barbarians', at different time periods created anarchy simply because there was no strong power to tame them in strategically important pockets from where they had originally sprung out. Denial of sanctuary or a safe haven to organize their clandestine activities is of paramount importance.

However, the Bush Doctrine requires to be more comprehensive in order to take a concrete shape. Otherwise, it won't deliver decisive outcomes. The stalemate in Iraq even after four years, reveals the weakness in the Bush Doctrine. Unilateral actions become extremely difficult if the terrorists move from one country to another, which is the case and this has been admitted by the above report on global terrorism. The net result of all these could be an uneasy compromise rather than continuation of war because terrorists can't engage in a prolonged battle with the mighty United States while the latter in the absence of a common consensus from its allies would find the costs and risks too high. Another important thing to note is that such a situation may hasten the rise of a rival power center. The real conundrum that America faces in the new millennium is: how to keep its allies bound together in the face of their growing divergence in trans-Atlantic perceptions on various international issues.

Some 'heroes', fired by the romanticism of their glorious national past and their 'caliphates' or driven by a sudden paroxysm to recreate an 'Abbasid' or a version of the erstwhile Persian empire may either rush in to have a 'charge' at the sole superpower or clandestinely brandish their weapons of mass destruction to be released at an opportune moment to precipitate a chain of anti-American rebellion in the Middle East. They know that no major power has got the capability to face up to the US leadership and that pressure must be put at some 'unexpected' points that must contain elements of 'surprise' at the same time. This is the Kennan Doctrine working in a reverse way. This would test the US will and patience and would divert the American attention from the traditional perception of international politics. The reasoning is simple: while the United States remains mired in countering some elusive and extremely mobile groups, another more friendly and compliant major power or powers would find time and space to intervene, regroup and ultimately to challenge the US world hegemony.

Such efforts at undermining the sole superpower are not that preposterous, as it may seem on the surface. Such acts are based on a cool and careful assessment of the US strength and weakness and the moment chosen speak volume of their real intentions: forcing the United States to retreat into its own hemisphere. They want to hammer continuously at the US soft belly: its traditional inclination to isolationism and not to entangle in other nation's affairs.

They know that if the United States is allowed some more time to consolidate the latter's Cold War gains, it would be impossible to contain the American political and cultural supremacy. In plain terms, they feel that the American advantages are their disadvantages. It is in this backdrop that the United States would have to decide on its future course: unilateralism or multilateralism? Unipolarity or multipolarity?

In his January 28, 1992 State of the Union address, President George H. Bush has laid bare the outline of the American foreign policy in the new millennium in unilateralist terms. "There are those who say that now we can turn away from the world, that we have no special role, no special place. But we are the United States of America, the leader of the West that has become the leader of the world. As long I am President, I will continue to lead in support of freedom everywhere....Strength in the pursuit of peace is no vice; isolationism in the pursuit of security is no virtue".

Case for multipolarity

Multipolarity means the existence of more than two power centers in managing international affairs. Multipolarism had dominated international politics since the days of the Westphalia with occasional interruptions, till 1945. Two most important conditions for multipolarity are that no major power enjoys a distinct military advantage over its rivals or that they are more or less at par and that an alliance of some major and minor powers are capable of preventing and defeating the emergence of a single power domination. However, the record of multipolarism is not impressive. Most of the wars in the last few centuries had taken place under such a kind of international order. European multipolarism has eventually coalesced into a monolithic entity in the post war period as the erstwhile great powers of Europe seek a common European identity through the EU and the ESDI (European Security and Defense Initiative).

One successful period of multipolarity lasted from the Concert of Vienna in 1815 following Napoleon's defeat till 1914. This was the golden era of multipolar international order despite the fact that it was precisely during this time that Europe underwent huge internal political upheavals and experienced recurrent conflicts. The relative peace enjoyed during the period is more due to overseas colonial expansion. It was the overseas colonies that acted as safety valves from the turmoil in Europe. For example, during the period of African colonization, countries of Europe sometimes acted jointly to subjugate the various ethnic groups and tribes of Africa.

Multipolarism gave birth to power politics. Each party hoped to gain more and they could do so only from a position of strength. Diplomacy and power politics thus became important tools for multipolarism. Allies and foes could trade places more often to attain their objectives or the same two arch rivals might enter into an alliance with a third common power center, as prevailed during the Bismarckian era. Obviously, multipolarity meant preponderance of national interests even to the exclusion of ideologies because it was basically an arrangement for the sake of 'convenience' between various imperial powers. Multipolarism works well between countries with geographical proximity and with different political and economic ideals. Whenever these ideological forces get the better of any particular power, multipolarism is at stake.

Imperial Britain, the strongest of the European powers in the nineteenth century offers one such example of skillful use of multipolarism, particularly in the European affairs. During that period, major European powers needed the support of as many allies as possible and hence they bothered little about the nature of governments or social systems in other countries until their 'interests' were hurt. That is why Bolshevik Russia had not much difficulty in getting recognition from European powers than from the far-flung United States. It is, rather, in the nature of ideologically driven countries to go in for a unilateral or single domination of the world as was done by Nazi Germany and the Soviet Union during the last century.

Europe, in the new millennium, knows that it can't match the US military capabilities yet it wants to leash the trans-Atlantic colossus, to some extent. Europe's main objective in restraining the American unilateralism is to create a condition in which it (Europe) either strives to blunt the 'impetuosity' and dynamism of the United States, or to make it more and more dependent on the European guidance that would make Europe a de facto co-sharer of world leadership. Europe justifies its actions on the ground that the United States happens to be its ally instead of being a foe and hence they have a right to influence the US actions. This may not be without merit but the big question is how long the United States would remain Euro-centric? It happens to be only superpower of the contemporary time and it may want to have its own ways. Multipolarity would not be the American cup of tea, at least, not before the American innings is played out. Till that time, the United States would naturally expect the 'freedom of action' from its allies that is commensurate with its unipolar status. We are just beginning to see the seed of an emerging US-led world order sprouting on a global scale. Putting brakes or trying to shackle the 'Samson' is bound to arrest the dynamism of the Western Civilization.

Countries of Asia are mostly ideologically driven because of the influence of nationalism and tradition. One of the major American foreign policy goals of the post Cold War era has been to iron out the 'rough' traditionalist 'edges' of the culturally sensitive Asian countries through the process of 'homogenization' and 'standardization'. Replacement of ideologies with para-ideologies (common interests and objectives) fosters co-operation and strengthens regional blocks as the influences of the nation-states keep on diminishing. This means that different blocks or regions instead of individual nation-states would attain significance in international politics in the coming years. In that sense, regional blocks instead of individual nation-states may be the defining feature of any future multipolar world order.

However, regional blocks may require a leading power for its proper functioning and it is quite likely that these individual blocks may come to depend on the whims and interests of a dominant partner within that block. Conversely, mutual gains may lead the members within a block to avoid conflicts and wars at all costs. This may lead the traditional enemies like China and Japan, or India and Pakistan, to be more tolerant of each other. For example, these countries hardly had any compunction in showering 'accolades' on each other in the recent Afro-Asian partnership meet in Jakarta in April 2005. But then again that euphoria and good will may be transient.

Nevertheless, one outcome of intra regional contacts is the strengthening of the respective regional blocks that could either act as deterrence both for intra or inter regional conflicts or may lead to more political and economic 'protectionism' vis-à-vis non-members within the same region. On the other hand, if some nations choose to form a regional block voluntarily or out of economic interests, they have the responsibility to ensure that the block does not disintegrate. These multi regional blocks may be stepping-stones towards a common global village. After all, regionalism denotes a more globalist orientation.

Given the fact of America's sheer size and capabilities in most key areas and the fact that the US participates in many overseas blocks, it is clear that no rival regional power center would go 'unchallenged' and 'unengaged' by the United States. The United States hopes to sustain these regional platforms so that their transition to a higher global form becomes easy. In any case, the United States wants to be an 'indispensable' nation. Another American policy objective for encouraging these regional blocks is to initiate a process in which national and cultural enmities would gradually fade under the impact of economic integration and the resultant benefits. The United States knows that this is crucial for legitimizing the American world leadership. If countries within a region can erase their ethno-religious and other cultural differences, then they would strive to extend this rationale on a larger scale. As a result, the suspicions created in the minds of others regarding the American identity and intentions would disappear. Such a process, in turn, would eliminate anti-American sentiments in many regions.

The US withdrawal

The next alternative is the American withdrawal from world politics back to its nineteenth century regional and hemispheric 'cave'. Some scholars strongly believe that this will considerably affect the progress of modern human civilization and render the international order anarchic. There would be widespread and constant wars, conflicts, and destructions, both at the regional as well as at the international level. This will not only undo the great works done by the centuries-old Western Civilization but would also throw the world back into the days of the medieval feudalism. Bereft of the improved communications networks due to lack of developments in science and technology (since the United States happens to be hub of creativity in the fields of science and technology) because of self-imposed American 'isolationism', industrial activities and free trade benefits would slow down considerably; civil societies would be greatly reduced and replaced by traditional villages and majlis. The vast contraction of commerce to its local level would mean that inter-regional contacts would become minimal. The world as a whole would look extremely different from what it is now at the beginning of the twenty-first century. An analogy would suffice to describe such a situation. The United States happens to be sun-the source of all dynamism and creativity in modern times. If the light of the sun goes out, then bacteria and infections will spread unchecked.

Such a situation in its miniaturized form is not without precedence in history. For example, the collapse of the Roman and the Persian Empire in quick succession more than one and half millennia ago plunged the world into what we call the dark Middle Ages. During the Great Crusades at the beginning of the second millennia every sort of brutality and inhumanity were in full display in their barest forms while the Mongols and the Tartars ransacked large parts of the world. A temporary reversal of British imperialism (loss of the American colonies) and the erosion of powers of major European powers like France (in the Seven Years war) triggered the French revolution and created some sort of uncertainty in Europe resulting in the Great Napoleonic wars.

Nevertheless, there is a difference now from earlier instances. Most of these chaotic situations in history occurred with recurrent frequency even before the system of nation-states came into being. With the onset of industrialization and the spread of modern Western Civilization, the domination instinct and ferocity of the individual despots or the tribal chiefs had been largely refined. Knowledge has replaced brute force. Gunpowder and cannons rendered a repeat 'long march' of the ruthless Viking raiders or the Hun horsemen impossible. Modern Huns or Vikings may be more intelligent and may change their tactics often, but it is highly unlikely that either a single or a grouping of the non-state amorphous entities could have the capability to recreate a New Dark Age. Modern 'barbarians' would rather end up in prisons or would be on the 'constant' run being hotly pursued by law abiding state powers. Dictators and autocrats may create rogue states, but they would be hardly competent enough to challenge major state powers. No nation would like to forego the advantages of interdependence merely to try its luck.

However, another important caveat is poverty and inequality in wealth distribution – the North-South divide – that may motivate people in the deprived regions to create conditions of lawlessness. All these are some of the tough jobs that the United States has taken upon itself to perform in the post-the Cold War decades. It wants to make sure that no region remains outside of modern economic activities and that the backward regions must develop their economies. For this to happen, these regions and countries must develop their economic and political infrastructures and must remain tied to a center for constant help and guidance. No dictator would be tolerated and all states must respect the rule of law and abide by the norms of civil rights and democracy. Such approaches have a common purpose – to prevent the recurrence of a 'second' Cold War, to defeat the forces of barbarism and to advance the cause of modern civilization. To that extent, the American policies are uncompromising as President Bush's new doctrine lays bare. Any American withdrawal from international politics would defeat that purpose.

The problem is that such actions may be taken as efforts towards Western 'Civilizational' dominance. But the choice today is one between civilization and barbarism in any of its forms and not between civilizations. The goals of various civilizations are the same: economic development, greater interdependence, and the preservation, protection and propagation of modernism. The same developments in science and technology that may tremendously augment the power of the civilized nations to fight off the forces of darkness have lowered the threshold of invulnerability of these states because of indiscriminate proliferation of key tools of 'destruction'. Thus, the fight between civilization and barbarism goes on. At present, it has devolved on the United States to assume that responsibility on a global scale. In that respect things are as plain and simple: Would the law abiding people of the world submit to the whims of a few fanatic zealots or would they be willing to cede some of their freedom to embrace the rule of civil societies and democracy under the US leadership?

Joint sharing of world responsibility with Europe

Joint sharing of the world leadership by, at least, two power centers within the same civilization or the dominance of the Western Civilization is another variant of multipolarism, albeit, in a narrow sense. The new millennium affords a unique opportunity for these two power centers to project their influences over world affairs from positions of strength, for the first time.

The Western nations including the United States want to keep a low profile in this angle of power sharing. They apprehend that too much emphasis on the Western Civilization would generate strong polarization along cultural lines. They just don't want to exacerbate that trend in view of the anti-western, anti-colonial and anti-imperialist sentiments in the developing world fostered and sustained throughout the whole of nineteenth and the twentieth centuries. Nevertheless, the gains registered by the Western Civilization must be protected. So it is almost a sine-qua-non that at least one power center belonging to the Western Civilization remains in charge of world affairs all the time.

The issue here is one of how the United States wants to conduct its policies with a view to preparing the ground for a future world order based on an informal and unwritten joint-power sharing with Europe. There are criticisms in some quarters that the US unilateralism happens to be a narrow concept because of its over-reliance on the use of force that defies the present day reality. That reality is that global affairs are increasingly defined by non-force parameters like economic integration and interdependence, a host of social and cultural issues ranging from economic inequalities to the spread of transnational diseases like AIDs, drug trafficking, ethno-religious conflicts that often transcend borders and that demands cooperation at a global level, proliferation of non government organizations, environmental and ecological disturbances, problems connected with international financial stability, movement of capital and labor and the problem of unemployment and labor exploitation, other welfare and humanitarian issues, and finally terrorism. No single nation, however mighty it may appear, can manage all these problems, alone. It may either be the responsibility of the world community of nations or even the joint responsibility of Europe and the United States, in the least, because modern civilization and its problems are the handiworks of the West.

One offshoot of this joint sharing of global responsibilities between the United States and Europe may be some 'exclusive' spheres of influence beyond their borders –a situation that has never arisen previously. Yet there is nothing to fear because it is extremely unlikely that transatlantic nations would go to war against each other even over major differences. First, while the European 'high-handedness' is a thing of past, never to return, the United States, in turn, simply need not subjugate Europe. Secondly, these two continents won't create a situation that would endanger the Western Civilization. Thirdly, there is the fear of a 'common' danger from the forces of religious fundamentalism and terrorism. Fourthly, the new millennium belongs to the days of post modernism, post colonialism, and post communism in which the 'domination spirits' have been so curbed and refined that the incidence of war between major powers has come down to a zero level. Fifthly, centuries of transatlantic ties have fostered a 'system' and character that is difficult to change. Transatlantic bonds have reached a 'critical mass' level that can lead only in one direction: cooperation between countries belonging to the Western Civilization. Lastly, and most importantly, Europe does not need to resort to war to marginalize the United States. That would go against the European logic to engage the United States in world affairs. The fact is that if the United States finds Europe either hostile or disinterested about America's world leadership, it would have little problem in reducing its European engagement and leave Europe to the vagaries of war, intra or intercontinental. It is thus in Europe's interest that the United States stays as a world leader. In that respect a multipolar world order or a power sharing between the US and Europe is distinctly on the cards. Zbigniew Brezzinski in an article, A Geostrategy for Eurasia, defined the American role in the post Cold War era in these words: "Europe is America's essential bridgehead in Eurasia. America's stake in democratic Europe is enormous. With the allied European nations still highly dependent on the US protection, any expansion of Europe's political scope is automatically an expansion of the US influence. Conversely, the United States' ability to project influence and power in Eurasia depends on close trans-Atlantic ties." This 'Eurasian' dimension can be extended to cover the entire globe.

Some the post Cold War 'case' studies

Iraq

Saddam Hussein tried to be smart, somewhat, as he took advantage of the 'void and uncertainty', created by the Soviet withdrawal, when Iraq invaded Kuwait in August 1990. However, it proved to be voodoo for him as he failed to fully grasp the lesson of the just bygone era: if the United States could restrain and oppose the mighty Soviets from extending the latter's influence to other regions, why should they allow a far inferior Iraq to do so? Containment of communism was not an end in itself. It had some purpose – to reduce and deny the Soviets any space in any other part of the world while enhancing that of America's own. The Truman Doctrine was more strategic than a mere ideological doctrine. Saddam completely failed to grasp this truth as he relied more on historical-cultural factors and anti-Israeli sentiments of the Arabs.

Two factors evoked America's prompt response to Iraqi occupation of Kuwait. First, the Middle East and the Gulf happen to be strategically important regions in terms of energy and geopolitics. The Great Game between Czarist Russia and imperial Britain in the nineteenth century and Germany's pre-world war overtures in this region had been the testimony to the above fact. Another important factor is the presence of Israel. In any other strategically less important region, viz., Africa, the United States might not have reacted with such a determination. But not so in the Middle East, where lay its two key allies: Israel and Saudi Arabia.

Could the United States have ignored Saddam's occupation of Kuwait when the world community of nations was slow and hesitant to react and respond? Or would any Security Council Resolution demanding unconditional Iraqi withdrawal from Kuwait be forthcoming without the American initiative?

The simple answer is that other nations were either too weak to redress the wrong or didn't have a comparable geopolitical stake as those of the United States, at that time. On top of it, there remained a 'watch and wait' approach in the hope that the United States would act first, out of its super power 'obligation'. The United States had to act anyway, now that there was no the Soviet Union to persuade Saddam to withdraw from Kuwait. The United States simply could not allow another M-E state to take charge of this region.

The Iraqi claim over Kuwait dates back to 1961 when Kuwait became fully independent from the British rule. In fact, Saddam was preparing his moral and military grounds to invade Kuwait since the end of the protracted Iran-Iraq war in 1988. Even the fall of the 'patron' super power (the Soviet Union) could hardly reverse Iraq's audacity to annul billions of dollars of loans incurred from Kuwait during that protracted Iran-Iraq war. Iraq, thus, had little alternative to recover its war-ravaged economy except through oil revenues. Iraq might have some justification as Kuwait made unlawful uses of extracting the crude from adjacent oil fields belonging to Iraq and was undercutting oil prices, thereby, causing a fall in Iraq's revenue from the sale of oil. Yet Iraq's unilateral decision to go to war instead of accepting arbitration from major powers (whose vital interests lay in M-E oil supplies) amounted to testing the American will and patience.

Saddam touched another raw nerve in the American foreign policy matters. He knew that the post-1945 dollar hegemony was at the root of the American supremacy. So if he could grab Kuwait – one of the major sources of world's oil supplies, this would give Iraq an additional strategic advantage to grab some other largest oil fields in Saudi Arabia and, more importantly, to regulate both the price and supply of oil to other parts of the world. In short, the far-reaching consequence of Saddam's policy was twofold: to shake off the very foundation of the American 'empire' based on dollar hegemony – an option that even the mighty the Soviet Union carefully avoided during the entire Cold War period, and secondly, to eliminate the Jewish state from the map of the globe.

Saddam backed up his ambitions with a more dangerous program of acquiring nuclear and other WMD's. In a sense, Saddam's strategy might have been brilliant but it was impracticable and most untimely because the United States, the sole world leader remained not only militarily far superior but it was just keeping a 'mysteriously' low profile in world affairs as it remained busy elsewhere in the immediate post-the Cold War period – in its efforts towards German unification and with affairs in post Soviet Russia. Saddam counted on another factor: European support or their neutrality in view of Europe and Japan's heavy dependence on Iraqi oil supplies. Saddam was either misled or he perhaps misinterpreted an American 'feeler' from the US Embassy source about

America's reluctance to intervene in the event of a possible Iraqi invasion of Kuwait.

President George W. Bush hoped to complete the unfinished job of his father through the second Iraqi campaign. Every other major power supported the US led campaign in 1991 Gulf to eject Iraq out of Kuwait. Naturally, the United States had to stop after liberating Kuwait without ousting Saddam from his throne. Among other things, President George H. Bush was led to believe by a CIA report that Iraq would plunge into deep anarchy and secessionist movements following Saddam's removal. The American indifference towards Saddam's indiscriminate bombing of the rebel groups in the North and South of Iraq in the aftermath of the first Gulf War amounted to giving Saddam rather a freehand in order to avoid Iraq's disintegration.

In the years following the end of the first Gulf War, the United States was upset as (1) Saddam flouted the terms and conditions of its 1991 surrender and continued his repression of the common people and the Kurds, (2) he sought to produce WMDs in a clandestine manner, and (3) he misled the UN inspection team and was believed to be supporting international terrorism. Saddam also diverted the revenues earned from the 'oil for food' program to beef up Iraqi defense instead of feeding starved Iraqi children and women. Clinton's America retaliated by bombing Iraqi targets, albeit for a brief period. The United States under George W. Bush thought about conducting another UN led campaign in Iraq to oust Saddam Hussein. But other major powers felt that the UN Inspection team working in Iraq be given more time. The United States had its own proofs and documents that Mr. Powell produced with much 'special effects" on a giant screen in the UN Security Council meeting. Yet it failed to convince France, Russia, Germany, and many other countries.

After much heated debate, the United States, finally, managed a workable majority so as to lend a semblance of legitimacy and a multilateral face (with the support of Britain and other smaller European power) to its proposed unilateral campaign that took place in March 2003. Although the American victory was swift, the much sought-after peace still remained elusive as Iraq got plunged into a situation of anarchy. The United States saw the specter of Vietnam revisited. As of now, more than 3,000 Americans have died in the post war reconstruction period in Iraq. Nevertheless, the United States achieved one of its principal policy objectives: ensuring steady oil supplies and preserving its dollar hegemony, for the time being. More importantly, the 2003 Iraqi campaign paved the way for chastising other rogue states in the region: Iran and Syria. In the previous chapter, an effort was made to explain the US actions in the Gulf in the light my theory of domination. From a geopolitical standpoint, the US post Cold War policies in the Middle East were aimed at denying any rival or major power any significant foothold In that region.

Haiti, Bosnia, Kosovo, and Somalia

The post-1945 US administration continued its early twentieth century policy of intervening in its backyards. The case of the American interventions in Guatemala, Cuba, Dominican Republic, Chile, and Panama had been discussed in an earlier chapter. However, the post Cold War US President Clinton seemed to have run short of ideas in tackling the Haitian imbroglio of the early 1990s. Previously, there used to be that patent American excuse: preventing the communists from forming a government in any other Latin and Central American country. But the post Cold War Haitian revolution denied Clinton that privilege. His predecessor George H. Bush, had already refused to intervene in Haiti except condemning the overthrow of the democratically elected regime of the Catholic priest, Jean-Bertrand Aristide, through a military coup led by General Raul Cedras. President Bush even ordered sending back Haitian boats containing 'economic' refugees from the high seas destined for the United States.

President Clinton, who developed an interest in the Haitian 'voodoo', as he had written in his autobiography, decried Bush's inhuman approach in his 1992 election campaign. But once in office, he, too, preferred to follow his predecessor's policy in regard to the Haitian problems. However, the failure of the ongoing UN efforts in 1993 and the mounting pressure from the Trans Africa Organization and the Congressional Black Caucus compelled him to send a small contingent of military force in October 1993. To the US humiliation, that attempt failed. A year later, President Clinton ordered larger forces to be deployed. Just before their landing, former president Carter persuaded Cedras to get out of the country and the 20,000 US forces entered the Haitian capital without resistance. Aristide was restored as the president of Haiti. The US forces joined the UN peacekeeping operations, in the meantime. Ironically, the American intervention in Haiti could not be justified by the post Cold War logic of establishing democracy, rule of law, and market economy, because Haiti was too small a country either to attract the US attentions or to influence the domestic politics of its other larger neighbors. As a result, the US and the UN forces left Haiti by February 1996.

The United States faced a similar situation in the Bosnian crisis in the 1990s. The problem surfaced as communism started to unravel in the Soviet Union and its satellite states in the East and the Central Europe. After the breakup of the Czech and the Soviet Federation, Yugoslavia was rocked by ethno-religious clashes when its constituent republics of Slovenia, Croatia, and Bosnia-Herzegovina demanded secession from that federation in 1992. Yugoslav president Slobodan Milosevic used force and repression to subdue these demands. The United States refused to participate in the UN forces overseeing aid distribution in Bosnia. The United States also prevented the implementation of the 1993 Vance-Owen peace plan to end the war in Bosnia on the ground that the plan was biased against the Bosnian Muslims. The conclusion of the Dayton Accord at America's behest a couple of years later, however, failed to guarantee Bosnian sovereignty as that republic was divided on ethnic lines. To make the matters worse, a more brutal form of the unrest followed, this time in Kosovo. The ethnic Albanians there sought independence from Belgrade and planned to merge with neighboring Albania. Milosevic, once again, unleashed a reign of terror through ethnic cleansing that led Clinton to send his troubleshooter, Richard Holbrooke, to broker yet another political settlement. Milosevic turned down the US offer leaving the NATO forces to unleash a month long aerial bombings of the industrial, military, and communications targets of Yugoslavia. Milosevic capitulated after sustaining heavy losses, yet again.

The American problems in intervening in the Balkan crisis were evident from the outset. First, the Balkans were no part of America and hence they could not be used as pretexts for self-defense. Secondly, the United States was yet to shake off its the Cold War syndrome in initially opposing Serbia, the Soviet ally, and in favoring Croatia and Bosnia. The United States, however, did not stick to its initial stand as it negotiated with Milosevic in giving shape to the Dayton Accord. Thirdly, geopolitical compulsion of the Cold War era had ceased to operate and the United States had little to do with fighting in a far-flung region like the Balkans. The United States was led to intervene because of the expositions in the media of the man-made atrocities perpetrated in that region. Perhaps, the United States, as Clinton had pointed out, feared the repeat of events leading to the First Great War in Europe. But this logic appeared weak in view of the fact that, unlike some eight decades ago, the post Cold War Germany had yet to attain the status of an independent power center and Russia was just humiliated in the Cold War. It may be that the United States hoped to send a message to Europe that the latter's problems can't be seen in isolation except as a trans-Atlantic problem. The case for intervention in Haiti was weak, that in the Balkans was more tenuous. How would then the United States justify its participation in the Operation Restore Hope in Somalia when that country was both geographically far off and not any part of Europe, even?

Somalia was under the grip of intense civil war in the closing years of 1980s and its economy was on the verge of a collapse. As the civil war intensified, the conditions of the homeless, women and children were shown on TV screens that moved the American public opinion in favor of the American interventions in Somalia on humanitarian grounds. President Bush tried to justify a very brief humanitarian intervention in Somalia "to open the supply routes, to get the food moving, and to prepare the way for a UN peacekeeping force to keep it moving". However, the United States withdrew following an urban battle to capture a local rebel leader Mohammed Aideed, in which eighteen Americans were killed. Somalia, like Vietnam, proved to be a permanent blemish on the American foreign policies with far reaching consequences. While the US-Vietnam war took place within a bipolar international set up so that blames could be laid on the Soviet and Chinese support for North Vietnam, Somalian crisis occurred at a time of the American domination of world affairs. The US withdrawal exposed the fact that the United States lacked legitimacy and motivation to intervene there. Yet the United States found a scapegoat in the UN peacekeeping forces. The United States declared that it wouldn't henceforth go abroad to enforce the observance of the UN humanitarian norms.

Conclusion

Taken together, all the above cases had shown that the post Cold War American foreign polices lacked direction, somewhat. The American foreign policies during the period under discussion neither followed the rule of classical realism that made national interests dependent on self-defense, regional disturbances, and territorial integrity nor did it have any ideological direction of the Cold War days. The American willingness to cooperate with the United Nations was to admit the indispensability of United Nations at that time. But as soon as the interests of the two diverged, as in Bosnia and in Somalia, the UN-US relations soured. The bonhomie of the immediate post Cold War years was over. All these interventions had one objective: to legitimize the use of force by the United Nations at the behest of the United States. 'Minor' transgression like the violation of sovereignty can't be avoided to ensure 'humanitarian' compliances.

All the above cases also revealed the limitations and bankruptcy of various multilateral organs like the UN, NATO, and the EU. In the second Iraqi campaign, it was the UN that had to learn the limits of its powers while NATO developed irreconcilable cracks in Kosovo and Bosnia as both the EU and the United States differed at every stage of the operations from aerial bombing to the issue of leadership. The American success in the Afghan campaign following 9/11 encouraged the United States to resort to use of force with greater risk and doggedness in the Middle East. More importantly, it was supposed to provide the foundation for the US unilateralist international order under the guise of a 'collective' security strategy contingent on rule of law, democracy, human rights observances and freedom.

But it is precisely the above-mentioned post-Cold War 'packages' of the United States that have soured the US- EU relations. The United States feels that use of force is necessary to spread the above-mentioned values in a more positive way. On the other hand, a more cautious Europe favors the use of force only when all other alternatives are exhausted. The US doctrine of preventive war to chastise rogue states that had sponsored terrorism and acquired weapons of mass destruction did not entirely convince its European allies. Europe felt and still feels that such a 'licentious' approach would tempt the United States to determine the nature of the threat and the enemy according to its liking. For Europe, it is also a matter of principle to respect the sovereignty of nations. Europe favors moral suasion while the United States feels that morality must be backed by hard force to have any practical meaning.

From the US standpoint, it would be a pity on America's part if that very country that has spent so much resources in unleashing waves of modernization, either fails to capitalize on its brilliant achievements or if any other major power runs away with all the attendant gains at America 's expense. Undoubtedly, it is the American dollar that still serves as the medium of international finance and trade and that has rebuilt Europe out of the debris of WWI; it is the American food that in no small way feeds many parts of the world; it is the American arms that form the main weaponry of most nations in the world; it is the American technology that draws others from the abyss of underdevelopment; it is the American universities that produce the best of talents for every other nation including the United States; it is the American soil that is the home to immigrants from every corner of the earth; it is the American hegemony that had so far prevented wars between major nations and is responsible for relative peace that prevails in the international arena; it is the American political ideals that happen to be the better guarantor of individual liberty and rights than any previous political systems; it is toward America that the rest of the world looks up at the solemn hour of necessity, be it natural or man-made disasters, enforcement of justice and arbitration and, in short, it is the American presence in international theater that allows people in every part of the world to breathe air of freedom and inject in them a real motivation to lead a decent and peaceful life.

The United States happens to be at root of most of the dynamism on a global scale and if this fountain dries up, entire human civilization would degenerate into anarchy and decadence. Even if we assume that with the American retreat, this will not be the end of the world, it can safely be said, that the world would lose much of its luster, creativity and freedom as no other great power is singularly capable of delivering so many goods, simultaneously. Greeks were philosophers; Romans were more militaristic; France, Britain, and Germany happened to be commercial, nationalistic and imperialists. None of them were interested in developing or enlightening the rest of the world, that is, they had no universal message and mission like the republican America.

It is true that the United States, sometimes, reveal brazenly expansionist and even imperialistic tendencies, but no country would bestow such benefits to others out of gratis. There is also another important consideration. Any good order needs to be consolidated and even *enforced* because like the water in a lake, human instincts and activities need to be channelized. Streams may be different but they flow to a common destination, the ocean. Likewise, twenty first century America happens to be that ocean to which every nation flows. Earlier, it was the mother country that played the role of the 'great ocean' and the colonies were the streams. Now it is the United States that forms the hub of global activities. Colin Powell aptly described that there was not a single country on the earth that is not touched by America and vice-versa and that a thousand cords bind the countries of the world with America.

So far, the previous American masterstrokes had their desirable effects and could be seen in their distinctiveness because, prior to the end of the Cold War, the United States projected its influence abroad from the solid ground of its shores. It is only after the end of the Cold War that the Eagle finds itself journeying into the mid-air. As an airplane prepares to take off, it is possible to feel the tremendous speed, may be some 200 miles per hour that it attains on land. Interestingly when the same plane flies at a far greater speed of, say, 800 miles per hour in the air, everything seems rather static. The same is true of the movement of a ship. One hardly feels that the ship is moving as one peeps through the porthole of the cabin. Likewise, previous major American foreign policies appeared masterstrokes because they were related to some specific enemies. During the post Cold War era, no major power could challenge the United States in the near future. That is why even the brilliant of foreign policies taken by the three presidents after the end of the Cold War, appeared lackluster but they had clear purposes as I have written at the beginning of this chapter.

International politics in the new millennium has become more inclusive and flexible. Unlike earlier hegemons, the United States has created a number of options and regimes in the post 1945 era that serves as several shifting points (to borrow from Kennan) to engage the rest of the world in such a manner as to deter them not only from coalescing into an anti-American alliance but making them more dependent on America for solving multifarious problems, at the same time. More importantly, such shifting points may allow multiple exit routes for the American foreign policies, thereby, making it more broad-based. Such an assured and open approach gives it an edge over its colonial and former Soviet counterparts or any other historical imperial powers. The American policy of 'constant engagement' is different from those of the policies of the erstwhile great powers who lacked both the American capability and the blessings of modern technology. America's strength lies not only in one or two core areas but also in most of the peripheral or the 'shifting points' referred above. These can serve as the loci in different circumstances and together they go to enhance and strengthen its core advantages. As a result, the relative power gap of the United States with its nearest rival keeps on increasing. This is what I meant by an extremely open-ended and flexible strategy in which the United States would always be the major beneficiary.

The new millennium offers a real possibility for continuation of the American hegemony on a global scale. There can be no retracting from this fact. Moreover, the United States happen to the superpower for quite some time that already gives it some additional advantage over others. The joint Anglo-American signing of the Atlantic Charter in 1943 determined the future direction of a global or international political system. The United States has thus a responsibility to complete that job. A return to pre-1939 days is not possible even if the balance of power politics or multipolarism of the earlier era returns. That the EU and NATO were created at the American behest after the end of WWII and in which the European nations took active interests is an indisputable fact. Trans-Atlantic relations are near permanent from which neither Europe nor the United States can withdraw of their own sweet will and not without serious consequences that may jeopardize the entire Western Civilization. That way the American assumption of world leadership was not a gift from Britain but an inevitability born out of the strategic realities of that time.

Likewise, the UN Charter was accepted by every other nation not at gunpoint but by consents. The UN Charter was not enforced by war but it was an aftermath of that war. It was a peaceful and voluntary agreement between all nations. Since a leadership is needed to oversee the proper working of international regimes and since the United States was the only power capable of performing that role at that time, (the other super power, the Soviet Union was economically and territorially devastated and moreover the Soviets had a political system that was new and needed more time to attain legitimacy before the Western eyes), it devolved on the United States to shoulder these obligations. This common consensus amongst various nations was tantamount to a tacit and unwritten agreement to accept the American leadership. That way the American legitimacy in world affairs was a near 'established' fact after 1945.

It is irrelevant that a written agreement would have legitimized the US global leadership any more than the fact that such an agreement couldn't have taken place openly. In that case, every other nation stood to lose their sovereignty the moment they formally acknowledged the US hegemony. Now the real problem in the new millennium is to realize that nations, in general, must enter into a sort of 'written' agreement to observe *democracy* and rule of law within their own lands even to the extent of accepting external 'supervision'. Recent 'terrorist' plans and actions clearly reveal that such an external supervision is absolutely necessary even in a smallest part of the globe. A written guarantee to observe, implement, and preserve democracy in one's land is not tantamount to the surrender of sovereignty in so far as it guarantees international stability, peace, and prosperity. Extraordinary times demand extraordinary policies. Since the new millennium began with a terrorist bang, most other nations, like in the post war years, would have to take an extra step in entering into a common agreement to counter terrorism. These countries must not only democratize their polities but also forego a bit of their sovereignty by agreeing to undergo regular supervision. But that would be a temporary measure. As soon as terrorism wanes significantly, such supervision may be relaxed but with a guarantee that they can be re-imposed if the situation so warrants.

It is in this backdrop that the American leadership in the new millennium is to be viewed. The emphasis is now both on performance and legitimacy. Of course, in the performance angle the United States has exceeded all expectations by tucking the undeveloped and developing nations along with other developed nations into a new economic order that unleashed the third wave of industrialization. For over six decades since 1945, no war has taken place among major powers. Even many wars were cut short, thanks to the American mediation. International trade has spread exponentially because of the American insistence at the GATT for lowering of tariffs. Many developing nations have registered phenomenal growth following the American economic model. On the debit side, there are some blemishes like the Vietnam War, the American dual stand in respect of human rights and undemocratic governments, and the American insistence on unilateralism even to the extent of violating the UN observations.

Once the American global leadership is accepted, it is virtually impossible to defy that country unless the latter commits some grave wrong to others or to humanity in general. So far, the American record is better than even its predecessor, imperial Britain. The American *world hegemony is a kind of international political and social contract rather than an act of usurpation of power.*

References and readings

American Empire, The Realities and Consequences of the US Diplomacy, Andrew J.Bacevich, MA, Harvard University Press, 2003.

Ralph Peters, "Our Soldiers, Their Cities", Parameters, 26 (1996), 43-50. Quoted in Lindsay Hastedt's the American Foreign Policy, Past, present, and Future.

Fraser Cameron, the US Foreign Policy after the Cold War, Global Hegemon or the Reluctant Sheriff? Routledge, 2002.

H.W. Brands, the Americans *and the Cold war,* NY, 1993.

Zbigneiw Brzezinski, *The Grand Chessboard: American Primary and Geostrategic Imperatives*, NY, 1997.

J.Baker, *The Politics of Diplomacy, Revolution, War, and Peace, 1989-1992,* NY, 1995.

Robert L. Hutchings, *At the End of the American Century: America's Role in the Post Cold War World,* Washington, 1998.

Robert J. Art, *A Grand Strategy for America: A Century Foundation Book*, Ithaca and London, 2003.

W. David Clinton, *The Two Faces of National Interest*, London, 1994.

William C. Hyland, *Clinton's World, Remaking the American Foreign Policy*, Westport, CT, 1999.

Ivan R. Dee, *The Imperial Tense: Prospects and Problems of the American Empire*, Chicago, 2003.

Zimmerman, W. Origins of a Catastrophe, NY, 1996.

Alterman, E. *Who Speaks for America? Why Democracy Matters in Foreign Policy*, Ithaca, 1998.

Boren D. and Parkins E., eds, *Preparing America's Foreign Policy for the Twenty-First Century*, Norman, 2000.

Bush, G. H. W, *All the Best*, NY, 1999.

Friedman, Thomas, *The Lexus and the Olive Tree*, NY, 2000.

Hass R.N., *Intervention: The Use of the American Military Force in the Post-Cold War World*, Washington, DC, 1999.

Helms, J. *Empire for Liberty: A Sovereign America and Her Moral Mission*, Lanham, MD, 2001.

Robert Kagan and. Kristol, K., eds., *Present Dangers: Crisis and Opportunity in the American Foreign and Defense Policy*, San Francisco, 2000.

J. Mearsheimer, *Back to the Future: Instability in Europe After the Cold War, NY, 1990.*

D.P. Calleo, *Beyond the American Hegemony*, NY, 1987.

Walter LaFeber, *Inevitable Revolutions: The United States in Central America, 2nd edition*, NY, 1993.

INDEX

www.ingramcontent.com/pod-product-compliance
Ingram Content Group UK Ltd.
Pitfield, Milton Keynes, MK11 3LW, UK
UKHW020114200726
13856UKWH00002B/534